CHARLES KRAY is the elder brother of Ronnie and Reggie – two of the most famous criminals in history. He grew up with them in East London, where all three were exceptional young boxers, dubbed 'The Fighting Krays' by local newspapers.

Boyhood brushes with the law left them with no love of policemen; but as they grew older Charles saw his brothers mix with increasingly dubious characters and, eventually, acquire an aura of fear and respect among the criminal fraternity.

He was with them when they built their empire; beginning with a billiard hall, growing to include a chain of gambling clubs and night spots, and ending with grandiose plans for international expansion. He knew and understood their unique personalities; was privy to their thoughts and decisions; and remained unfailingly loyal to his family even when he knew the twins were doing wrong.

In this remarkably candid autobiography, he reveals what it was like to be a member of this family, and asks the question: Where did we go wrong?

Charles Kray's co-writer Jonathan Sykes hails from the West Riding of Yorkshire, where he spent his childhood and youth in a little town called Brighouse in the foothills of the Pennines. He left grammar school with Matriculation certificate, served a spell as general dogsbody on the local newspaper, then journeyed south in search of fame and fortune. As an actor with Unity Theatre in the late thirties, he made a minor impact as Kostya Dorokhov in 'The Aristocrats' and as Agate Keller in Clifford Odet's 'Waiting for Lefty', following these small successes with a walk-on part in World War II which was, he says, 'the easiest and worst-paid job I have ever had'.

During the post-war years he travelled the World, working for bread and writing for fun, turning his hand to anything that showed a profit either in cash or experience. Now in his mid-fifties he lives with his wife and daughter in West London, devoting his time to writing.

Crime, ciminals and the law have always fascinated him and he admits to having enjoyed writing Charles Kray's biography, a book which, in his opinion, cried out to be put down on paper.

ME AND MY BROTHERS

Charles Kray

with
Jonathan Sykes

EVEREST BOOKS LIMITED
4 Valentine Place London SE1

Published in Great Britain by Everest Books Ltd, 1976

ISBN 0905018 141

Copyright © Charles Kray and Jonathan Sykes 1976

This book is sold subject to the condition that it shall not, by way of trade or otherwise, be lent, re-sold, hired out or otherwise circulated without the publisher's prior consent in any form of binding or cover other than that in which it is published and without a similar condition including this condition being imposed upon the subsequent purchaser.

Printed and bound in Great Britain by
REDWOOD BURN LIMITED
Trowbridge & Esher

Without courage there cannot be truth; and without truth there can be no other virtue.

(Sir Walter Scott)

To betray others, even if we are all wrong, is dishonourable, and a dishonourable life is not worth living. Dishonour is without hope, whereas suffering can always end.

(Anon)

FOREWORD

Charles James Kray was born on the 9th of July 1926. The proud parents were Charles David Kray and his wife Violet, a pretty, blue-eyed blonde of eighteen, two years younger than her husband. They were typical East End newlyweds and they lived at 26 Gorsuch Street in Shoreditch.

Seven years after the birth of Charles James, Violet Kray presented her husband with a pair of bonny twins. The family home was now at 68 Stean Street in Haggerston. The twins were named Reginald and Ronald in order of appearance (Reginald being the elder by one hour) and they were the apples of their mother's eye.

Almost forty three years later, on the 5th of March 1969, Charles James Kray was taken down from the dock of the Old Bailey, London's Central Criminal Court, to begin a sentence of ten years imprisonment passed on him by Mr. Justice Melford Stevenson after a jury of twelve good men and true had found him guilty of complicity in the murder of Jack 'The Hat' McVitie. Among others sentenced with him, after the longest trial in the history of the Old Bailey, were his brothers, the twins Reginald and Ronald Kray. They were committed to prison for life, with a recommendation from his lordship that they should serve a minimum of thirty years.

What happened between the 9th of July 1926 and the 5th of March 1969? What was the chain of events that led to Charles Kray's appearance in the dock and caused the learned judge to say 'I am satisfied that you were an active helper in the dreadful enterprise of concealing traces of the murder by your brother'? What forces were at work during those forty three years which transformed Charles Kray and his brothers into a target for a specially created department of the Metropolitan Police, culminating in the lucrative employment of twenty three counsel (including nine QCs) in a criminal trial the cost of which was in excess of £150,000?

There has been considerable speculation about these events, most of it ill-informed and some of it highly sensational. It has been said of Charles Kray that, as the elder brother of the twins, he exercised a deterrent influence on their tendency to violence. Some of the ponces, thieves and other criminal riff-raff who claimed to be acquainted with the activities of what was referred to at the trial as 'The Firm' have said that Charles was the guiding genius who directed the twins' activities for his own personal gain. There are others, among them mature and experienced men of business, who found Charles a very likeable character with more than his share of natural charm and good manners.

There was no doubt in the mind of Mr Justice Melford Stevenson as he passed sentence on Charles Kray. He was satisfied, on the evidence presented before him, that the elder brother of the Kray twins had been 'an active helper in a dreadful enterprise'. It was this same judge who, almost four years later, was to be the subject of defiant abuse screamed at him by George Ince, then on trial at Chelmsford Crown Court accused of the murder of Mrs. Muriel Kathleen Patience at her home adjoining the Barn Restaurant near the Essex town of Braintree. A further coincidence was that the case ended in deadlock, the jury being unable to agree on a verdict, and at a second trial under Mr. Justice Eveleigh George Ince was acquitted on the evidence of an alibi provided by Dolly Kray, Charles' wife.

In the light of recent controversy in which the name of Mr. Justice Melford Stevenson has been linked with adverse comment on the professional behaviour of certain members of the Bar, it is interesting to note that there was evidence of friction in the interchanges between his lordship and counsel for the defence, Victor Durand Q.C.

Whether or not the Krays have sought publicity, it has inevitably found them. The East End has always produced its own breed of boxers who literally fought their way out of the slums. Charles and his brothers were no exception. All three showed considerable promise, and when the twins turned professional at the age of seventeen under the managership of one Jack Jordan, the fight cognoscenti of the East End predicted a brilliant future in the ring for both of them, particularly Reggie who, at the age of twelve, failed by a narrow points margin to become the Schoolboy Champion of Great Britain.

It is important to note that the childhood of Charles and his brothers was spent in part against the background of the second World War. Charles was thirteen and the twins six when war was declared, and for the next five years Violet Kray and her sons, in common with millions of others, were in close contact with the supreme violence of international mayhem. The family was evacuated to Hadleigh in Suffolk where they were the guests of a Mrs. Styles, but after a few months Violet Kray collected her children round her and back they went to the East End. For the rest of the war they lived in the small house at 178 Vallance Road in the middle of the increasing devastation which went on around them, fleeing to the shelter of the railway arches when the sirens announced the coming of the German bombers.

Father Kray was a notable absentee from the family home. In the first place he had no liking for the business of killing Germans – or anyone else for that matter. Also, and perhaps more importantly since he had to provide for his family, his talent for dealing in gold and silver flourished in time of war. People were not so concerned to lay up treasures on earth when death waited round the corner. So Violet Kray, with some help from her sisters May and Rose, bore the responsibility of caring for her three sons.

As the war entered its final stages Charles became of age for military service. He joined the Navy, and for the next year or so was stationed in Cardiff and Plymouth, where he represented the Navy in the welterweight division, fighting in inter-services competitions with a considerable degree of success. This was remarkable, for at the age of fifteen he had contracted rheumatic fever and it was feared that he might suffer for the rest of his life from a consequent heart condition.

I first met Charles James Kray while he was still serving the few remaining months of his sentence in Maidstone jail. I went to the rendezvous with an open mind, though I had already committed myself to the project of writing his life story. I had never met his brothers, the twins Reginald and Ronald, though naturally I had read everything I could about them and had seen them from time to time in the course of my work.

Charles Kray today is a fit and healthy forty-eight, almost seven years of prison life behind him. At this our first meeting I found him to be a highly articulate and very intelligent man who had obviously derived as much benefit as possible from such facilities as the prison authorities provided. He was widely read and spoke good French, what he had to say was said quietly but with conviction and, what surprised me most of all, he had earned full remission on his sentence of ten years imprisonment.

To anyone acquainted with the penal system of this country it would appear almost impossible that a man who had been convicted of a crime which merited a ten year sentence should behave impeccably within the rigid confines of prison discipline. It is astonishing but true that Charles Kray was never brought up before the governor of any of the prisons in which he was incarcerated for any breach of the innumerable rules and regulations to which he was subject while a guest of Her Majesty. At no time was he discovered to be in possession of prohibited articles or goods (the list of which is almost endless). He did not forfeit one single day of remission for good conduct. These facts, in my opinion, indicate a level of determination which is well-nigh superhuman.

In the following pages he tells his story, largely in his own words and with a minimum of correction and editing. It is the story of a man on whom the accident of birth conferred a strange and terrible responsibility, a man who often had to make the choice between his sense of morality and loyalty to his brothers, a man caught up in a chain of events which led to the Old Bailey and a long prison sentence. It is a story told by one of five people who alone have the knowledge and the authority to tell it. He is, and always has been, the devoted son of Violet and Charles David Kray and the loyal elder brother of the twins, Reggie and Ronnie Kray.

This is the story of Charles James Kray. When you have read it, ask yourself one question.

In his place, what would I have done?

Jonathan Sykes
London 1976

ONE

It was six o'clock in the morning when they came for me.

I was wakened from a deep sleep by the ringing of the doorbell and heavy knocking. Dolly, my wife, sat up in bed.

She said 'What's that, Charlie?'.

I didn't say how the bloody hell do I know, but put on my dressing gown and went downstairs to find out.

I turned the knob of the Yale lock and opened the door to the full extent of the safety chain, which proved itself no match for the combined weight of the Old Bill. There were three of them – later on I was told that there were others round the back – and they were in the hallway and standing up very close to me so that I couldn't move. It was all so perfect and so quick it must have been well rehearsed.

I said 'Just a minute – what's wrong?'

'Let's go in to the lounge, shall we' said one of them, and they crowded round me and sort of ushered me through the door. When they got me inside they sat me down and the one who seemed to be in charge took the phone off the hook.

Of course I would have been a bloody fool not to realise that something was up. These three were obviously carrying guns. They didn't wave them about or anything like that, but they were armed all right. Well, by this time Dolly had come down and my little daughter Nancy with her, and I couldn't help but laugh when this little three-year-old told them to put the phone back on – and one of them did just that.

I asked them again what this was all about and the top man said that I was being arrested on a charge of conspiracy to defraud and anything I said would be taken down in writing etc, the usual caution. I said what are you on about, defraud, I've never defrauded anybody in my life, but the only reply I got was to be told to get dressed because they were taking me down to the nick.

Gary, my son, came down the stairs looking a bit puzzled, but he didn't ask any questions, just stood there wondering what was going on. He was a quiet boy, and he just stood there.

By this time the Old Bill were beginning to look a bit embarrassed, but that didn't stop them from standing over me while I washed and dressed and all the time they made no attempt at conversation. I wanted to have a shave, but they told me not to bother. One funny thing happened which didn't seem to have much to do with anything, and that was they took all the money I had and counted it in front of me and put it in an envelope. It wasn't much, just a few pounds and some loose change.

Dolly hade made some tea, and she asked the three fellows if they would like a cup and they said they would, so we stood around drinking the tea. I didn't say any more to them apart from what I had already said, because I wanted to know more about the reason for nicking me, but they didn't volunteer any further information.

After a little while one of them said that we'd better be going, and suddenly produced a pair of handcuffs and asked me to hold out my hands. I was flabbergasted. I told them there was no need for that, but he didn't reply, just went on with the job of trying to put them on me. This was where the thing turned into a farce, because the handcuffs wouldn't fit, they were much too small and even by pinching the flesh they couldn't be made to fasten properly. The bloke in charge looked rather put out, but I think they realised that I wasn't going to be any trouble, and when I told them that I had no intention of trying to get away they stopped trying to get the cuffs on and put them back where they came from.

I was still not too disturbed about things, because I was quite sure that whatever was wrong would be cleared up as soon as I got down the nick and got hold of my solicitor. My conscience was quite clear. I knew that I had never defrauded anybody in my life, and anyone who said I had was a bloody liar. Yet somehow, in the back of my mind, I had an uneasy feeling that all this business, three coppers carrying guns and treating me with a lot of caution as though they expected me to shoot my way out of trouble, wasn't in keeping with arresting a man on suspicion of fraud. Another thing, these fellows were not Metropolitan Police, I could swear to it. The London bobby is unmistakeable. Anyway, there was no point in playing guessing games, I would know all about it soon enough.

I said cheerio to Dolly and the children, told them not to worry because I would be back soon, and went out to the police car with a copper on either side of me holding on to my sleeves.

I looked back at my home through the rear window of the car. I was not to know it then, but the next time I would see the place would be more than six years later and in very different circumstances.

That was the morning of Wednesday the 9th of May 1968.

Going back to the beginning, to the time when I was a small child, I remember how it used to be. There was just the three of us, Mum Dad and myself. We lived in a little street just off the Hackney Road, Gorsuch Street it was called, a real East End street where the people used to sit around on their doorsteps in fine weather. There was no television then and very few radios.

Dad was a dealer 'on the knocker', going round calling at houses and buying up anything of value, clothes, old gold and silver and so on. He must have been good at it because we were never short of money and, though he was away from home quite a lot, my Mum saw to it that I was well clothed and fed. I remember I had a lovely sailor suit, which was fashionable at the time, when the other kids in the street had no arse to their trousers.

When I was old enough to go to school I went to Laburnum Street School nearby. As I remember I wasn't a brilliant scholar, but I took to the sporting side like a duck takes to water and was crazy about football. One of the teachers – his name was Hawkes – was my favourite, and he taught me a lot about the game so that, even at a very early age, I was quite a useful player. My Dad used to come along to some of the school games and yell encouragement from the touchline. He saw to it that I never went short of sports gear such as shirts, shorts, shinpads, boots and the like, and though I may not have been the finest player on the field I was certainly one of the best dressed.

Dad was very interested in sport, but loved boxing above everything else. He used to go to the contests which were put on regularly at Hoxton Baths and other places, and sometimes I went with him. There was something about these bouts that fascinated me and I used to sit in the crowd in my little sailor suit with eyes like saucers as a couple of hungry fighters knocked hell out of each other for a few pounds and any 'nobbins' that came their way. 'Nobbins' were the coins tossed into the ring by an appreciative crowd at the end of a good fight when both men had given of their best.

Dad came of a large family, four brothers and three sisters, and had been born and bred in the East End. His father, my grandfather, was well known in Hoxton as a street trader and a man who was afraid of nobody. They called him 'Big' Jimmy Kray. I used to help him set out his barrow in the local street market and he would give me a few coppers for sweets. I liked him. He could tell good stories about the famous boxers he had known, Jimmy Wilde and Ted (Kid) Lewis, a Hoxton boy who became a world champion. Sometimes I used to imagine myself as one of these beings, a champion of the ring, a Lonsdale belt round my middle, the roars of the crowd, the lights and the smell of sweat and resin – then I woke up.

By East End standards I had a wonderful childhood. Looking back on it now, with the knowledge that in the thirties there was real hunger among the working people of the country, millions earning no more than a pittance and millions more on the dole, I consider myself one of the lucky ones. But in the teeming streets of Hoxton I couldn't close my eyes to facts. Young children roamed those streets, ragged and hungry, neglected by their parents, stealing from barrows and shops not for extra spending money but only to get something to eat. Many who became thieving villains in later life started their criminal career by stealing in order to keep alive. I certainly was one of the lucky ones.

This isn't to say that I led a sheltered life. Laburnum Street School was only public in the sense that anyone could go there and Hoxton wasn't a respectable suburb. There were fights outside the pubs on Saturday nights where tired kids with dark circles round their eyes waited for their fathers and mothers and scattered when the violence broke out. Policemen walked about in pairs and often looked the other way when a couple of villains decided to settle their grievances with the aid of knives or iron bars. The brutality and savagery of their elders rubbed off on the children, and it was not unusual to see a pair of ten-year-olds set about each other with all the ferocity and much of the skill displayed by the hungry fighters in the boxing ring.

As was to be expected, I was involved in a few incidents, but I was quite big for my age and very fit through football and running so, apart from collecting the odd black eye and the occasional bloody nose, I didn't suffer too much. What I did discover in myself was a natural ability as a boxer. Mum didn't approve of fighting, so I had to take care to tidy myself up before going home if I had been having a bit of an argument with one of my schoolfellows.

When I was about five there was a smallpox epidemic in the area, and both Dad and I caught the infection. Smallpox is nothing to laugh about even when it occurs in places where there are good hospitals and plenty of expert medical attention. In the crowded areas of Hoxton and Shoreditch the epidemic claimed a lot of victims, but fortunately Dad and me were not among them.

Shortly after that we moved to Stean Street, the other side of the Kingsland Road and nearer to the school. I liked it there. Just down the street was a stable yard where the horses that drew the delivery carts were kept, and the old chap who looked after the yard was very nice to the kids in the neighbourhood. He would let us play in the yard, providing we didn't get in the way too much. I used to spend a lot of time sitting on the wall that enclosed the stables watching the old man mucking out the stalls and grooming the huge animals when they came in after the day's hauling. It was all very exciting to a small boy.

Sometimes Mum told me off when I came indoors with muddy shoes and smelling of manure, but she told me off in a nice way. I thought she was the loveliest woman in the world. Even when I behaved badly, as all children do, she was never really angry with me and didn't scream and yell like some of the other mothers in the street. Another thing, she was always neat and clean and nicely dressed and I was very proud of her when she took me out shopping or over to see her sisters in Bethnal Green, my aunts May and Rose.

Its not easy to look back over the years and describe things as I saw them then, through the eyes and mind of a child. A six year old in 1932 was a very different person from a six year old today. Ask a modern child where he or she came from and ten to one the answer will be: 'Out of mummy's tummy.' As far as I was concerned at that age, both birth and death were a mystery to me, and I didn't know all that much about the in-between part. So when Mum began to put on weight and slow up a bit I had no idea what was happening. I have a vivid memory, however, of that one particular day when I was more or less turned out of the house and told not to go back indoors again until I was called. Aunt May and Rose were there, and there was a lot of coming and going which I watched from the wall round the stables. Then, in the early evening, I was called

18

and went up to Mum's bedroom and there they were, my twin brothers.

Of course I asked Mum where they had come from, and she said she had bought them. The next question I asked seemed an obvious one.

I said: 'But Mum – why did you buy two?'

It was the 24th of October 1933. I was just over seven years old.

It is often said, that, when a second child appears in a home, the elder and, till then, only child tends to feel resentment about the new arrival. In this case it was not one but two, and I didn't feel resentful at all. In so far as I can remember my exact feelings at the time I was pleased, which was perhaps partly due to the fact that Mum was so overjoyed with these two little bundles. I really didn't mind being thrust into the background to some extent, even though I had been an only child for long enough to take my Mum's love and care for granted. But there was no doubt about it, the twins attracted attention wherever they were taken in the brand-new shiny double pram, wearing identical clothes over their identical bodies. At that time they were so much alike that only Mum could tell the difference. I know I couldn't, and as for other people, they had no chance.

I read somewhere that young babies are just a loud noise at one end and a total lack of responsibility at the other. It's true there were a lot of nappies about, but the twins were very good babies where the crying stakes were concerned and I didn't have any disturbed nights. I used to look at them sometimes as they lay in their cot and they would look at me with round dark eyes, very calm and somehow in a grown-up sort of way as though they knew all about me and what was going on around them. Of course that was impossible, but I couldn't get rid of the feeling that they knew more than they ought to.

It was a good thing that the twins didn't cry very much in the night, because I was in the same room with them. We only had the upper part of the house at Stean Street. Mum's brother and his family were downstairs. Since there were only Mum, myself and the twins for most of the time, Dad being away on business, we weren't really pushed for space and the twins were no trouble to me.

Mum's sisters, May and Rose, came to visit us quite a bit. They were mad about the twins, and begged to be allowed to take them out in the pram. It was quite a sight to see, May and Rose fussing over the twins like a couple of motherly hens with their chicks, and the twins sitting in the big double pram and accepting it all as though it was their right. They got a lot of attention, which was perhaps not a good thing in the long run since, as they grew older, they came to expect people to make a song and dance about them and were rather put out if they didn't get it.

Still, we were a happy little family, Mum, myself, the twins and Dad on the occasions when he was there with us. I don't want to sound snobbish, but we were a cut above our neighbours. Apart from the fact, as I have mentioned before, we had sufficient money coming in at a time when most families were on the poverty line, we had a sort of local fame which derived from the Lee and Kray families. Dad's father was well known in the area and commanded a lot of respect, and 'Cannonball' Lee, Mum's father, was by way of being a legend in his own lifetime. Both these men had never worked for a boss and they had an independence that was envied by others who had to do what they were told and go where they were sent.

Grandfather Lee was an outstanding personality in an area where there was some competition. He was a mixture of showman and minor tycoon, always ready to turn his hand to anything, a fine athlete and a rabid teetotaller. He didn't get on too well with Dad, who liked a drink, but he was very fond of me and the twins. In his day he had been a bare-knuckle fighter. I was fascinated by his hands which were all broken and twisted like the roots of an old tree, but he could do anything with them, carpentry and things like that, really fine workmanship.

Going forward in time, Grandfather Lee died while I was away in prison. He was ninety six. Grandma Lee died two years after him. I think they were both affected by the trouble me and the twins had got into. When we were arrested the police went to the house and searched it and even took away the old couple's pension books. They were returned, of course, with the explanation that the authorities wanted to identify them as relatives, but it all seemed rather queer to me. I was very upset at the thought that I would never see the old chap again. He and Grandma Lee didn't come to visit us in prison, the journey would have been a bit too much for them at their age, because Ronnie was, I think, in Durham and Reggie and me were in Parkhurst.

I have fond memories of Grandfather Lee. One of his tricks was to take a white hot poker and lick it without burning his tongue. He explained to me that it was all a matter of saliva in contact with the white hot metal, but to me it was just plain magic. I remember he made a model plane, a biplane it was, and there was a parachute attached to it, and he demonstrated how the chute would open in case the engines failed.

One occasion I remember very clearly. Mum's brother, my uncle Johnnie, had a coach business and one day he took a party down to Southend for the day. As he was getting the party into the coach ready for the return journey, suddenly there was Grandfather Lee with his bicycle. The old chap had cycled forty two miles – he was seventy five years old. What's more, he was ready to cycle back again. Johnnie would have none of it, but he said later that he almost had to manhandle the old chap into the coach.

Going back to the days at Stean Street, we were marked out as a family not only because of background but also because of the twins. They were always beautifully dressed and people would stop my mother in the street just to get a good look at them. They were as famous, in their own way, as the two grandfathers. Sometimes, when Mum was busy with the family washing (no launderettes in those days), I would take the twins out in the pram and felt quite proud when neighbours leaned over them and said what bonny little things they were and how well they looked.

Suddenly, however, when they were about two years old, everything began to happen to them. They were at the toddling stage. Ronnie developed some sort of illness which caused him to go blue in the face when he got excited, and sometimes he would fall down and scream in pain. The doctor discovered he had a double hernia and so away he went into hospital for an operation. While he was absent, Reggie was obviously fretting, and I got a foretaste of what was to happen frequently in later years, the close mental and physical relationship between them. In the end, Mum had to bring Ronnie out of the hospital before he was ready to be discharged, but once the twins were together again everything was all right. Then came a succession of the usual childish ailments, which they suffered together, except for one occasion when Ronnie, who seemed to be the more unfortunate one, caught diphtheria. This phase passed in due course and they developed into normal healthy kids, running around and getting into the sort of mischief that children do. There was one thing, though, that was very noticeable. They seemed to be quite content with each other's company and didn't play in the street with the other toddlers.

I was now about ten years of age and becoming more involved in the sporting side at school, which took up most of my spare time. There was football every Saturday during the season and I went in for running and boxing too. I left Laburnum Street School and went to a more senior one in Scawfell Street just off the Hackney Road and quite close to the recreation ground, one of the green patches so rare in the East End of which we schoolboys took full advantage, even though the adjacent gasworks gave off fumes which couldn't have done our breathing apparatus much good. It was a big chance for me. I had been one of the bigger boys at Laburnum Street, but I was now very much one of the tiddlers in a bigger pond. One of the older boys by the name of Gregory was a first class all round sportsman and I admired him tremendously. He played for the school in goal, was an outstanding wicket-keeper at cricket and was also a very fine boxer. To my delight he took an interest in me and taught me the finer points of ringcraft and also gave me hints on how to improve my football. It was largely due to him that I was selected to play for the school when we won the finals at Heaton Manor, Hackney.

This was a great occasion. I played at right half and playing at inside right was a boy named Gibbins who later played for Tottenham Hotspur. I met him in Liverpool Street one day just after the war. Dad and I were just going off on our rounds (I was working with him then) when we met this chap. I asked him how he was getting on and he told me that he was with the Spurs. I said was he on the ground staff and then suddenly it came to me that he was one of the players, I had read about him somewhere. Was my face red! Anyway, we both laughed about it.

It was just after I went to Scawfell Street that I had my first serious street fight. I forget the other boy's name and also the cause of the fight, but we slugged away at each other for the best part of an hour until we were both too tired to raise our arms. We were surrounded by adults who made no effort to separate us, but that was part of the East End way of life where violence was never far below the surface and settling a disagreement with fists was the accepted thing. It was also accepted that, once the fight was over, you shook hands and forgot all about it, which is what me and the other kid did. The only consolation we had for the cuts and bruises we inflicted on each other was that we had provided some entertainment for the crowd. Since then I have taken a bit of stick in the ring as a professional boxer. Give me that, anytime. The rounds only last three minutes.

Talking about settling arguments with fists, that was what the local villains did. If there was something at issue between a couple of rival gangs they would each put up a champion for what was called a 'straightener' and the two men would then fight it out at a chosen spot – a certain woodyard in Hackney Wick was a favourite place – and honour was satisfied. Sometimes the fight didn't take place and the rival gangs would gather in a nearby pub to have a drink together all nice and friendly. Then, suddenly, a chance word would start the whole thing up again, and there would be razors flashing, broken glasses used as weapons and blood all over the place.

Some of these villains were quite proud of their scars. There was one who was nicknamed 'Tramlines' whose face looked like an aerial survey map of the famous marshalling yards at Hamm. One look at that fearsome face and other villains were either moved to put a few more stripes on it or give the owner a wide berth.

When war came to the East End and the German bombs shattered the humble homes, shattering the inhabitants with equal impartiality, it seemed only a fitting climax to the years of bloodshed and violence that had flourished there.

The couple of years leading up to the outbreak of World War Two saw a rather important change in the lives of the people who lived in the East End. There was more money about, the queues at the Employment Exchange dwindled as more workers were drawn into the factories and the docks and the cash registers at the pubs began to rattle with greater frequency. Dad's business boomed as his clients threw out the old gear to make room for the new, though there was still a healthy sale for whatever Dad brought back from his trips. The twins were now in excellent health, all their little illnesses behind them. The coming war was being talked about on all sides, though I for one didn't understand all the chat about Hitler and his plans to conquer the world. What I did see at first hand was the capers of Oswald Mosely and his Blackshirt mob, marching through the Mile End Road and Whitechapel where a lot of Jews lived, holding meetings at street corners and causing trouble wherever they went. One of the leaders was a chap called William Joyce, a tough-looking merchant with a deep scar down one side of his face. As everyone knows, he went off to Germany after war broke out and broadcast from Berlin. He was nicknamed Lord Haw Haw and after the war was hanged as a traitor.

About this time – I would be twelve or so – Dad came home with a new pair of football boots for me. They were the latest style and very expensive. I couldn't wait to put them on. We had a match at the recreation ground that Saturday afternoon, and I trotted off with my gear, the boots dangling over my shoulder by the laces. I was going through the railway arches when three kids snatched the boots from me and ran off. I was determined to get the boots back and ran after the kids, shouting at the top of my voice and refusing to be shaken off even when they dodged round corners and went over walls. I think they must have got fed up with me following them for they dropped first one stocking which had been tucked inside a boot, then another stocking, then one boot and then the remaining one. I was at the recreation ground in time to change for the match and we won the game. I told Dad all about it when I got back home. He patted me on the shoulder and said: 'You're a trier, son, a real trier.' I never felt closer to him than at that moment.

I must say this about Dad, that he was a very good father even though he was away for quite long periods at a time. Of course he liked his little drink, but he wasn't the sort of man to spend money on booze and leave his wife and family short. Mum never had to go out to work as so many other East End wives did and as a consequence me and the twins were well cared for and not left to roam the streets and get up to the sort of mischief that brought other kids in the neighbourhood up against the law. Mind you, we were not namby-pamby, we had our share of normal childish high spirits and I am sure that we tried Mum's patience on more than one occasion. I'd like to say here and now, though, that she was an angel and no children could have wished for a better Mum. She was always there when we needed her. I'm sure she had no ambition in life but to bring up her children as nicely as possible in the circumstances in which we lived and as families go in the East

End we were among the most respectable and respected.

Mum had a remarkable personality. She was always calm and quiet and very rarely raised her voice either to us children or anybody else, but she had a knack of getting her own way by the strength of purpose with which she tackled all her problems. When Ronnie was brought out of hospital Mum was convinced in her own mind that he would be better off at home with his twin brother and she just marched into the hospital and brought him out. Of course she had to contend with doctors and nurses who told her it would not be wise to remove the child from the care of trained staff, but Mum knew best, not in an ignorant and pig-headed way but because she really believed that Ronnie needed his Mum and his brother. That was something the hospital could not provide. Ronnie came home and Mum's action was justified, because the twins together again, recovered their health miraculously.

Another thing about Mum, once she had set her heart on doing something she would steadily work towards it and not allow anything or anyone to stand in her way. She didn't go at things like a bull at a gate but surmounted all the obstacles in her way by sheer perseverance and will-power. I knew that, for a long time, she had wanted a house of her own with a front door that wasn't shared and her own back garden. When one day Aunt Rose came to see us with the news that her next-door neighbours were leaving, I was sure that our next address would be 178 Vallance Road. It was.

Because this house was to be the Kray family home for some twenty five years, I would like to describe it as I saw it on that late summer morning in 1939. The road itself runs between Whitechapel Road and Bethnal Green Road for a distance of just over half a mile and is roughly parallel to Commercial Street which lies to the west, as do Spitalfields and Liverpool Street Station. Aldgate Pump, the boundary between the City and the East End, was not far away and Cheshire Street market where 'Big' Jimmy Kray traded from his barrow was just around the corner. The trains from Liverpool Street to Bethnal Green thundered along the raised track behind the house, a noise to which we were all accustomed and which didn't bother us in the least. We had lived perhaps not within sight but certainly within sound of the traffic from Liverpool Street all our lives.

The house was one of a row of terrace houses and was far from being a palace. On the ground floor there were two rooms, a kitchen and a scullery with a door that gave out on a small garden and the outside lavatory. Upstairs there were three rooms one of which looked out on Vallance Road. From the windows of the other two rooms we could watch the trains as they ran to and from Liverpool Street. When we went there it was only a house. Mum made it into a home.

I don't think that Dad, deep down, approved of the change as it brought him under the disapproving eye of his teetotal father-in-law, but he had other things to think about, for almost unnoticed in the excitement of moving the Second World War had broken out. The fact that on the third of September 1939 a somewhat discredited old politician broadcast that England was at war with Germany, underlining the gravity of the situation with the sounding of an immediate (and unnecessary) air raid warning, meant very little to us children. Apart from sandbags being packed around public buildings, gas masks being issued and a bunch of public-spirited citizens dashing around in makeshift uniforms, there was no change in the scene we had known all our lives. There were certainly no waves of enemy bombers raining death and destruction on our homes as we had been led to think. That was to come later. For the present the usual comment was that it would all be over by Christmas.

For Dad, of course, there were certain important matters to be considered. He was of military age and, although the authorities did not seem anxious to send him overseas to kill Germans immediately, he knew that it was only a matter of time. On the one hand he saw his wife and children reduced to living on a private soldier's family allowance while he would be deprived of many of the things that made life worth living such as his booze and baccy. On the other hand he saw no reason why he should not go on the trot. After all, he had been trotting all his working life. In addition he had never called anyone boss, and not even the prospect of being employed by the British High Command attracted him. So Dad made his decision early and when the time came he put it into practice.

So far as me and the twins were concerned the outbreak of war was a non-event. I had just celebrated my thirteenth birthday and the twins were coming up to their sixth. My schoolwork together with the football, running and boxing that went along with it, took up most of my time. The twins were happy as mudlarks. Their aunts May and Rose were almost next door, Grandfather Lee and grandma were within easy reach and Uncle Johnnie, Mum's brother, ran the cafe across the street. They could always be found in one or other of these places except at meal times. Then they would be home. Mum's cooking, then as now, was too good to be missed. She was a great believer in seeing that the family ate good and nourishing home-cooked food, and I am sure that this laid the foundation of our fitness when we took up boxing seriously as professionals.

At this point I would like to make a few comments on some of the things that have been said and written about the twins' childhood. A lot of it is guesswork and some of it pure fantasy. John Pearson, in a book titled The Profession of Violence (published in 1972 when we were in prison) tries to make out a case that the twins even in those early days showed signs of becoming criminal psychopaths. Now I am not a highly educated man. The educational system in Hoxton and Bethnal Green was never designed to turn out philosophers and scholars, but I have a certain amount of intelligence. In support of some of the outrageous statements he makes he quotes an obscure Dr. Lange of Munich (I can't resist this – no doubt an associate of Dr. Strabismus whom God preserve of Utrecht) who, in 1929, took up where Sir Francis Galton left off in the study of 'biological inheritance as a vital factor in the formulation of a criminal'. This Sir Francis Galton conducted his researches in the enlightened 1870s. Yes, you are quite right, over one hundred years ago!

Bear with me while I turn myself into Charlie Kray, late of 'Oxton and Bethnal Green and deliver my comment.

'What a load of fucking cobblers.'

For the record, and as I saw them, the twins were a couple of normal East End kids who got up to the usual pranks that kids get up to all over the world. As a family we were close and united. Mum and Dad are still together to this day after nearly fifty years during which they have suffered hardships and aggravations far greater than those of most couples. It was said that, if you kicked one of us, the others limped. Is that a crime?

One thing that prison does for a man is to give him time to think and, what is more important, get to know himself. After more than two thousand three hundred solitary nights locked up in a cell not much bigger than a large lavatory, nights during which I have tried to find answers to many questions only in the end to become more aware of my limitations, I have reached some conclusions. I will deal with these later.

Another thing that prison does for a man is to give him access to books – and, of course, the leisure to read them. Most prison libraries carry a fairly wide selection of reading matter, and then there are the 'floaters', books brought into the precincts of the jail against the rules. The Profession of Violence was a floater, but the information I gathered about Sir Francis Galton came from impeccable sources, the prison library no less.

This eminent Victorian authority quoted by Pearson was born in 1822 and died in 1911. He was a cousin of Charles Darwin, who I believe knew more about apes than human beings. He was a Fellow of the Royal Society and he invented a system of identification by fingerprints. He also applied mathematics to biological problems. A waggish fellow inmate at Maidstone, when I told him about this, remarked 'Ah! Fucking by numbers'.

The background against which Sir Francis made his remarkable discoveries embraced such novel social and economic innovations as the first steam railway from Stockton to Darlington, the first crossing of the Atlantic by steam, the establishment of the Metropolitan Police, the Chartist riots, the declaration of war by France and Great Britain against Russia, the assassination of U.S. President Abraham Lincoln and the first flight by a heavier-than-air machine made by the Wright brothers. They were not twins. If they had been, Sir Francis would probably have made something out of that. He died in the year in which members of Parliament received their first wage packets.

Once I got my teeth into this research lark I found it fascinating and turned my attention to finding out something about this Dr. Lange (whom God preserve) of Munich. Unfortunately there was nothing in the prison library, perhaps because this character was not so famous as the eminent Victorian.

I want to make a point here, and I am not being facetious or indulging in sarcasm. This fellow Pearson, by quoting outdated and probably suspect authorities, was well on the way to convicting the twins before they had reached an age when they could make any sort of decision for themselves. It could be laughable if it weren't such a serious matter. In this age of jet travel, nuclear fission and landings on the moon when enquiry into the motivations of human beings has become a highly scientific business even yesterday's theories can be old-fashioned today. To put the proposition that a couple of kids were pre-destined to a life of crime and violence on the basis of theories advanced by a steam-powered scientist in a past century, backed up by the limited researches of a little-known Munich doctor poking about among the records of the Ministry of Justice in Bavaria, is just so much eyewash.

The truth of the matter is that my brothers were marked out as different from the rest because they were that rare phenomenon, identical twins. Because they were different they were regarded with distrust and suspicion like any rarity in the animal world. In the stories of the Wild West, the fastest gunslinger was always a target for the up-and-coming youngster who wanted to win an instant reputation. Many an English gentleman has looked out of his window on a Spring morning and said: 'It's a fine day. Let's go out and kill something.' By the same token, and on more than one occasion, a bunch of Bethnal Green kids would set out to clobber the Kray twins for no other reason than that they were the grandsons of 'Big' Jimmy Kray and John 'Cannonball' Lee, and they were different.

These are the facts of life in the East End, a breeding place of violence, where any attempt at peaceful persuasion is taken as evidence of weakness, where violence begets violence which in its turn breeds greater violence. I have seen it with my own eyes, and I am not impressed in the slightest by the pronouncements of a Victorian gent whose knowledge and experience of the East End stopped at Mansion House. As for Dr. Lange (whom God preserve) of Munich, all I can say is that his discoveries may have some relevance to Bavarian criminal twins born at the end of last century and that's about all.

I am not saying that the twins were little angels. Far from it. They were tough and incredibly fearless. When arguments between them came to the point of fighting, they fought, but when they were attacked they tore into the opposition like hellcats and didn't stop until they had won. I really believe that they would have died rather than be defeated. It was strange and just a bit frightening to see these two, only just out of the toddling stage, shape up like miniature prizefighters. Of course they were influenced by Grandfather Lee who told them tales of the great fighters he had known in the days when he would go up to Victoria Park on a Sunday morning and fight with bare fists for a few shillings. I would sometimes go down on my knees and spar with one or the other, just for fun and to show off, demonstrating how to block a left lead or avoid a right hook. They learned quickly and occasionally I would be on the receiving end of a punch which surprised me by its power and accuracy.

Looking back, I am sorry in a way that I had any part in introducing the twins to boxing, yet if I hadn't done so someone else would. Bethnal Green and Hoxton, with a tradition of producing good fighters, some of whom became champions, had more than its share of ex-pugilists looking for good young prospects, another Mendoza or Kid Berg or Ted Lewis.

I feel I may have given the impression that the East End was just an area full of fighters and villains, but this is not really the case. There were decent, hardworking men who did their best to bring up their families in a proper and respectable way in spite of the environment, who went to work as dockers and labourers, brought their pay packets home every Friday night and kept out of the pubs. The mothers, fighting a daily battle against dirt and disease, also bore a great responsibility for the welfare of their children and the maintenance of the home. Among these people one found warmth and friendliness and a ready desire to help one's neighbour.

This was the background against which our family lived its day to day life. We had our roots in Vallance Road, and evacuation when the bombs began to fall could not drive us away for long.

When we packed our belongings and set off for Hadleigh in Suffolk, I looked back at our home. I knew we would be back there soon and that the house would still be standing.

TWO

There were hundreds of us crowding the platforms at Liverpool Street station, kids of all sizes and colours, identification labels tied to their clothes, some with their mothers, others in groups with an adult in charge. The real war had started and bombs were falling on London.

Evacuation had begun to get under way after a period during which whoever was responsible for making the arrangements seemed to be in two minds what to do. For a fourteen year old boy this was an unforgettable and terrifying experience: the nightly wailing of the air-raid siren, a frightening sound in itself; then the thrum-thrum of aeroplane engines which seemed to fill the sky; then the whistling sound that became a roar; then the explosion and the blast which rolled through the narrow streets, shattering windows and blowing down doors for miles around.

The district close to the docks, which included Hoxton and Bethnal Green, was a target for the bombers. Grandfather Lee, who seemed to understand the tactics of the German High Command, said that it was obvious that the Germans would try to do as much damage as possible to the ports in order to stop the flow of imports. The river Thames was a perfect guide to the enemy planes. On moonlight nights it was a silvery path leading to the heart of dockland. The wardens who rushed about blowing whistles and shouting 'Put that bloody light out' were powerless to black out the Thames.

Although I was very frightened at times, which is understandable, I also found some things exciting. The twins, for example, thought it was all a wonderful game as they trooped to shelter under the railway arches with Mum and me. When Dad was at home he stayed indoors or went down to the pub. No shelters for him. 'If it's got my name on it it'll get me,' he used to say.

Grandfather Lee was in his element. Although he was over sixty he knocked up a makeshift stage under the arches and led the community singing, did his famous bottle-walking act and tried his best to keep people's minds off the hell that was going on in the streets. On one occasion he fell off the stage, but this remarkable old chap was on his feet again and carrying on as though nothing had happened.

There were some terrible happenings too. When the bombing started somebody in authority decided that all the tube stations should be closed to prevent people using them as shelters. That decision was soon reversed by the people themselves, who tore down the barriers and took the stations over. There was a tragedy at Bethnal Green Junction when a crowd stormed the station and rushed down the stairs in panic. Hundreds of people were killed and maimed, among them Billy Corbett the boxer and several of Dad's friends. His brother and sister-in-law had a miraculous escape, managing to get out of the crowd, before they fell over each other on the narrow stairway.

Funnily enough the twins didn't seem to be all that disturbed by what must have appeared to them as strange behaviour on the part of the adults in their little world. They were usually hand in hand as they toddled off to the shelter with me and Mum, or they would hold on to each other's clothes when a bomb dropped nearby. Even when the anti-aircraft guns opened up with a racket that almost lifted the top off your head they showed no signs of fear, and certainly didn't burst into tears as so many other kids did. Somehow they seemed to feel security in each other. Mum behaved as she always had done in emergencies, being very calm and coping with every situation as though she had been at war all her life – which in a way I suppose she had.

The upshot of all this was that someone somewhere came to the conclusion that women and children could not be expected to take this hell on earth much longer, which is how we came to be on the platform at Liverpool Street on the first stage of our journey to the little village of Hadleigh in Suffolk, about fifty miles from London. We didn't have a lot of luggage. The house and everything in it was left in the care of Mum's sisters, May and Rose. I don't think Mum wanted to leave Vallance Road but she realised that it was something that had to be done for her children's safety and as usual that came first.

Apart from odd visits to Southend and Clacton for a day trip or a short holiday, me and the twins had never been far from our home ground, so this was a real adventure, to be going to a strange house among strange people in a country village away from the crowded and narrow streets of Bethnal Green. By this time a large part of that area of the East End had been reduced to rubble, but there was still a lot left standing. Out little section of Vallance Road had escaped serious damage although we had lost all the windows and a parachute mine had landed on the railway line just behind the house. If it had exploded that would probably have been the end of the Lees and Krays. Come to think of it, Fate plays some queer tricks. I wonder if there's a Selection Committee somewhere Up There which decides who goes and who stays.

Dad was left behind in London. His business was booming in spite of (or maybe because of) the perils of war, and as he said, someone had to earn the wages. He promised to come down to see us in Hadleigh as often as he could and that was that.

Hadleigh, when we got there, was a new world to us. We were billeted on a lady called Mrs. Styles, who was a widow with a nephew a few years older than me. He became a pilot in the Fleet Air Arm later in the war and was killed in action. Mrs.

Styles husband had been a doctor in the area, and her home was a solid, Victorian house with its own large garden. To us it was a palace. We had to overcome a few problems during the settling-in stage, but Mrs. Styles was kindness itself and very understanding.

The twins took to the country life. Plenty of fresh air and good grub (food shortages were not so apparent in rural districts) put colour in their cheeks and gave them the energy they needed to scour the fields and woods for miles around. As for myself, I decided that I should do something to earn a bit of money and after some nosing around I got a job helping out in the local fish and chip shop which meant a small income and a good feed every night. Later on I became more ambitious and went to work full time at Price's factory where they made mattresses and I made the tea. It wasn't a bad life, but I missed my athletic hobbies, particularly the boxing. Still they were a pretty good crowd at the factory and I got on well with most of them even though we didn't have much in common.

One thing the twins and I liked was when the snow came and we could go sledging. We used to set off with Mrs. Styles' nephew and his sledge for the nearest hill as soon as the snow was deep enough. The twins would clamber on to my back as I lay full length on the sledge and off we would go, the wind whistling past, to end up more often than not in a heap at the bottom of the run, the three of us a tangle of arms and legs and the twins laughing their little heads off. We had a lot of fun.

Dad came down to see us fairly often even though travel wasn't all that easy. He became quite a favourite in the local pub with his news of what was happening in London. I think he enjoyed the break but he was always ready to be off again. His visits unsettled Mum to some extent. She missed her family and friends and the life of Vallance Road, but she never complained.

The invasion scare started in the spring of 1941. Stories began to circulate of the imminent landings of the Germans on the East coast. Since all news was heavily censored there were neither official denials or confirmation of the rumours and in consequence they spread like wildfire. I could see that Mum was becoming increasingly worried, not for herself but for us kids, so I wasn't very surprised when one morning she told us to get our things together because we were going back home. Mrs. Styles tried to persuade Mum to stay in Hadleigh but her mind was made up and nothing could make her change it. Don't get the impression that Mum was pig-headed and obstinate. She gave a lot of thought to anything that might affect the well-being of her family, came to a definite conclusion and then went on to put the conclusion into practice.

It was later found out that the invasion rumour was so much hooey, but at the time it was very real to Mum as it was to many people in the East coast area. Fear is contagious and spreads very rapidly. A lively imagination could picture Panzer troops sweeping through the quiet village, dive bombers striking from the skies and bullets, which are no respectors of persons and cannot discriminate between soldiers and civilians, flying about all over the place. Mum wasn't going to have any part of this. If the time ever came when she would have to fight Germans it would be in her own backyard with her family at her side.

So we left Hadleigh more or less as we arrived plus a few mementoes of our stay there. I had no strong feelings either way about returning to Vallance Road. If anything, I was pleased at the prospect of once more meeting my mates and taking up boxing where I had been forced to leave it. The twins weren't so happy. They had fallen in love with the countryside, and the memory must have been lasting for, when many years later they decided to buy a house, they chose one in Bildeston only a few miles from Hadleigh. That, however, is only by the way; the story of the house at Bildeston will be told in another chapter.

The house in Vallance Road was still very much the same as we had left it some seven months ago. The temporary plastic sheets that had replaced the windows had in turn been replaced by glass and May and Rose had kept everything clean and tidy. Within a few days it was as if we had never been away. There were still bombing raids, of course, but nothing like so concentrated as before. The Germans had their hands full in other places such as Greece and North Africa.

We, in a smaller way, had our hands full too. Dad got his calling up papers and promptly went on the trot. For the first time in our lives me and the twins came into close contact with the police, who also had their hands full, because Dad wasn't the only man in the district who had decided that the British Army wasn't big enough for him and General Montgomery at the same time. I must say, in all fairness to the police, that they didn't pursue the matter of Dad's disagreement with the armed forces all that seriously, but they did call at the home from time to time in the hope that they might catch Dad off the trot and on the hop. We kids had our instructions and, like the three wise monkeys, we followed them to the letter. It was a real: 'When did you last see your father?' situation.

At that age (I was almost fifteen) I didn't see the position in terms of a moral dilemma. Dad did what he considered best for himself and us and that was okay by me. Dad reasoned that he didn't start the war so why should he help to finish it, and in any case the professionals involved in carrying on the war wouldn't want their efforts loused up by an amateur like him. It was a specious argument, but I wasn't concerned about that. My Dad was my Dad, he'd done his best for me all my life. Now I was in a position to do my best for him and I lied like a bloody trooper.

It wasn't all that good for the twins, though. Of course the Law didn't bother them much, they were too young to provide any reliable information, but I could see that they were beginning to look upon a copper's uniform as something that concealed the enemy. Aunt Rose didn't help all that much either. If she happened to be about when the Law paid a visit she made no bones about marking their card for them which made things a bit uncomfortable for all concerned. When she was roused she could use language that would make a market porter blush. On these occasions the twins, if they were present, would stand side by side and watch the proceedings very gravely with identical inscrutable looks on their faces. They took everything in and whatever they thought they kept it to themselves. I think that even at that early age, getting on for eight, the seeds were being sown that made them distrustful of uniformed authority in later life, but I could be wrong. The old Bethnal Green chant, 'All coppers are bastards,' was in vogue long before they were born.

I had now reached an age when it was time for me to go to work. With so many able-bodied men in the army there was no shortage of jobs for a willing youngster. The Ministry of Labour fixed me up as a messenger boy in the shipping department at Lloyd's just over the City boundary and within walking distance of Vallance Road. I would cut through the back doubles into Commercial Road, pass Aldgate East station and arrive in Leadenhall Street at half past eight ready to start work. From then until five thirty, with an hour's break for lunch, I was everyone's dogsbody. Saturday was a half day off from noon. For my labours I got eighteen bob a week, which I handed over to Mum every Friday night.

Actually this weekly charade was more a gesture than anything else. I don't think that Mum needed the eighteen shillings, but she encouraged me to be independent. One way and another I had all of it back during the week what with lunch money and odds and sods for this and that. However, I felt that I was doing my bit as the man of the house in Dad's absence.

The work I was doing wasn't so hard that I didn't have the time and energy for boxing. I went down to the local institute three nights a week for training and Grandfather Lee had fixed up a punchbag in the top back room which I leathered to some tantivy whenever I had a chance. The twins took a close interest in these performances. Now and then I let them stand on a chair in turn and have a go, but I stopped that when I found out that they were using each other as punchbags when

I was out at work.

Mum wasn't very keen on my boxing, but she became reconciled to it when she saw that I didn't collect a flat nose and a pair of cauliflower ears. I suppose she remembered her young days when her father came home from Victoria Park on a Sunday, after a bare-knuckle fight, with a face like a disaster area. I explained to Mum that amateur boxing wasn't a dangerous business, that the gloves we wore were like feather pillows, and she seemed satisfied. Anyway she didn't put a stop to it.

One thing that boxing did for me, in a sort of negative way, was keep me out of bad company. Most of the kids in the Vallance Road area in my age group used to get up to all kinds of skullduggery. When they weren't breaking into shops and factories they were groping the neighbourhood girls in quiet spots under the railway arches, and some of them boasted of their sexual adventures in terms that left nothing to the imagination. There was more licence in wartime than there had been before, which is saying something, because the East End kid normally knew what are called the facts of life at a very early age and what's more put them into practice. Teenage marriages were the rule rather than the exception, and the majority of child brides walked down the aisle or into the registry office looking very thick round the middle.

Somehow I didn't fancy this furtive scuffling and groping and panting in dark corners, added to which my mates at the institute told me terrifying stories of the way masturbation and copulation sapped your strength and even more horrifying tales of the dreadful diseases that could be caught, diseases that eroded the marrow from the bones and brought on premature blindness. As well as this, I suppose I was a bit of a romantic with the idea of saving myself, pure and clean, for the girl I would one day marry. The result was I kept myself out of entanglements with the opposite sex and put my excess energy into belting the opponent in the opposite corner.

I thought of these things as I lay in bed in Bethnal Green

hospital. I had kept myself fit, I hadn't smoked or touched alcohol, and here I was, stretched out and unable to do anything for myself, struck down by rheumatic fever at the age of fifteen.

At first I had thought it was nothing to worry about. I had a sore throat and felt rather out of sorts. Mum made me gargle with salt and water but it did no good. In the end she took me up to the hospital where they wasted no time in putting me to bed with strict instructions that I was to lie there absolutely still. I wasn't even allowed to get up to go to the lavatory. I was choked. Day after day, night after night I lay there, using a bottle when I needed to pass water and a bedpan for the other thing.

This sort of enforced idleness almost drove me mad. I had been accustomed to dashing about and doing things and the prospect of lying on my back as helpless as a new-born baby for God knows how long appalled me. Mum came to see me as often as the rules of the hospital permitted, so did my aunts and several other people, but it wasn't much consolation to me as I counted the hours and minutes between visits. What disturbed me more than anything else, however, was that I discovered that I might become a permanent invalid with a heart condition. I honestly thought very seriously of doing away with myself.

As it turned out the issue was decided for me in a most dramatic fashion. At the end of several weeks in bed, during which time there had been a few air-raid alerts but no bombs anywhere near the hospital, we had a direct hit. There was pandemonium and the nurses began to evacuate the ward which contained quite a few old men. I had been flung out of bed, and nobody paid any attention to me as I walked, very unsteadily, out of the ward and down the stairs. In view of the dreadful warnings I had been given I expected to drop dead at any moment – but I didn't and like Felix the cat I kept on walking.

Mum had me out of hospital and back in my room in Vallance Road the next day. For the next week or so Dad, who risked being picked up by the Law, slept in the room with me and stayed there during the days until one morning I felt well enough to get up, which I did – and from that moment on I never looked back. Even today I can't believe my luck. From what I have heard from doctors I must be something of a walking miracle.

It wasn't long before I was back at work again in my blue uniform with the red collar, dodging around the City streets and diving into the nearest basement when the air-raid warning sounded. All the messenger boys had been instructed to go to an air raid shelter when a raid was on, but we preferred the office basements where there was always a cup of tea and some biscuits or a bun. Also, there was no bossy warden to shove us back inside if we wanted to leave before the all clear.

One of my jobs was to take over the switchboard when the operator went to lunch. I was fascinated by this man, who had lost his sight in the First World War. It was a fairly big board with something like fifty extensions but he handled the plugs and cords as though he had eyes in his fingertips. I used to walk him to the bus stop at the end of the day's work and he gave me a shilling every Friday which I didn't look for but which came in very handy.

As soon as I was really well again I went back to boxing. I had graduated from the junior club, the Coronet, shortly before I was taken ill and now I was with the bigger boys of the Crown and Manor youth club in Hoxton. I also joined the local branch of the Naval Cadets over at Hackney Wick, where there were very good facilities for training. I began to take the game very seriously. As I have said, as a family we were not on the poverty line, but we weren't rolling in it either, and professional boxing was a way to extra money. A good amateur could sign professional forms as soon as he reached the age of seventeen and, depending on his ability and his success in drawing the crowds, would be able to pick up as much as ten pounds for fighting four three-minute rounds in a supporting contest. There was always the 'nobbins' to be considered on top of the pay, though the boxers sometimes came off second best to their helpers in this particular area. It isn't easy to pick up coins when you're wearing six ounce gloves, and there are no pockets in boxing trunks.

I don't remember how many fights I had as an amateur, but I was always bringing home prizes, cutlery, glassware and so on. I also picked up a few cups and medals some of which Mum has to this day. The twins cast their eyes on the loot and thought they might as well do the same. They began to come out with me when I did my roadwork in the early morning before going to work and it was a sight to see, these identical little figures trotting along beside me, full of professional mannerisms, doing side-steps and shooting out left leads and right crosses. They were now attending Daniel Street School (which later became Daneford Street), where there was boxing as part of the sporting side, but in the evenings they would go into the back room upstairs, which was fitted out as a rather primitive gym, and put the gloves on with each other. They hadn't yet reached their ninth birthday but they really handled themselves like experienced fighters. It was amazing.

I know I am devoting a lot of space to the boxing activities of me and my brothers, but this is because it was such an important part of our lives at the time. Furthermore I believe that the success of the twins in the ring had an effect on what was to happen to them in the future, and to a great extent shaped their lives.

A world champion heavyweight (I think it was Gene Tunney) once said that the boxing ring is the loneliest place in the world. I agree with him because I've been there. A canvas-covered square surrounded by ropes, fiercely lit, the rest of the place in near-darkness, in the other corner the man who is going to beat you or be beaten by you and the referee who is just a presence with a voice. The timekeeper's bell rings. For the next three minutes everything in you is concentrated on that other man, you are in close physical contact and the third man in the ring somehow becomes a shadow who occasionally taps you on the arm or shoulder or head, or says break, which you automatically obey. You circle round, looking for an opening, you do your best to score points or put the other man on the canvas, but all the time it is concentrate, concentrate, concentrate.

This is what professional boxing is all about. It's the way to fame and fortune for any poor boy who is prepared to dedicate himself to the game. When you put your man on the deck for a count of ten or win the fight on points and the referee raises your gloved hand and the crowd roars, then you feel like a king – and the more it happens the greater you feel, until after a time you get the idea that you are invulnerable.

There is one thing to remember and that is a pro must watch his behaviour outside the ring. To get involved in street fights is to risk damage to his hands, which are, after all, the tools of his trade. Then there's the question of his licence, which can be taken away from him by the Board of Control if he is convicted of an offence of violence. Most important of all, magistrates take a serious view of a pro giving an ordinary citizen a right-hander. In their opinion a boxer's fists are almost, if not quite, lethal weapons, and it has not been unknown for a Bench to send a pro to prison for beating up some drunken daredevil who wanted to boast that he had stuck one on Jimmy So-and-so, the pride of Stepney.

I didn't realise it at the time but these were the doors I was opening up for the twins when I took them along to the Robert Browning Institute. They were about ten years old. The Institute at the time was allied with the famous Fitzroy Lynn Club which included in its list of members such names as Tommy McGovern, Dicky and Danny O'Sullivan, Freddie King and (no relation) Ronnie King, the Gill brothers from Bethnal Green, Charlie Tucker and the heavyweight Albert Darvil who came from nowhere to take the A.B.A. championship from the holder, Scribham, and literally became famous overnight in amateur boxing circles.

Ted Bunnett and Charlie Sims were resident trainers at the Institute, which was in Trafalgar Street, Walworth, not far from the Elephant and Castle. It was Charlie who watched the twins as they put on an exhibition bout. At the end of a couple of minutes he turned to me.

'Are you telling me these kids haven't been in the ring before?'

I said 'Yes.'

'Bloody amazing,' he said. 'Bloody amazing!'

That was the start of the twins' amateur boxing career. They represented the Air Training Corps, of which they were members, and their school, Daniel Street. It is, by the way, coincidental that my son Gary was at the same school under its changed name, Daneford Street, with John H. Stracey, who is, as I write, a current contender for championship honours.

During the next three years the twins fought regularly in local and national contests with outstanding success. In the London Schools contests they ran out of opposition for three years running and were obliged to face each other in the finals. There was some controversy about this state of affairs, but it didn't affect the twins. Nobody was going to take the honours from either of them, and since it had to be one or other, then let the best man win. In the even, it turned out two to one in favour of Ronnie with Reggie the victor at the third (and last) meeting.

This was a contest to remember, for they never faced each other in the ring again. I sat with Mum and Dad at the ringside in York Hall, Bethnal Green. I had had a word with the twins beforehand in the dressing room and told them to take it easy, put on a good show, but I had a feeling that Reggie wanted this one to be his, that he had made up his mind to settle the issue at the third meeting. Anyway, there they were, these two diminutive figures sitting in their corners, identical in appearance, surrounded by something like a thousand cheering schoolkids, the announcements were over, the bell rang and the fight was on.

I have seen (and taken part in) some fights in my time, but never a one to equal this. It was a classic. Reggie, the skilful boxer against Ronnie, who would die before giving up. They were both utterly absorbed and entirely committed to winning. More than once I wanted to stand up and shout 'Stop it, stop it!', but somehow I couldn't bring myself to do it, and anyway I had my hands full with Mum and Dad who were both on the point of getting into the ring and putting an end to the fight. The judges may have had some difficulty in awarding points early in the contest due to confusion as to who was who, but there was no doubt about the eventual decision. Ronnie's face was covered in blood in the third and final two-minute round and Reggie was awarded the fight by unanimous verdict.

Afterwards, in the dressing room, Mum gave them both a real coating, making it more than plain that they would never appear in the ring against each other again as long as she was able to prevent it. The twins burst into tears – they were only thirteen-year-old kids – and promised Mum that it was the last time, while Dad and me stood by feeling a bit awkward.

I can't resist another tilt at our old friends Sir Francis Galton and Dr. Lange (whom God preserve) of Munich. If they had been present in that dressing room their high-flown theories about the 'inner laws of heredity' would have taken a swift kick up the arse. They would have been privileged (and I use the word in its strongest sense) to witness a united East End family take a family decision on a family matter in the good old East End way, with a bit of shouting, a few tears and, in the result, a closer and greater understanding brought about by that greatest of all 'inner laws' – family love.

Oh, yes – I can hear you saying it. What's Charlie Kray doing, talking about family love! Has he gone soft in the head or something?

All right, I'll tell you what I'm talking about. Whoever you are, wherever you come from, if you are a member of a family cast your mind back to something that happened to the family, something that maybe was trivial to the outsider but important to you. Then, when you've swallowed the lump in your throat and wiped the tears from your eyes, think . . .

Because we're all human.

Except perhaps for Sir Francis Galton and Dr. Lange (whom God preserve) of Munich and a few others I intend to name.

With that bit of spleen out of my system, I'll get back to the nitty-gritty.

I'd just come home to Vallance Road after a spell in the Royal Navy, about nine months as a rating with most of my active service spent in the boxing ring. I became a matelot by the simple business of volunteering. I was advised at the Naval Cadets that it would be better for me to volunteer for the Navy before I was called up for National Service, when I would be liable to be posted into any section of the Armed Forces, but I fancied the Navy so in I went.

My boxing reputation preceded me. No sooner was I out of the train than I was in the gym with the PT instructor for a try-out and from then on my career was mapped out for me. I was a natural welter-weight, about ten and a half stone, and I had developed a useful right hand which put paid to a few aspiring representatives of the Army and the Air Force in the inter-services competitions in which I represented the Royal Navy. Of course there were occasions when I met up with somebody who carried heavier armament which taught me to appreciate the old saying, 'You can't win 'em all.' Still, I did my best and got my rewards in the shape of the perks that come the way of boxers in the Forces such as freedom from many of the irksome restrictions of a sailor's life, the little extras over and above the normal rations, the admiration and support of my fellow matelots and, above all, the opportunity to increase my boxing skills in actual contests.

The war was over by this time, but during the demobilisation period men had to be kept occupied and also entertained. Boxing shows were popular, and I found myself fighting on an average once a week, first in Cardiff and later in Portsmouth. Whether it was the tension of these contests or a legacy of rheumatic fever I don't know, but I began to suffer from blinding headaches which the MO diagnosed as migraine. The upshot was that I went before the Medical

Board and was discharged from the Navy on health grounds.

Back in Civvy Street the headaches disappeared. I teamed up with Dad once more and fell back into the routine of work and training and, after a short while, it was as though I had never been away. Mum, as usual, was doing wonders with the rations. As for the twins, they had come on rapidly during the time I was away. They were fighting regularly representing Daniel Street School, the Air Training Corps and Robert Browning Institute, which meant a very crowded programme for a couple of kids who hadn't yet reached their fourteenth birthday. As was to be expected they had become well known in the area, the famous fighting twins of Bethnal Green with their pictures appearing regularly in the East London Advertiser over the records of their victories. I had signed as a pro in the welterweight division and made a good start by victories at Watford in Eddie Mallett's competition (where I picked up fifteen quid) and over Jack Allen, a Whitstable welter. The judges at Watford included Jack Solomons, the famous boxing promoter, who congratulated me on my performance.

I'd like to mention here what I consider one of Reggie's best performances in the ring. Before the war, probably the finest amateur boxing club in the East End was the Webbe Boys' Club. When it was re-started after the war ended, the first show was held at Shoreditch Town Hall, and both Reggie and Ronnie took part representing the Club. Ronnie had a decisive win over a boy called Thompson from the Crown and Manor BC, but the fight of the evening for me was the set-to between Reggie and a Jewish boy from Eton Manor called Gold. I don't remember his first name. This boy was good. He later represented Israel in the Olympic Games where he did very well.

I was in Reggie's corner that night. He had already fought three rounds in the preliminaries and another three in the quarter finals and must have been a bit tired, but he went out from the corner like a rocket and really set about Gold. Reggie was a shade ahead on points at the end of the first round, then

Gold made up the leeway and went ahead in the second. The third round was a sizzler. Both were intent on winning and by the end of the round were exhausted. In my book the fight was a draw, but there can be no such decision in amateur boxing, and the victory went to Gold. The points margin must have been a narrow one.

This boy Gold went on to become schoolboy champion of Great Britain in the finals at Hull. Reggie, fighting in another weight class, was runner up.

All our fights received the maximum publicity, mainly due to the news value of that rare happening in boxing circles, the appearance of identical twins on the same programme. We weren't bad at winning, either.

We became known, the three of us, as the Fighting Krays.

I'd like to look back, with the benefit of hindsight, at that period in the lives of me and my brothers when our boxing exploits marked us out as different from the normal run of East End youngsters.

Looking at myself objectively, I see myself as an easy-going, happy individual, travelling around with Dad 'on the knocker', getting on well with most people, slow to take offence but well able to take care of myself if the occasion arose. I took up professional boxing because I had a talent for, and considerable experience in, that particular trade, because it offered the possibility of picking up prize money and because there was always the chance that I might reach championship standard if I pegged away and got the breaks. I certainly didn't use the ring as an escape valve for some feeling of violence in myself that had to find an outlet, and you can take it from me that very few professional boxers are violent men. In the ring they have a job to do over a specified number of three minute rounds with intervals of one minute, they go in and do that job, they collect their wages and that's it. There are exceptions, of course, but take my word for it, they are few and far between.

I am now going to stick my neck out and say that the

unsavoury face of the noble art is presented not by the fighters, who go into the ring and give of their best, but by the hangers-on, the shady characters who cluster on the outskirts of a successful fighter's entourage, who are tolerated because of some past and tenuous friendship and who bring to what is fundamentally a fine and honourable sport a faint, objectionable odour of criminal activity. All of which is a bit of a mouthful for a self-educated ex-pugilist, but it expresses my feelings precisely.

I didn't have much contact with that sort of thing during my professional career. Although I was one of the Fighting Krays, my brothers were the ones who attracted most attention. They were up in front, not just the grandsons of 'Big' Jimmy Kray and John 'Cannonball' Lee but public figures in their own right with columns of print and news photos to prove it. Yet, and I must tell the truth as I saw it, they did not seem to be unduly affected by their local prominence. They attended school regularly, they didn't keep late hours – if they had they wouldn't have won their fights as they did – they didn't throw their weight about among the other kids in the neighbourhood. The Headmaster at Daniel Street School spoke well of them and the vicar of the local Church, St. James the Great in Bethnal Green Road, who knew them well, had only one complaint about them. They were not regular members of his congregation.

What I am trying to get at in telling my story is the truth, and if there had been to my knowledge anything in the behaviour of my brothers which gave an indication of what was to happen in the future, then I would disclose it. I'm not saying that my brothers were little angels. What I am saying is that they were typical products of their generation and environment, brought up within the confines of the same social and economic conditions as thousands of other kids, with a home background as stable as was possible at the time and a mother who was devoted to their welfare.

The only difference between them and the thousands of other kids is that they were identical twins and were introduced to boxing at an early age. If that is the explanation for their actions when they reached manhood, then I wish to God I had never taken them to the Robert Browning Institute and asked them to put the gloves on for Charlie Sims. I also ask myself the question (and I know they'll forgive me for saying this) why aren't Henry Cooper and his twin brother behind bars?

That's a ridiculous argument, isn't it? Of course it is. That is why I believe the reason is not in the Bavarian criminal twins theory or all the glib psychoanalytical twaddle about psychopathic twin personalities. It's a simple, ordinary explanation that can be understood by simple, ordinary people who, given the facts, can safely be left to draw their own conclusions.

One thing stands out a mile. Somewhere along the line something went wrong. What it was and how it happened will be made clear to the best of my ability. I don't propose to tell a pack of lies or try to whitewash anybody because it wouldn't serve any useful purpose.

I haven't yet dealt at any great length with the criminal side of the environment in which we grew up. It is a well-known fact that Bethnal Green, Hoxton, Shoreditch and the surrounding areas contained the highest percentage of criminals in the Metropolitan Police records. In our manor of Bethnal Green there wasn't much to choose between the police and the criminals; they were merely on different sides of the same fence, they all knew each other, they maintained a sort of truce with reservations and, providing some semblance of law and order was maintained, and a certain number of convictions obtained, nobody grumbled. In a way it was quite a gentlemanly business with the rules very properly observed by both sides. 'Straight' people had no part in the game and the only unsavoury contributions to it were made by the informers or 'snouts' and the 'bent' coppers who were tolerated as necessary evils.

Naturally we Krays were known to the police. It wasn't

because we were felons, but 'Big' Jimmy and the Southpaw Cannonball were characters and Dad was listed as a deserter from the Armed Forces; I was a professional boxer and the columns of the East London Advertiser were rarely without some mention of the twins' boxing exploits, suitably illustrated of course. Yet the Old Bill didn't bother us unduly. For example, it was a well-known fact that, when I left the house in the morning, I had a rendez-vous with Dad, and any copper who wanted to make a bit of a name for himself had only to follow me and ten to one he would be in a position to make a pinch; but I only had one spot of trouble, which was when a couple of the local law pulled me off a bus in Bethnal Green Road and accused me of being my father. It didn't take them long to discover that I had a cast-iron alibi – they were twenty years out of date!

There was one incident which sticks out in my memory. There was a police constable who lived in Vallance Road – in fact he was the *only* police constable who lived in Vallance Road – who, during the war, was a special, one of those public-spirited citizens who believed that the best way of helping the war effort was to keep an eye on the members of his own team. When the war ended he became a regular. For some reason he seemed to have a down on me, and frequently stopped me and made me turn out the contents of my bag which invariably contained nothing more sinister than the proceeds of the day's collection. The world has its complement of annoying bastards and this was one of them. It seemed to amuse him to see me empty the bag on the pavement and then stuff the gear back into it after he had shoved it around with his foot. I swallowed this performance a few times but finally one day I lost my temper.

'All right – turn out the bag,' he said.

I said: 'Bollocks!'

'Turn it out – or I'll take you down the nick.'

I moved a few paces back and beckoned to him.

'Come on. Under the arches, mate!'

Everybody knew what that meant, including him. Under

the arches was a favourite spot for settling differences.

He said: 'And what will you do there...'

I said: 'I'll beat your fucking brains out!'

He weighed about fourteen stone to my ten-and-a-half and he knew I meant what I said. He turned to walk away.

He said: 'Just watch it, that's all. Just watch it!'

I had no further trouble with him. Some time later he committed suicide. Nobody could stand him, including his wife and kids, and I suppose he got to the point where he couldn't stand himself.

That was the way of it in Bethnal Green. You couldn't allow too many liberties or you might as well move out of the district.

If I said here and now that we had no contact with the criminal element you would call me a liar and you'd be quite right. The three of us had been at school with boys who grew up to be thieves and tearaways. More than once we were offered bent gear (stolen goods) but we refused it, not on moral grounds but simply because it was not good business. The Old Bill had no time for receivers (known as dabblers) for a very practical reason. They gave the thief a quick way of getting rid of the loot and stood in the way of the recovery of a lot of property a proportion of which was looked upon by the Old Bill as their 'perks'.

This was the way it worked. A blag mob would pull a job and the Old Bill, tipped off by some snout or other, would catch them bang to rights in possession of the loot. The mob would be tried and convicted and the stolen property would be returned to its lawful owner, less a few easily negotiable articles or a bit of cash which had unaccountably gone missing. The lawful owner would be so pleased at the return of the major part of his possessions that he would say nothing, the blag mob would know nothing and a couple of the Old Bill would spend their next holiday in a three star hotel instead of a bed-and-breakfast gaff.

We certainly weren't three starry-eyed innocents, we were perfectly aware of what went on round us, but we were able to stand aloof from the lawbreakers and assorted villains on two counts. First, the business provided us with an adequate income and second, we took our boxing seriously. You can't hang around on street corners or in cafes until the early hours of the morning and then get up at six a.m. for roadwork, and sparring with the Old Bill is a very negative form of training for a fight. In a way we occupied a unique position. The Old Bill didn't bother us because they knew we were straight. The hard cases in the neighbourhood, with a few exceptions, gave us no aggravation because they knew they were on a hiding to nothing if they came any of the old nonsense. Of course there were times when we had to prove a point by direct action and this happened now and then but not very often.

There is one feature of East End life that outsiders find difficult to understand; the age-old feuds between one area and another, the causes of which took place so long ago that they have been forgotten. Only the enmity remains. There had always been feuding between the rival factions of Bethnal Green and Watney Street, an area on the other side of Commerical Road not far from the scene of the notorious Sydney Street siege. Sometimes at week-ends a group of bored young toughs would take it into their heads to stray into enemy territory looking for some excitement in the form of a punch-up with the traditional opposition. There was no rhyme or reason in this, it was just habit, and it was all juvenile and senseless. Nevertheless it was there.

In the main the youths of Bethnal Green sought their amusement in the dance halls and cinemas of the Whitechapel and Mile End Roads, while their counterparts from Watney Street favoured the Commercial Road area. Inside the V formed by Whitechapel Road to the north and Commercial Road to the south with its point at Aldgate East was neutral territory. If a gang of youths from Watney Street were seen in Whitechapel Road on a Saturday night (or vice versa) it was a certain sign that there was going to be trouble.

It was one of those Saturday evenings in early June when even Bethnal Green can look beautiful. I forget where I spent the evening, but I know I came home later than usual. Mum was in the kitchen, rather worried because the twins weren't in. I persuaded her to go to bed, which she did, and about an hour or so afterwards the twins turned up. They looked as though they had been dragged through a hedge backwards. I asked them what was up, but they behaved as though I wasn't there, went into the kitchen and washed and tidied themselves and went to bed.

A couple of days later I found out what had happened. The twins had gone to meet a friend in a cafe in the Commercial Road, they had been seen and instantly recognised by a yobbo from Watney Street and, when they came out of the cafe, they faced a mob-handed collection of Watney Street hooligans bent on teaching these Bethnal Green Krays to stay on their own manor. According to reports, the twins didn't wait for the usual exchange of insults leading to jostling and finally confrontation. They sailed into the gang, laid six of them on the pavement stone cold, and stood there as the rest scarpered.

Something like this was bound to happen sooner or later. The story was told and re-told, embellishments were added, until finally what had been a brief encounter when nothing more lethal than fists were used became a full-scale gang fight, bicycle chains and the lot, with the twins blamed for leading a Bethnal Street band into forbidden territory.

I think it was then that the twins tasted real power for their first time. They were accustomed to victory in the ring, to defeating a single opponent, but this was different. With only their hands, backed by a refusal to recognise the odds against them, they had scattered a bunch of young toughs who outnumbered them six to one, causing considerable damage to several of them in the process.

There was another aspect of this incident. The twins could no longer remain aloof from street fighting. Watney Street could not take this defeat lying down, and reprisals were planned. The young villains of Bethnal Green went into action against the enemy with gusto, and inevitably the twins were drawn into the conflict since it was against them in particular that revenge was sought. As one of the Fighting Krays I was also embroiled to some extent and I was obliged to keep my eyes open and be prepared in case some of the Watney Street lot took it into their heads to sort me out.

All this, I am convinced, marked a turning point in the twins' life. The transition was rapid and inexorable. Their schooldays were over and they had collected all the honours possible as schoolboy champions. They had time on their hands and began to spend it in pursuits which they kept secret from Mum, Dad and me. They stayed out late and neglected their roadwork which is an indispensable part of a fighter's training schedule and, as I was soon to discover, they made a habit of dropping into Aunt Rose's house before coming home to remove the traces of the street battles in which they were becoming involved.

I did not take my responsibility as the elder brother lightly. I tried to talk to the twins, but I might as well have saved my breath. Literally overnight they had become men and left their boyhood behind, and in that new man's world they made their own decisions and faced up to the consequences. They had not yet reached their fifteenth birthday!

During that long, hot summer of 1948 I had many things on my mind. There was still a war-time flavour in the air for, even though bread rationing ended in July, there were shortages of things like sugar and meat. Dad and me still had to exercise a bit of care as we went about our business, as he was still liable to be picked up as a deserter. Yet my main worry was over the twins. I foresaw a packet of trouble in the near future.

There were grounds for my worries. During the war and for the following couple of years the streets of the East End had been comparatively free of violence. Many of the youths who could have caused trouble were away in the country during the war as part of the evacuation scheme, and young men of military age were either in the Forces, drafted into industry or on the trot. But now, along with the relaxing of many of the controls which had been so necessary in wartime, there seemed to be an increase in licence. Teenagers in groups roamed the streets looking for excitement and street battles were on the increase. That the twins were concerned in these outbursts of violence was pretty evident – in fact they could only have opted out by leaving the district. Additionally, because they were tough and incredibly fearless with a natural talent for leadership, they were out in front when the battles were on. There was nothing that I, or anybody else, could do about it. The process of violence, once started, marches on, and the rest is in the hands of Providence.

As summer passed my own and very private life entered a new phase. Just after my discharge from the Navy I had met a girl with whom I fell very deeply in love. She was the youngest of four sisters (there were two younger brothers also), father being a respected Poplar man who had been in the Merchant Navy, worked in the London docks and graduated to a position in the Customs & Excise. Her name was Dolly Moore. She was beautiful and very understanding – she had to be, with a boy-friend dedicated to boxing and early nights – and we had decided to marry.

Both Mum and Dad approved of her and the twins accepted her as a future sister-in-law. The only snag was the fact that a young married couple had no chance of setting up in a home of their own at that time unless they fancied living on a bombed site. Mum solved that problem in characteristic fashion. The gym on the upper floor of 178 Vallance Road was dismantled, the room re-decorated and furnished and Dolly and I started our honeymoon there after we married on Christmas Day 1948.

Exactly one week later I stepped into the ring at Leyton Baths for my first professional fight, a four round supporting bout against a welter named Jack Allen who came from Whitstable. I leave to the imagination the ribald comments from my friends at the ringside. Suffice it to say that oysters were freely mentioned in several contexts, all of them unprintable.

I cruised home an easy winner on points.

THREE

Shortly after my release from Maidstone I accepted an invitation to appear on Thames Television's programme Today.

In the hospitality room at the Euston House studio the producer of the programme pressed a very large gin and tonic into one of my hands and a typed sheet containing a list of the questions I was likely to be asked into the other. He must have forgotten to give a copy of the list to interviewer Bill Grundy. When I got in front of the cameras the questions I was asked bore no relation to those on the typewritten list. I shall know better next time.

Brother Grundy, after some preliminary skirmishing, informed me that he was himself the father of three boys and that the eldest had considerable influence over his younger brothers. Did I not, he asked me, have some influence over *my* younger brothers, and if so, why didn't I use it to control them during their early years? This was a rhetorical question. I started to say that the twins were very stong personalities, but he was off on another tack before I had got the words out of my mouth. I could have told him that the twins were not the sons of a television personality and that they were brought up in another era and a different life-style – but maybe he knew these things without being told and wasn't really interested in my answer.

The point is that the answer is the same today as it was

twenty seven years ago. Even at the age of fifteen my brothers were really grown men taking their own decisions and acting on them. If they came unstuck they wouldn't come crying to me or asking my advice about what they should do, but take the consequences and make the best of it. Remember they had been boxing ever since they were ten years old, and in the ring there is neither time nor space for family conferences as to whether you should belt the other fellow in the guts or on the chin. Advice is given before the fight and in between rounds, but for the rest you are on your own.

When the twins finished their schooling they went to work in Billingsgate fish market. This was their own choice. The work was heavy but well-paid and there was another angle which didn't escape my notice. Fish, as the advertisements say, is Nature's brain and nerve food. Humping cases of it also puts muscles in places where most people only have places. It was the same as doing weight lifting, only it was paid for. As a consequence the twins, who had never been exactly puny, stripped off as true lightweights, just under the nine stone mark which, taking their height into consideration, meant that they didn't carry an ounce of surplus fat. They were still fighting as amateurs but developing along slightly different lines. Reggie was the boxer, cool and scientific, seeming to have a built-in knowledge of ringcraft. Ronnie lacked some of the finer points but his courage and pertinacity were beyond question.

For the three of us, during that early period of my marriage, boxing was our whole life. As a professional I was much in demand by the local promoters because I always gave of my best and they could be assured of a crowd-pleasing performance from me. I fought in the welterweight division, which didn't receive the publicity (or the pay) of the heavies, but I was on to between five and ten pounds a fight which in those days was a fair amount of money even after my manager, Ted Bebber, had taken his percentage.

The money wasn't the most important consideration. Dad and me were making a good living on the knocker, for he was a skilful buyer and sometimes brought off a very profitable deal in the old jewellery line which boosted my wages. But I was in my early twenties, fit and strong, and there was always the chance that I would be noticed and taken up by one of the leading promoters, as had happened to some of my contemporaries who went on to fame and fortune. So I took on everything that came my way, promotions at the famous Mile End Arena where many a future champion had slung his first right-hander, Hoxton, Stepney, Leyton, West Ham, there I would be with my bag of boxing gear, often accompanied by the twins who would watch points from the ringside and learn techniques which they later put to use when they signed professional forms.

I gained a reputation as a useful and reliable fighter, but somehow the big break never materialised. I suppose I didn't have that little extra touch of class which takes a man out of the ruck of supporting bouts and into the champions' league. But I was proud of my skills and the local fame I enjoyed as a professional boxer in my own right and as the eldest of the three Fighting Krays.

To get away from boxing for a moment and into the social scene of the area in which we lived, we were often called on to assist in the various functions organised by the local church (St. James the Great in Bethnal Green Road) and the youth clubs of which the twins were members. These do's were an important feature of the life of the East Enders, an escape from the daily round of work and bed, and they threw themselves into the festivities with gusto. There were all kinds of jobs to be done as part of the organisation of such affairs, knocking up stalls for jumble sales and so on, and the three of us were well to the fore in these activities. We made a friend for life in the vicar of St. James Church, the Rev. Hetherington. The twins liked and admired him and would go to considerable lengths to oblige him whenever he asked a favour of them.

That was the way of things for us, the family life at Vallance Road built around Mum and my wife with Grandfather Lee and Mum's sisters in the background and Uncle Johnnie's cafe opposite, with Dad dropping in from time to time, all very cosy and seeming to be as solid as the Rock of Gibraltar. Although rationing of certain necessities had not been ended, the days of war had become a dim memory. We ate well, slept well and everything went well. It was almost too good to last – and it didn't.

As I have mentioned earlier, as a family we enjoyed fairly good relations with the police. We were all known to them as straight, honest people. Even Dad's little escapade was accepted tolerantly with the passage of time. There is a delicate balance between the police and the residents of a tough manor which is largely preserved by the older and wiser members of the force. Every nick has its Sergeant Dixon (the fatherly television copper at Dock Green). By the same token there are to be found the young and comparatively inexperienced officers, passionate guardians of what they believe to be law and order, avid for promotion, whose zeal in carrying out their duties may be commended by magistrates but are often frowned on by their superiors.

One of these eager beavers was Police Constable Donald Baynton who was on duty in Bethnal Green Road on a certain Saturday afternoon in October of 1950. Seeing a number of youths who appeared to him to be obstructing the pavement he told them to 'move along, please', though he may not have used those exact words. One of the youths made some kind of comment whereupon P.C. Baynton, the sort of man who would stand no nonsense, gave him a violent push. He was immediately on the receiving end of a right hook to the jaw, because the youth who was pushed was my brother Ronnie, who didn't take kindly to being pushed by anyone, not even a police officer in uniform.

Of course Ronnie was arrested. He went quietly with the officer, having realised immediately that his action in slipping over a right hook, although automatic, was hasty and ill-advised. What happened thereafter was a prime example of a molehill growing into a mountain in a very short space of time.

Reggie had followed the pair at a discreet distance as they made their way to Bethnal Green nick and had waited outside, confident that Ronnie would soon come out. It wasn't Ronnie who came out, however. It was P.C. Baynton, looking like the cat that has stolen the cream. He told Reggie to get the hell out of it or he (Baynton) would give him what had just been given to his brother, accompanying the threat with the significant gesture of smashing his fist into the palm of his other hand. Reggie called him a dirty name and turned and ran, not in fear but with the aim of luring Baynton round the nearest corner, and out of sight of the nick. Once round that corner, Reggie faced the gallant constable and coolly and scientifically gave him the beating of his life – I saw the result later that day – then went home.

I was indoors when Reggie came in and told me the story. I didn't waste any time in going down to the nick to find out what was happening, and when I saw Ronnie I went spare. He was in a dreadful state, his face a mass of cuts and bruises and only just conscious. The Old Bill had given him the full treatment, the sort of going-over they dished out to hardened tearaways. I swear it made me feel sick just to look at him. I didn't mince my words, and only left the station when they threatened to nick me as well, but I promised them that I would be back with a doctor and they would hear more about it.

When I got back to Vallance Road the local inspector from Bethnal Green was there with the eager beaver. I must say that Reggie had made a good job of this fellow, who looked almost as bad as Ronnie, and I couldn't help feeling that rough justice had been done. However, that doesn't satisfy the law and Reggie, having been identified as the assailant, was duly arrested. I told the inspector that I had seen with my own eyes what had happened to Ronnie, I intended to cause as much trouble as I could and, if they tried to do the same to Reggie then all hell would be let loose.

To be quite fair the inspector was ignorant of the fact that Ronnie had been beaten up and he gave me his word that nothing would happen to Reggie and also that he would enquire into the whole affair. I knew, by the way, that this inspector had been on friendly terms with Dad. He was actually a very nice and reasonable sort of man.

That was the sequence of events but the damage had been done. Ronnie, although he didn't refer to it, never forgot what transpired that Saturday afternoon in Bethnal Green nick, grown men standing round him, fists and boots going in, the ineffectual attempts to protect himself and the indignity of finding himself on the floor over and over again. He took it and didn't complain, but the resentment was there. Reggie, too, was not unaffected by the proceedings. He had taken on a grown man, a tough copper bigger and heavier than he was, and had left him lying on the pavement spark out – and he had done this with his fists.

In the end, of course, reason prevailed. The Old Bill had more important things to do than start a feud with a local family. They got hold of Dad, not to nick him (which they quite easily could have done) but to let him know that they didn't propose to make a song and dance about the incident unless they were forced to. The implication was quite clear. If I kept my mouth shut there would be no comeback. If I kicked up a fuss, then they would make a start by nicking Dad and then come down on the family like a load of bricks and do their best to make life unpleasant for us. There was nothing I could do but swallow it. The twins duly appeared before Mr. Harold Sturge at Old Street, no mention was made of Ronnie's injuries, they were both given probation and the magistrate commended P.C. Baynton for his courage. I've no doubt the station inspector also had words with the young constable, in fact he may well have been transferred to another manor for we never saw him again.

I have given considerable space to this particular event because it was the first time I had been directly involved in any trouble concerning the twins. There had been a fight outside a dance hall in Mare Street, Hackney the previous March and the twins had been gathered in with some others.

The case went to the Old Bailey, not because the twins were involved but because one of the victims had been badly damaged by a weapon, a length of bicycle chain. The twins were discharged, as I felt sure they would be. I knew them well enough to be convinced that, if they wished to give anybody a hiding, they would do it with their hands and not with bicycle chains.

To my mind there were a lot of questions to which I didn't know the answers. Had someone in the nick made a remark about the twins after their discharge, perhaps to the effect that they were a pair of fucking nuisances and someone should do something about them? Did the gallant young constable recognise Ronnie and Reggie and set out to make a reputation for himself? Did a couple of colleagues set about Ronnie in the absence of senior officers? Did Baynton deliberately provoke Reggie? Who knows?

I don't intend to make excuses. Ronnie was in the wrong when he punched the policeman, but the later events point up a conclusion that will become more apparent as my story unfolds. It is that violence begets violence which in turn breeds greater violence until finally the situation becomes out of control and everybody is left wondering what went wrong – and where.

I mentioned earlier that imprisonment gives a man plenty of time to think and to get to know himself. It also puts him out of circulation and gives his enemies carte blanche to even up old scores without fear of reprisal. In addition the coast is clear for all kinds of cranks and publicity hunters to spread the most incredible stories in print and by word of mouth.

When Nipper Read and his Avenging Angels rounded up The Firm at 6 a.m. on Wednesday the 9th of May 1968 there was no shortage of characters to leap upon the Kray bandwagon. Public bar oracles with shady pasts gargled through mouthfuls of free pints, 'Oh, yers, knew the twins when they were kids, I did. Proper terrors they were, always going about with knives and guns, terrorised folk. Good riddance, I say.' Henry 'Buller' Ward, sneak thief, ponce, bully and the biggest toe-rag I ever met, publicly proclaimed that he had often thought of doing away with the Krays either by running them down with a motor-car (he was such a bad driver he would have missed us anyway) or lying in wait with a rifle on the arches overlooking 178 Vallance Road. People who knew us told what they knew with embellishments and some who had never even seen us invented the most hair-raising stories.

If what was said and printed were to be believed, the youthful Krays spent the great majority of their time creating mayhem in Bethnal Green and adjacent manors, rushing around armed with various weapons of offence ranging from bicycle chains to shooters, waging war on the police and frightening innocent citizens out of their lives.

Which is a load of rubbish to which the facts give the lie. Anyone who knows anything about boxing (amateur or professional) is aware that the sport calls for total dedication. What with earning a living, roadwork, gym sessions and appearances in the ring, there is no spare time for hooliganism or anything else, except the good night's sleep which is essential to physical fitness.

I want to say, right here and now, and I would swear it on a stack of Bibles, that at no time during our youth and early manhood did we use a weapon of any description. If we were involved in any trouble we relied on courage and the ability to use our fists to get out of it.

Actually, we didn't need anything else.

It was a big night at the Albert Hall on December 11th 1951. Topping the bill was a ten-round contest between Tommy McGovern, lightweight champion of Great Britain and one of my contemporaries at the Robert Browning Club, and Allan Tanner of British Guiana. Of the seven supporting bouts, five of them featured fighters from Bethnal Green; bantam Ron Johnson, middleweight Jimmy Davies and the three Kray brothers, myself at welterweight and the twins at lightweight.

It was the first time the three of us had appeared together on the same bill.

There was a capacity crowd. The special ringside seats at three guineas were packed, as were other seats at prices ranging from two guineas down to the humble half-dollar. A large Bethnal Green contingent had made the journey from the East End to cheer on their local lads and perhaps pick up a few bob on the side, though betting was strictly prohibited!

For me and my brothers this was the crowning point of a year that had been full and rewarding. On July 1st, the day on which the state of war between Great Britain and Germany officially ended, the twins started their very own private war (in the nicest sense) by turning professional. Two days later Dolly, my wife, presented me with a son and heir whom we named Gary.

The twins started their professional career in fine style with five joint appearances in which they brought off the double every time, to the great delight of their manager, Jack Jordan, the Bethnal Green fight fans and, naturally, the Lees and the Krays. The fifth double I remember vividly. It was a charity tournament at the Lime Grove Baths organised by Alf Mancini junior in aid of the dependants of Wally Davis. That Grand Old Man of Boxing, Patsy Hagate, acted as Master of Ceremonies. Since it was a charity do, the rounds were of two minutes duration instead of the usual three.

Reggie was booked to meet a fellow called Steve Cooney, but he withdrew at the last minute for some reason or other and Bill Sliney of King's Cross came in as substitute. This lad was very clever, much more experienced than Reggie and managed by Dave Crowley who didn't make a habit of picking losers. I thought Reggie was overmatched, but I needn't have worried because he put on an impeccable performance and gained a points decision. Incidentally, Ronnie was to meet this same Bill Sliney on the Albert Hall bill some six weeks later.

Ronnie's fight that evening was a real turn-up for the book. He was fighting George Goodsell of Cambridge, a useful lad with a big punch into which Ronnie walked before the fight was really started and he went down for a count of nine. The only person in Lime Grove who wasn't convinced that it was all over bar shouting was Ronnie. He came up off the deck and filled in the remainder of the first round with a two-fisted assault on the surprised Goodsell that brought the crowd to its feet. In the second round it was Ronnie all the way, though I could see that he hadn't fully recovered from that knock down in the first round. Round three was a sizzler. Ronnie came out of his corner like a thunderbolt, hammered Goodsell with combination punches that rocked him back on his heels and put him away for the count with a right that would have made a hole in a brick wall.

Three weeks later the twins were in action again, this time on a full professional bill at the National Sporting Club, which had just moved back into the lush surroundings of the Empress Club in Berkeley Square. Reggie did his usual first-class job on Bobby Wood from Northampton, a faultless performance against a really useful lad and one that was greatly appreciated by the dinner-jacketed audience. One gent was so impressed that he went up to Reggie as he was leaving the ring and thrust a bundle of notes into his hand which turned out to be twenty-five quid.

Ronnie was out of luck on this occasion and ended the run of double victories by being disqualified in the second round. He was fighting a chap called Sherlock from Oxford, who seemed to be in a hurry to get back there or to get away from Ronnie, I'm not sure which. Anyway he back-pedalled round the ring, chased by a very frustrated Ronnie who literally had to grab him to get a punch in. The referee cautioned Ronnie twice in the first round for holding, and disqualified him before the second round was more than a few seconds old. I thought it was a pity that the twins' unbroken run of victories should be ended by a disqualification. So did the British Boxing Board of Control which fined him fifty bob.

Talking about money, it is interesting to record that the twins received seven pounds each for the Lime Grove show and twelve pounds ten shillings for the NSC effort, both less manager's commission of twenty-five per cent. Ronnie's take home pay for chasing Mr. Sherlock round the ring for just over three minutes amounted to six pounds seventeen shillings and sixpence, not a princely sum by any standards. Still, he got a consolation prize in the shape of half of Reggie's nobbins.

Then came the big occasion, Jack Cappell's promotion at the Albert Hall a fortnight before Christmas of 1951. In those days when Jack Solomons reigned supreme over the fight game, a boxer had really arrived when he appeared either at the Albert Hall or Harringey Arena. It took me eighteen victories in twenty contests to make the Albert Hall. For the twins it was their seventh joint appearance as professionals and they had celebrated their eighteenth birthday in the October. This was a remarkable achievement and the only time in the history of British boxing that any fighter had made it to the Albert Hall after only six fights and at the age of eighteen. The twins made it a double.

Behind the bright lights and the yelling crowd at an international boxing tournament there is always a human story. The twins had already been booked to appear when John Sharpe, the matchmaker, had a brilliant idea, which was to get me on the same bill as my brothers. I had decided some time before this to quit the ring and in fact I had not had a fight for several months, but a young welter from Aldgate by the name of Lew Lazar was looking for another victory to add to his unbeaten record. Although I was a bit rusty after my long lay-off I was quite fit, I could do with a little extra money for Christmas so I took on the bout for a purse of twenty-five quid and the chance of upsetting Lew Lazar's applecart.

So there we were, the three of us, sitting in the dressing room, ready to go out and do battle. We had the first three fights on the bill. Ronnie was the first to go against Bill Sliney of King's Cross, who had been decisively beaten by Reggie at Lime Grove in October. In the first round, after a clash of heads, Ronnie emerged with a cut eye, but he had clobbered Sliney to such effect that the King's Cross lad wasn't all that anxious to come out for the second round. His manager and second Dave Crowley, persuaded him to carry on and in the result Ronnie, who as has been mentioned before, would die rather than give in, lost on points.

Reggie was next, drawn against Bob Manito of Clapham. There was no doubt about the outcome of this fight and Reggie sailed away to a points victory in his habitual cool and scientific fashion.

It was my turn. From the dressing rooms to the ring at the Albert Hall is a long walk which even the cheers of the Bethnal Green fans couldn't shorten. Gloved up in my corner I waited for the announcements to finish, went to the centre of the ring to get the final admonitions from the referee, back to the corner and last minute advice from my trainer and second, Harry 'Kid' Berry, and the fight was on.

I was an experienced professional fighter, I knew all the tricks of the trade, but I learned one important lesson that night, which was never to step into a ring unless you are fighting fit. My timing was all to pot, I ran out of wind, I couldn't put my punches together and Lew Lazar was all ready to knock seven shades of shit out of me. I took two counts of nine in the first two rounds, but pride wouldn't let me stay down. In the third my opponent wound one up from his ankles which connected with my guts and that was it. I couldn't breathe, I was down on my hands and knees and the referee got to ten before I did.

It was my twenty-first pro fight, my third defeat and I never donned the gloves again in public. Nor did the twins. Reggie, who would have been a champion, and Ronnie, who might have been, received their calling-up papers for compulsory military service. The first appearance together of the Fighting Krays marked the end of their brief and meteoric career.

I took my twenty-five quid (less manager's commission) and, amongst other things, bought my six-month-old son a white fur coat for Christmas. He didn't say much but I am sure he was delighted. It was a good Christmas at Vallance

Road, Mum and Dad, Dolly and me and the twins and our relatives, all happy and jolly together.

My wife Dolly has not been prominent in this narrative so far. I suppose that, in common with the rest of the male chauvinistic pigs (a contemporary label attached to married men which has only recently come to my attention) I tended to take for granted the female involvement in family life. But just as Mum was a good mother, so Dolly was a good wife in the best East End tradition, deeply concerned for the welfare of her husband and, when our son came along, totally committed to his well-being.

I remember very vividly a couple of incidents, one before our marriage and the other after the event, which should have given me a lead to Dolly's subsequent behaviour while I was away in prison. While we were still courting Dolly often spent the night at Vallance Road, and would share Mum's bed in the upstairs part of the house. I slept in the same room as the twins downstairs. One night there was a hell of a crash – it was about 3 a.m. – and I got up and went into the hall to find Dolly in her night clothes, smothered in blood from a deep cut on her face. It transpired that she had suddenly leapt from the bed and dived through the window, frame and all, obviously in the throes of a nightmare, bounced off the scullery roof and landed up in the yard. She could have been killed.

The other incident was, in a way, rather funny. I was fighting at Watford in a welterweight competition put on by Eddie Mallett and judged by John Lewis, the Labour M.P. for Bolton, Jack Solomons and Benny Huntman. Dolly was at the ringside, and I was in the dressing room, having qualified for the semi-final. She watched the man I was to meet knock out his opponent in the first round and promptly fled from the hall. She came back when it was all over to find that she needn't have worried. I won the competition and the fifteen pound purse. I have never known to this day whether she was concerned about my probable fate at the hands of the KO merchant or my prospects of missing the prize money.

Me and my brothers were never actively engaged in the

noble art after our Albert Hall appearance, although at a later time we met and entertained many famous fighters; Joe Louis, Rocky Marciano, Sonny Liston, Billy Walker, Henry Cooper and so on. When we wished each other a happy new year on the first of January 1952 I was just another ex-pugilist now a full-time wardrobe dealer and the twins, who had turned in their jobs at Billingsgate, were in that vacuum between being called up for military service and being informed where to report and when. They came out on the knocker with Dad and myself to fill in the time but they couldn't be expected to show much enthusiasm. They were finally ordered to report at the Tower of London for service with the Royal Fusiliers, and off they went one morning early in March, not knowing quite what to expect but confident that they could deal with it whatever it might be.

They were back home in time for tea and, according to Mum, they were in a foul temper and refused to comment on what had happened. When Dad and me got back in the evening they had gone out, they returned home after we had gone to bed and the next morning the police were round to pick them up as deserters. I discovered later that they had taken exception to a corporal's attitude, one of them had punched the NCO on the chin and they had severed their connection with the Royal Fusiliers on the spot.

I could understand and, to a certain extent, sympathise with them. The twins would take orders but only from someone who was in their opinion competent to give them. I had never known them to disobey a trainer's or manager's instructions, they had the true self-discipline which is the mark of a good fighter, but when the second lowest form of animal life in the Army came the old acid they dealt with the matter quickly, efficiently and without wasting time and energy in argument. I could visualise the scene, the twins quietly taking things in, poised and self-assured, the corporal not quite certain how to deal with these two strange identical objects and falling back on the standard Army procedure. 'If you don't know what do do, shout.' No wonder they thumped him. I would probably have done the same thing myself, though I'm an easy-going sort of chap.

Still, whatever the rights and wrongs of the matter, the twins were in it right up to their stubborn necks. From then on it was Reggie and Ronnie Kray versus the Army, because they had made up their minds that they wanted no part of an institution that, to use their own expressive description, 'gave a prick the right to make cunts out of people'. But the Army was not easily persuaded that it wanted no part of Reggie and Ronnie Kray and it was at this point that the irresistible force met the immovable object.

Reading back over the last couple of paragraphs I feel that I might be guilty of a lack of objectivity. As I have said, I do not intend to use the whitewash brush, yet facts are facts. My brothers were hard men, conditioned to rebellion against uniformed authority and utterly fearless. In the context of the battle between the Army and the Kray twins somebody had to lose. There was no possibility of compromise. The big question was who would be the winner.

The Army is a large organisation proceeding along well-ordered lines as laid down in King's Rules and Regulations. In order that a Commanding Officer may be in no doubt about the action he should take in any given situation the Regulations provide a comprehensive list of crimes together with the appropriate punishments. Reggie and Ronnie spent an uncomfortable week in the guardroom, were released into the ranks and promptly went on the trot. This time they didn't make the mistake of heading for home, not because they were uncertain about their welcome but simply because that would be the first place the Old Bill would look for them. I'd like to make it quite plain, by the way, that I would have done all I could to help them no matter what the cost. So would Mum and Dad. That's what families are for.

Spring had come to Bethnal Green and also to other parts of London, which was a help to the twins. It's much more comfortable to be hunted in fair weather – ask any fox – and there's something about a touch of sunshine that tends to raise one's spirits. Another thing that helped them in some small measure was that the carrying of identity cards 'to be produced on demand by any person authorised to require such production' had been abolished earlier that year, in February I think, almost seven years after the cessation of hostilities!

When I sat back and thought about the situation and put things in the proper perspective it seemed to me to be such a waste. On December 11th 1951 my brothers were promising young boxers, just past their eighteenth birthday, with one blot on their record for which they had been put on probation. Now, in April of 1952, they were wanted men, on the run, forced into a position in which they had to survive by stealth and cunning and thrown more and more into association with criminals. Of course, the right and proper thing to do, as I pointed out when I saw them from time to time, was to give themselves up, take their medicine and serve out their time in the Army, where they would have facilities to carry on their boxing careers. I argued that they would only be twenty years of age when they would have completed their military service.

It was a waste of breath. They had made up their minds that they wanted none of the Army and that was that. It was inevitable that, sooner or later, they would be picked up – and they were. They had celebrated their nineteenth birthday in freedom but a fortnight later P.C. John Fisher, who knew the twins by sight, saw them in Burdett Road and challenged them. He collected a few swift, sharp punches for his pains and the twins got away, but not for long. The Old Bill caught up with them in the early hours of the following morning, they were duly introduced to the magistrate at Thames Court, Colonel W. E. Batt, who awarded them a month's imprisonment (at the same time awarding P.C. Fisher the sum of seven-and-six) and for the first time in their lives the twins saw the inside of a prison as convicted persons.

That wasn't the end of their troubles. After their sentence they were collected by a military escort and carted off to Canterbury to face a court martial for desertion. They promptly escaped from there, along with a couple of other fellows called Morgan and Bryant, and set off for London on foot. It was winter and they made it as far as Eltham on the outskirts of London, where the four of them were captured, wet, cold and dispirited, by a police motor-cycle patrol. Their journey back to Canterbury was much more comfortable even in handcuffs. The Army was taking no chances with these young desperadoes.

The outcome of all this was that they were tried and sentenced to nine months detention in the glasshouse at Shepton Mallet, the notorious military prison in Somerset where, during the war, a detainee had been brutally beaten to death. I don't think I need to say how the twins reacted to the strict discipline enforced by violence at that establishment. By the time I was able to get down to see them they had gained a formidable reputation. Even the toughest guard thought twice before taking them on. I know it sounds improbable, a couple of youths not yet twenty setting a highly organised military prison by the ears, but it was a fact, as I heard from the CO himself. I was asked to step into the CO's office by a Sergeant-Major. He was a regular Colonel and seemed to be a very decent sort, asked me to sit down and have a cup of tea, offered me a cigarette and started off by telling me that he knew I wasn't responsible for my brother's actions but would like to have a chat with me about them.

First of all he said that what he found difficult to understand was the fact that the twins resolved everything by physical violence and it was impossible to get through to them with words. I explained to him what life was like in the East End, how if anybody threatened you then you hit them first – and hard. This was the world my brothers had been brought up in. I don't think he completely understood what I was trying to get over to him, but he asked me if I would have a word with the twins, I promised I would, and we parted on quite agreeable terms.

I went in then to see my brothers and told them that I had had a chat with the CO, which didn't impress them in the slightest. You can't argue with people in this place, they said, all they understand is a poke in the face, and that's what they'll get from us. There was nothing I could do or say to alter the state of affairs. Actually, Ronnie was much more concerned in telling me how he had put one over on a certain MP who'd been leaning on him rather hard. This chap was outside the cobbler's shop where Ronnie was working at the time, and Ronnie cut his hand slightly, smeared blood over his face and then rushed out to the MP, shouting 'I've done it now, its all over, better get in there!' The guard rushed off, blowing his whistle, but by the time he had returned with reinforcements, quite sure that there had been a murder, Ronnie was back in the shop, his face and hands wiped clean. When they asked him what had happened, Ronnie put on an innocent look. 'Nothing's happened,' he said 'this fellow must be going round the bend. Been working too hard or something.'

Curiously enough there was one chap there, a sergeant, who could do anything with them because they respected him. When he was on duty there was no trouble with the twins. I saw this chap on one of my visits (which weren't frequent because of the distance from London) and he reminded me of the twins' manager, Jack Jordan. He never had any trouble with them either.

It was the twins versus the Army for the rest of their term in Shepton Mallet, after which they were discharged with, needless to say, a bad record. They emerged into Civvy Street with a clean balance sheet, all debts paid but many old animosities remembered, took up life once more in the homely surroundings of 178 Vallance Road and began to look around for something which would earn them a living.

While they were away two important and unrelated events had taken place. On February 4th 1953 the kids of Bethnal Green were able to spend their pocket money on sweets without having to produce coupons at the same time. Whether it was to honour the anniversary of the death of King George the Sixth, who had died in the previous February, or to act as a curtain-raiser to the second important event of that month, was never explained. However Her Majesty Queen Elizabeth the Second, on the 23rd of February, saw fit to grant amnesty to all those who had failed to rally to the colours in the dark days of World War Two, and Dad was free to emerge from the shadows and return to Vallance Road from which, by the way, he had never really been absent, in spirit at least.

During that year important events crowded thick and fast. Iron man Stalin went to meet his Marxist maker, the indomitable Queen Mary died shortly after, Winston Churchill was made a Knight of the Garter, the Duke of Edinburgh received his pilot's wings and Everest was conquered by Colonel John Hunt. The Queen was crowned in one of the few television spectaculars not presented by Lew Grade, Bank Rate was reduced from four to three-and-a-half per cent (no kidding), sugar rationing was ended, the Kray twins and the Army parted company for ever and, during the mildest December in twenty years, I celebrated the fifth anniversary of my marriage. Gary, my son and heir, didn't have much to say about these momentous happenings, but then he was only seventeen months old.

The New Year of 1954 saw us together as a family once more. I was still living at Vallance Road, the housing situation being much the same as when I married.

About this time I had some trouble of my own to attend to, in which I collected the first blot on my record. I was out in the van one day and pulled up at a garage for petrol. There was some building work going on and I noticed some zinc sheeting lying on the ground. I had a word with the bloke who seemed to be in charge, he said it was scrap, I gave him fifty bob for it, shoved it in the van and, so far as I was concerned, that was just another little transaction in the day's work. I was wrong. The next day the Old Bill paid me a call, I was nicked for stealing the zinc, nothing I said made any difference and I was fined five pounds at Stratford Court for larceny. This was the first conviction ever recorded against me. The second was when I came up at the Old Bailey with my brothers fourteen years later.

Naturally I went along to this garage to find the chap who had sold me the zinc, quite prepared to take five quids worth out of his miserable hide, but he was nowhere to be found. I did discover that, whoever he was, he had no right to dispose of anything on the site. I should have had more sense, but it's easy to be wise after the event.

My brothers, after a bit of nosing around in the employment market, decided to go into the wardrobe dealing business. I lent them some money for stock and off they went on the knocker. They did quite well, but they obviously didn't regard this sort of thing as their life's work and were constantly on the look-out for something more their style. I don't know what their style was, and I don't think they did either – until they came across the billiard hall. It was in Eric Street off the Mile End Road, just behind Burdett Road where they had clobbered 'three half-crowns' P.C. Fisher. It was also in Watney Street territory, but that didn't bother the twins, who had already taught the Watney Street gang a lesson and were quite capable of attending to any further education that might be required.

This billiard hall, which was called the Regal (it had once been a flea-pit) boasted fourteen tables and a manager whose business sense was in the inverse ratio to his love of playing snooker. The place was filthy, the tables neglected and the takings minimal. The twins went to the owner with the proposition that they would smarten the place up and put it on a paying basis, out went the snooker-playing manager and Reggie and Ronnie Kray took their first steps into the entertainment business.

The story went around that there had been some strongarm work in the background and that the twins had deliberately instigated brawls in the hall as a means of persuading the owner to come to terms with them, but I doubt that. The twins were not so devious. If they wanted something they would go and ask for it and keep on until they either got it or decided the game wasn't worth the candle. I saw the place myself and gave the twins a hand with the painting and general sprucing up, and it was obvious to me that the owner had got himself a good deal. He drew a few quid every week instead of next to nothing, business boomed and there was no trouble and hence no damage to equipment, unusual in this very tough part of the East End. The twins dealt firmly with any rowdyism, so firmly indeed that the hooligan element either behaved themselves or kept away. Everybody was happy, with the exception of the ex-manager who now had to pay the table charges instead of getting his games for free.

As the weeks went by and the twins settled into their new and congenial role it looked as though everything was coming up roses. There was, however, one thing that I found disturbing. Some of the characters who had been in the glasshouse turned up at the billiard hall as soon as the news got around that Reggie and Ronnie Kray were to be found there. These merchants dropped in either to chat about old times (which wasn't so good) or to bend the twins' ears for a handout (which was worse). On the surface everything seemed to be fine, so I subscribed to the policy of letting sleeping dogs lie and minded my own business. I knew anyway that the twins would not entertain the idea of turning down old mates who had helped them to chivvy the guards at Shepton Mallet, it was all part of their code of accepting people for what they were, not for what they had done. I'm rather that way myself – maybe it's a family characteristic.

One day in the early part of 1954 I called in at the billiard hall to see how things were going. I had been away on business for some weeks, having decided to give the London suburbs a rest and go further afield. Nobody expects an East London billiard hall to look like a tea-shop in Horsham, but I was surprised at the high percentage of tearaways and villains among the clientele at the tables and generally hanging about. There was one really dangerous fellow who seemed to be very much at home, an ex-boxer by the name of Bobby Ramsey who had at one time been a very promising lad indeed. Unfortunately he fell in with the wrong sort of people and for some time was associated with Jack Spot, one of the 'guv'nors' of the West End. Ramsey was much older than the twins and certainly had some influence on them. When I told them that this character was bad news they laughed it off and told me they were quite capable of handling Bobby Ramsey and half-a-dozen more like him, and it suddenly came to me that they were right, that they weren't my kid brothers any more but men in a man's world, and outstanding men at that.

I suppose in a way they admired Ramsey. He had been a successful boxer like them, he had travelled, he could talk with conviction of the men he had known who had made it to the top from humble beginnings by making their own rules and forcing others to obey them. He probably painted rosy pictures of the life these top jollies led, glossing over the terms of imprisonment which were a natural hazard of their dangerous profession and emphasising the rewards which lay around waiting to be picked up by those who were determined enough to go after them. I sincerely believe that Ramsey, more than anyone or anything else, was a decisive factor during a crucial period in my brothers' lives in leading them into further trouble with the law. I don't mean that they were easily led – on the contrary – or that Ramsey deliberately set out to lead them into a life of crime. Not a bit of it. Ramsey was a catalyst, a focal point of combustion, the spark that started a fire.

Look at it like this. Here were a couple of young fellows, identical twins with an identity of thought and opinion who had tasted the intoxication of victory in the boxing ring from a very early age, who had emerged the winners in street fights against considerable odds, beaten the Old Bill and the Army on their own ground and, at the age of twenty-one, were making a success of running their own business, small as it might be. The time they had spent on the run, the month in Wormwood Scrubs and the nine-month gestation period at Shepton Mallet became, in retrospect, minor irritations. The income from the billiard hall, supplemented by other sources some of which may well have been slightly illegal, enabled them to dress well, eat, drink and smoke and hand out the few odd quids to those less well endowed with the wherewithal than themselves. Small wonder, then, that they considered themselves kings on their own small patch and began to think of themselves as invulnerable.

This state of affairs, by the very nature of things, could not last for long. It only needs one bad apple in a basket to start the contamination which turns the rest rotten. There was a dreadful inevitability in the way in which the Regal billiard hall in Eric Street became a meeting place of thieves and villains. There were no fights and no disorder on the premises, as these occurences would have attracted the attention of the Old Bill, but it was there that the plans were made which were brought to fruition elsewhere. The twins at first maintained a neutral position and, so long as their clients caused no trouble, they were welcome. In any case some of them were friends from the old days of Wormwood Scrubs and Shepton Mallet. In all probability the twins were in the habit of helping some of these merchants through a sticky patch but, like good businessmen, they saw to it that whatever went out came back with interest if a particular individual had a good tickle. Immoral, yes, illegal, perhaps, but money is money wherever it comes from. Ask Sir Denys Lowson.

The twins seemed to be sitting pretty, but when you're mixed up with thieves and villains trouble is never far away. It came in the shape of a mixture of Bobby Ramsey and the Watney Street mob. Ramsey had got himself into a battle with some of the mob in the course of which a chap called Charlie Martin had tried to bend an iron bar over his head, actively assisted by a local tearaway, Jimmy Fullerton. The bar didn't bend but Ramsey's head did, and he was absent from the billiard hall for some little time recovering from the encounter. One night in August he turned up at the hall with a mate of his, a club owner by the name of Billie Jones, a middle-aged man but a tough nut. He had heard that Martin and Fullerton were drinking in the Britannia, a local pub, and he declared his intention of going there and giving them a taste of what they had given him. Ronnie, to whom the very mention of Watney Street was like a red rag to a bull, elected to make one of the party. Why he took with him a small revolver, which was kept in a drawer behind the bar, goodness knows. Ramsey had a collection of weapons in his car, including a bayonet.

Reggie was not at the hall that evening. Had he been there I am sure that he would have persuaded Ronnie to stay out of the affair which had all the makings of a serious business – which in fact was what it turned out to be. The trio got to the Britannia and found they were on a false trail for Charlie Martin and Fullerton were not there. But sitting at a table was Charlie Martin's younger brother Terry, and on the principle that one member of the mob was better than none at all, he was dragged outside. Ramsey, who had the bayonet tucked inside his trousers, set about young Martin and made a right mess of him. It was all over very quickly. Terry Martin hit the deck, the boots went in and, as a final gesture, Ramsey thrust the bayonet up Martin's anus. Then Ramsey jumped into his car followed by Ronnie and they shot off.

Had it not been for an unforeseen circumstance this incident would have been just another happening in the gang warfare which was a feature of East End life. In the normal course of events the victim would have been carted off to hospital, everyone concerned would have kept their mouths shut and Charlie Martin would have been left with the job of planning a spectacular revenge. As it turned out, a police patrol car stopped Ramsey for speeding, the blood-smeared bayonet was found in the car together with a crowbar and a chopper and the fat was well and truly in the fire. Ramsey and my brother Ronnie were nicked on the spot.

At the station they were searched as a matter of course, and the loaded revolver was found in Ronnie's pocket. It hadn't been fired, but that made no difference. Then a report came through from the London Hospital that a man had been admitted with serious stab wounds. One of the Old Bill put two and two together, an officer got to Terry Martin before his brother Charlie had a chance to see him, the young man talked and the case against Ramsey and my brother Ronnie was as good as proved.

As a matter of course the Old Bill pulled Reggie in. They were not going to be caught on the mistaken identity lark. They knew all about that one, and the pattern was set for the future. If either of the twins fell foul of the law it automatically followed that they were both nicked.

The rest is history. At the Old Bailey on November the 5th 1956 Ramsey was sentenced to seven years imprisonment. His mate Billie Jones got three years and Ronnie got the same sentence as Jones. Prosecuting counsel Victor Durand made it plain to the jury that Ramsey, who was the only one to plead guilty to the charges, was the instigator and prime mover in the attack on Terry Martin. Reggie, who had taken no part in the affair whatsoever, was quite properly acquitted.

Of much greater significance than the sentencing of Ronnie to three years imprisonment was the fact that these identical twins, who had literally spent their lives in each other's pockets, now had to look forward to leading separate existences. At that time I could only guess at what might happen, but events proved stranger than my wildest speculations.

FOUR

I think it's about time I started saying something about myself for a change. It's true, of course, that compared with the life led by the twins, colourful and full of incident, my own existence was pretty humdrum, just a junk dealer with a wife and a small son living in an East End manor. Yet there are rewards in that area which I suppose are only appreciated by those who receive them, rewards which seem small in relation to the effort put out to acquire them but which can be deeply satisfying.

I'm willing to bet that the richest man in the world didn't feel any happier than I did when I came home after a good day with a load of gear that I knew would fetch ten times as much as I had paid for it. I don't think I am bumming my chat (slang for blowing my own trumpet) when I say that I didn't fail as a husband and father in giving my wife and son everything they wanted within reason and the limitations of my pocket. I was always on the lookout for ways and means of bettering our condition of life, which is, after all, the driving force that has brought man from barbarism to civilisation.

During the seven years or so that I lived at 178 Vallance Road I was constantly searching for a place which Dolly and I could call our own, where we could live a proper family life with our son and any others that came along. I'm not saying that we were unhappy. Mum was, as always, kind and understanding and treated Dolly like a daughter which, in a sense, she was. Dad, bless him, was a proper jewel. Although not what you would call a demonstrative man, he had very deep feelings. He, I think, knew better than anybody how desperately I wanted to set up a home, for he had been in the same position himself when he married, living with relatives and not able to call the place his own.

We had been having a difficult time with Gary. He developed an eye condition which needed surgery and Dolly was under considerable pressure. She was (and still is) a highly imaginative and neurotic woman. She foresaw the worst, Gary losing his sight and spending the rest of his life in the dark world of the blind, but happily her fears were groundless. Just the same it was a great strain on all of us, and Ronnie being away didn't help.

One thing that happened as a result of Ronnie's removal from the active list was that Reggie and I became closer, which led to my retirement from the wardrobe dealing profession, and my first steps into the entertainment business. Reggie was a real go-getter who had always looked upon the billiard hall as a potential money-spinner but had set his sights on more ambitious projects. The East End at that time had its quota of drinking clubs, usually sleazy thieves' dens in which respectable people were rarely seen more than once. Probably the only decent club in the area was Harry Abraham's place bang opposite the billiard hall and even that wasn't up to much, though it was conducted very properly. Reggie's ambition was to open a really nice club where villains would be excluded and the respectable East Ender would be able to bring his family and enjoy himself with a bit of music, singing and dancing in the time-honoured way.

Early in 1957 Reggie came across just the place for his purpose. It was an old house near Poplar Town Hall and about a couple of hundred yards from Bow police station. It was in a sorry state of repair but the rent was low and Reggie took it like a shot. We pooled our resources, brought in a few mates who knew something about building and decorating, we both took our coats off and mucked in and when we had finished it looked a picture, something the East End had never seen before, bright and shining with a well-stocked bar and a small stage with an area for dancing. We called it the Double R but it was inevitable that it became known as The Twins' Club.

From the opening night it went with a bang. We let it be known that villains and hooligans were not welcome and that trouble makers would be dealt with very severely. Reggie, who had a natural flair for mixing with people without putting on airs and graces, was the perfect host, and we were lucky in getting hold of a first-class chap to run the bar with me and also act as compere, introducing the acts and 'calling up' the amateur talent, which was plentiful and surprisingly good. His name was Barry Clare and everybody loved him. He was as queer as a three dollar bill, but that side of his life he kept out of the club, which really was his whole existence. He worked like a Trojan, nothing was too much trouble for him, he was involved in everything and to a great extent some of the success of the club was due to his efforts. He came to a very tragic end, which I will refer to later.

During this period, when the Double R was becoming more than just a spot on the East End map and Reggie and I were making plans to expand, Ronnie was not forgotten. He was in Wandsworth prison, only a short drive away on the other side of the river, and we all visited him as often as the regulations permitted. Naturally we made sure, in so far as it could be arranged, that he had as many creature comforts as we could provide. A prison is not a Harley Street clinic and visitors who turn up with flowers and fruit are soon made aware of that fact. Nevertheless, just as there are bent coppers there are also bent screws (warders) and I do not think I am betraying any trade secrets when I say that Ronnie was at the receiving end of more than the regulation food and amenities. The methods by which this was made possible have been described ad nauseam in the memoirs of many an old lag, so I see no reason why I should describe them in detail. Suffice it to say that this was a practical problem which was dealt with in a practical manner by very practical people. Ronnie was a well-behaved prisoner, he took his medicine like a man – we looked forward to his release with full remission for good conduct and meanwhile got on with the job of building up something for him to come out to.

The first year during which the Double R was open for business coincided with a yearning on the part of some West End playboys (and playgirls) to mix with their less affluent brothers and sisters east of Aldgate Pump. The Prospect of Whitby was old hat, just another tourist trap, Charlie Brown's and the exotic Orient of Limehouse had had their day, but, said the cognoscenti of night life, what about that cute little place in Mile End with Queenie Watts and that darling Barry Clare calling up the little scrubbers to scream their songs into the microphone and, my dear, the villains you meet. The so-called villains were respectable Cockneys, but that made no difference. If people want to believe something they'll believe it no matter how you try to persuade them otherwise, and the West met the East and found that they got on very well together.

In that first invasion I met a few characters to whom I took a liking. There was Tommy Yeardye, a gentle giant and a current boy friend of Diana Dors; Jackie Collins, sister of the actress Joan Collins and definitely one of us; the diminutive 'Dandy Kim' Waterfield of the impeccable dress and ubiquitous Bentley; who brought with them their many friends and had a good old West End time at East End prices.

Inevitably there was the other side of the picture. Some of the East End yobbos and hooligans regarded their exclusion from the club as a personal insult. 'Wot, bar me? I can fucking go anywhere I fucking want to' was their attitude, and from time to time they would turn up mob-handed and demanded admittance. We had an answer to that in the twenty-odd stone of 'Big Pat' Connolly on the door, and few unwanted visitors managed to pass him by. There was, of course, the odd trouble maker who managed to get into the bar, but either me or Reggie were quite capable of dealing with that situation.

I remember one time when Queenie Watts was doing her stuff and a bloke tried to take the microphone from her in the mistaken belief that he was a better entertainer. It wasn't the only thing he was mistaken about. Reggie took the mike from him and returned it to Queenie, who went on with her number. Then this merchant, who obviously didn't know the difference between kindness and weakness, decided that he would like to dance with our mother who was sitting quietly at a table minding her own business. He was trying to pull her to her feet when Reggie stepped in, this time determined to stand no nonsense. There was no fuss, no bother, a right hand went over, the offender collapsed and was escorted to a less comfortable seat on the pavement outside. He wasn't really a villain, he just had too much to drink, and he came back a couple of days later to apologise for his behaviour.

There was another occasion I remember when Reggie dealt with the matter and I was put in my place. I ought to explain that we kept the usual club hours, three p.m. to 11 p.m. daily and noon to three p.m. and seven p.m. to ten p.m. on Sundays. During the afternoon business was fairly quiet and the watch on the door not too strict, and one day three burly coalmen barged in wanting a drink. They were covered in coal-dust and leaned against the newly-decorated wall. Reggie went up to them and asked them to leave, they became belligerent and one of them aimed a punch at Reggie. I came out from behind the bar to lend a hand, but it wasn't necessary. Reggie floored the three of them, showed them the door of which they took immediate advantage, then turned to me and told me to stay behind the bar where I belonged and leave him to take care of any trouble.

There were a few similar incidents, the most serious being when the Upton Park mob were refused admittance. They sent a real rough nut along to cause trouble, a villain who had recently left the Moor after a nine year sentence for carving up a Chinaman in Limehouse. He was dealt with very severely and we had no further trouble from Upton Park. This was one of the few times when Reggie really let himself go, in the process of which he taught the villain a lesson that he would remember for the rest of his life.

I was by now really enjoying myself. The work was exacting but I had never been an idler and anyway the rewards were worthwhile. What I found attractive was the business of meeting people, chatting to them, cracking jokes and finding that work could be a pleasure.

Mum and Dad spent several evenings a week at the club and so did my wife, Dolly, who took to this new life style as if she had been born to it. She spent a good bit of money on clothes and hair-do's and suchlike, but I didn't begrudge a penny of it, she looked lovely and I was proud of her.

The Double R had become established and was doing a bomb when I had another stroke of luck. I was chatting to one of the members of the club and he happened to let drop that there was a flat going vacant down by the river in Narrow Street. I was round there like a flash. It wasn't a palace, just a two-bedroomed flat on the second floor of an ancient block called Brightlingsea Buildings (where the hell did they find these names?), built for dockers and their families around the turn of last century. But that didn't matter. It was a home of our own at long last. I had sufficient money to furnish it comfortably if not luxuriously and we couldn't move in quickly enough.

I remember being asked some time later why I did not move out of the East End when I had the chance and the cash. I said, half-jokingly, that I couldn't bear to leave the manor, and realised afterwards that it was true. My father and his father before him were part of that life of market stalls and dealing, independent men with a built-in instinct for survival that carried them through crisis after crisis, men whose personal philosophy was as important to them as religion is to a churchgoer. I suppose it was in my blood. I was part of the East End, the East End was part of me and that was all there was to it.

As I mentioned before, the Double R was a raving success, but Reggie and I did not intend to mark time. What we had done at the club could be repeated in other directions. Working on the simple philosophy that it is easier to take a pound from each of a thousand people than a grand from one man, we decided to go into gambling.

In this modern day and age, with betting shops in almost every street, it is hard to realise that, less than twenty years ago, the modest punter who put a couple of bob on a horse with a street bookmaker was a law-breaker. It was a farcical situation in which furtive little men hung around on street corners taking money wrapped in slips of paper while the Old Bill wasted precious man-power on keeping them under observation and nicking them at regular intervals.

Looking back now on the gambling situation as it existed in 1957, a mere nineteen years ago, all one can do is laugh. Heavy gamblers who sometimes staked thousands of pounds on the turn of a card were ferried around London and the Home Counties to secret addresses where they were able to indulge in their favourite games of chemin de fer or poker. All over the country small groups gathered in basement clubs to win or lose a few bob on games of chance. Betting and gaming was a multi-million pound industry, and the authorities thought they could put a stop to it by creating a nation of petty criminals. Comic opera wasn't in it. Even Gilbert and Sullivan would have been hard put to it to manufacture such a nonsensical situation.

Actually the official mind, which is usually several years behind public opinion, was soon to change its attitude towards gambling and recognise the right of the man in the street to have a little flutter. Reggie and I anticipated this move, but gambling was still illegal when we expanded into a spieler across the road from the Double R. This did such a roaring business that we went into a couple of other places and very soon we were making money hand over fist. In many parts of the world we would have been hailed as public benefactors but in London we were law breakers. Not that we gave a monkey's, we knew what we were doing and were quite prepared to face the consequences.

This was the beginning of the good life. We were able to afford nice cars, good clothes, evenings out in the West End where we were intoduced around the night spots by the upper crust patrons of the Double R. Dolly and I met many people in these places whom we liked and who seemed to like us, and I found that my lack of education and manner of speech (of which I have never been ashamed) was no bar to being accepted by those who, in their infancy, had sucked silver spoons instead of dirty dummies.

Reggie and I learned a lot of things from our West End visits which we were able to put into practice in our own places. The punters who patronised them weren't slow to recognise this fact. They knew that they could be assured of a fair deal and freedom from aggravation in any of the Kray spielers, for we adopted the same principle that had proved successful at the Double R. We looked after our clients and dealt swiftly and severely with the troublemakers, not because we wanted to but because we had to.

While all this was happening our brother in Wandsworth was not forgotten. Whatever else happened he would have his share of the business when he came out, and it looked very much as though he would be joining the family for Christmas 1958. Though Wandsworth was a hard nick, he kept out of trouble, qualifying for full remission for good conduct during the first year of his sentence. He had no lack of visitors and we maintained the supply of little extras which helped to make prison life tolerable. I must admit to being surprised that Ronnie was taking his porridge so well. Of the three of us he was the most uncompromising and the first to resent what he called 'liberty-taking', and he had a deep-rooted hatred of uniformed authority which stemmed from the time when he was beaten-up in Bethnal Green nick when he was little more than a boy.

Because of what was to occur, I must now make my own feelings quite plain. I have spent the best part of seven years in jail, where I experienced every stage from maximum security in Albany on the Isle of Wight to minimum discipline in Maidstone. I know from practical experience what Oscar Wilde was talking about when he said: 'Every day is like a year, the days of which are long.' I know the effect on the mind of uncertainty about what is going on in the outer world, the long, long nights of worry over the significance of a cancelled visit or a censored sentence in a letter. I know, above all, that once a man is in prison he is no longer his own man but a creature of the system, wholly the property of those who are charged with the punishment of felons. No matter that he is a person of influence in the outside world with powerful friends, in prison he is a name and a number and nothing else. The moralist says that's part of the punishment. I say that it doesn't alter the facts.

The facts, so far as Ronnie was concerned, were as follows. He had served a year of his three year sentence as a model prisoner without a black mark on his record. I don't say that he was an angel – few prisoners are – but he had kept out of trouble, which in itself is no mean feat. Suddenly, in the course of a day, the whole situation was altered.

I had better make the point here which has been made over and over again, just in case it needs any further elaboration. A prison is a small world in itself. The inhabitants, warder and prisoner alike, are confined in this world, save that the warder has some freedom of movement outside his working hours. But the jealousies and antagonisms which arise in any community are sharpened in prison life by a rigid code of discipline which confers absolute power on prison officers, whether they are fitted to carry that responsibility or not, while giving the prisoner little else but the right of acquiescence. That right he may exercise to the fullest extent.

From what I have said of my brother Ronnie it will be readily understood that he was not the acquiescent type. He had his place in the prison hierarchy and made sure that everyone understood it. His attitude was quite plain and simple. Leave me alone, he said, and I won't cause any trouble. Unfortunately this attitude was interpreted by some of the screws as an open challenge to their authority. Wandsworth was a hard nick and the screws were hard men. The challenge was bound to be accepted.

It was. A trivial incident sparked off a situation in which Ronnie gave one of the screws a right-hander. The heavy mob, a hand-picked bunch of really tough warders, took the matter in hand. All the courage and fistic prowess in the world is no match for truncheons and weight of numbers. Ronnie was subdued, but he had to be put in a strait-jacket before he finally gave in.

This was the beginning of a nightmare situation. A convict has no civil rights but the authorities are under a statutory obligation to protect his physical and mental well-being. In the case of my brother Ronnie this took the form of sending him off to the psychiatric wing at Winchester prison for observation and report on his mental state.

There was nothing that Reggie or I could do about it. Even if we'd had all the money in the world – which we hadn't – officialdom had the last word. The result was predictable. Confronted by a human being who behaved like a caged animal (principally because he was treated like one), the headshrinkers of Winchester certified that Ronald Kray was insane.

We reacted to the news in various ways. Dad, always the Cockney optimist, said it was a load of rubbish, Ronnie was 'working his ticket' and setting the authorities by the ears as he had done at Shepton Mallet. I was very disturbed, because I realised the implications – Ronnie might be kept in prison indefinitely. Mum, of course, was very upset, but she was sure that things would turn out all right in the end. Reggie's feelings could be imagined. Here was his identical twin labelled a madman so what did that make him? Was he also tarred with the same brush? Or was the doctor wrong in his diagnosis?

Such questions cannot be answered. Under the rules there can be no independent second opinion and, although Reggie and I did everything that was legally possible, we got precisely nowhere. We visited Ronnie regularly and, powerless to do anything for him, were obliged to watch his gradual deterioration into dependence on drugs, massive doses of tranquillisers which dulled his mind and affected his memory. There were times when he couldn't recognise us, his own brothers and parents, and at those times I felt despair and hopelessness. Whatever the crime he had committed, surely this was not a fitting punishment. And there was always the nagging doubt. Was my brother really mad or had the authorities chosen this way of turning him into a tractable prisoner, robbing him of his will and power to reason in order that they might control him more easily?

Something had to be done to take Ronnie out of this nightmare. Reggie and I had money and friends. We considered the wildest schemes which in the end had to be abandoned. The insurmountable obstacle was the high stone wall of Winchester jail. So time went by, Ronnie was fed regular doses of a tranquilliser (which we discovered to be Stemetil) and we continued our efforts to help him in every way we could.

At this particular juncture in my story and with the benefit of hindsight I want to make an important point which has a direct bearing on the final tragedy which involved me and my brothers. I knew nothing of medicine but I knew where to get information, and I had to know about this drug Stemetil, when and how it was used and what the long-term effects could be. I took myself off to a friendly Harley Street specialist and asked him point blank what it was all about.

What I heard horrified me. Cutting out the technical jargon, such as references to the use of prochlorperazine and phenothiazine in certain cases of mental disturbance, the gist of the matter was that my brother Ronnie was being treated for schizophrenia with massive doses of a drug normally used for the relief of vertigo and vomiting (!). Moreover, and I quote the learned specialist, 'The precise mechanisms of the action of this drug are not yet fully understood.'

When I told Reggie about this he went up the wall. His twin

brother being subjected to this treatment by a bunch of prison doctors was too much for him to swallow, and the same went for me. We decided that, no matter what it cost, Ronnie was coming out and to hell with the consequences. That high stone wall was going to be breached even if we had to blow a hole in it. Fortunately for all concerned that wasn't necessary. The authorities at Winchester, having done their best (or worst) for the patient, decided to transfer him to Long Grove mental hospital near Epsom, a mere fourteen miles from London. Someone up there must have heard our prayers. The rest was not a matter of divine intervention but simply practical organisation.

No job was ever cased more thoroughly than the springing of Ronnie Kray from Long Grove. In the course of several permitted visits, Reggie and me and our friends were able to learn more about the workings of the institution than was known by the principal of that establishment. When the time came for Ronnie to have it away it was a piece of cake. Wearing a blue suit similar to the one he knew Ronnie would be wearing, Reggie, accompanied by a friend, went in on a visit. Then 'Reggie' (who was really Ronnie) went down to the canteen to get tea, walked out through the open gates and, by the time the deception was discovered, Ronnie was on his way to London and freedom in the car that had been waiting for him. Reggie talked his way out of the ensuing inquest and, strangely enough, no official action was taken against him though it was obvious that he had assisted in the escape of a prisoner.

There was another facet to the situation which was suggested by a journalist by the name of Norman Lucas, one of the many pressmen who tagged on to us in the hope of a bit of sensation. He came up with the information that, under the lunacy laws, any certified person who escaped from a mental institution and remained at liberty for longer than fourteen days automatically became sane and would have to be re-certified before he could be returned to the looney-bin. No wonder they are called the lunacy laws! We checked on that piece of information and it was correct.

In fact, Ronnie remained free for five months during which time he moved from one district to another, living in flats rented by various friends. Away from the confines of the mental hospital he became more like his old self, but there was still something about him that made me uneasy. I put it down to the fact that he was no longer under the influence of drugs because that was the only explanation I could think of. The real explanation came later.

While on the subject of Ronnie and his state of mind, and because this book is primarily intended to get at the truth and put the record straight, I want to refer again to various matters which were made public in print once me and my brothers were safely under lock and key.

I have made previous mention of one John Pearson, self-styled official biographer of the Kray twins who took three years to produce a book including half-truth, innuendo and outright falsehood which purported to be the story of the rise and fall the Kray twins. If I were to deal separately with each inaccuracy there would be no space in this book for reference to anything else. As it is, I will merely say that the same kind of slipshod research which made me three years younger, changed my name from Charles James to Charles David and challenged the pharmacists on their ability to spell STEMETIL (which he refers to as STEMATOL) is only too evident throughout this sensational cops and robbers saga.

'A brave and disturbing book' said the Daily Express, 'First-rate journalism' said the Evening News, 'It's an exciting read' said The Times.

I am not a literary critic, but I will admit that the book in question is extremely well-written. That it happens to be about three other people than me and my brothers is, I suppose, incidental.

That's enough about Mr. John Pearson, the Gnome of Rome. May he never fall in the Tiber.

To return to Ronnie, my purpose is to put the record

straight about his sexual proclivities which have been the subject of considerable printed comment. Ronnie was, and is, bi-sexual. He didn't hang around the public lavatories in Leicester Square, he left that province to knights of the theatre, minor politicians and senior civil servants, but like Oscar Wilde, though in less theatrical context, he found pleasure in the company of beautiful boys. That there should be no social stigma attached to sexual practices which existed in ancient and highly civilised societies (when our forefathers painted themselves with woad and put to sea in coracles) was made plain by that Sportsman of the Year Sir John Wolfenden in his famous report on homosexuality.

To be blunt, what has always annoyed me about the comments on Ronnie's sex-life is the snide insinuation that what is acceptable behaviour in many pillars of the Establishment somehow becomes unsavoury when practised by a lad from the East End. After all, in these enlightened days, a man's sex life is his own affair.

During Ronnie's period of freedom Reggie and I carried a double responsibility. In the first place we were now operating a successful club and a number of spielers, which made considerable demands on our time. Secondly but more importantly, we had to keep an eye on Ronnie's well-being. For five months we shuttled him around from flat to flat, keeping him on the move and a couple of steps ahead of the Old Bill. It was expensive and, in retrospect, sometimes amusing, like the time we acquired a cracking furnished flat in the St. John's Wood area and took Ronnie along to his new quarters. He walked in the door, gave the place a comprehensive once-over and walked straight out again, saying he would rather be in Vallance Road, It was typical of him that he took no account of the fact that we had laid out a small fortune by way of rent in advance and deposits against breakages and other contingencies. He didn't like the pad, and that was that. He saw no reason why he should stay there.

The stories that circulated to Ronnie's whereabouts were legion. He was reliably reported to be in the Bahamas, New

York, Malta, the Cote d'Azur, southern Spain and God knows where else. Actually he never went farther north than Finchley or west than Fulham, which is neither romantic nor sensational but just happens to be the truth. He paid a few surreptitious visits to Vallance Road to see Mum, the first of which proved rather awkward because he wanted to see Aunt Rose, the news of whose death while he was in Winchester had been kept from him. On this occasion he didn't say much but went out into the yard and stood there for a long time looking up at the railway arch. I believe that the knowledge that he would never see his Aunt Rose again hit him harder than he'd ever been hit in his life.

What with our increasing business interests and keeping an eye on Ronnie, Reggie and I had our hands full. We had a trusted manager running the billiard hall which returned a small but steady income. The Double R was doing a bomb. Apart from the regular East End clients there was the influx of free-spending customers from the West End. We had a few visits from Billy Hill, a legendary figure who was known as the guv'nor among the Mayfair mobsters and had done quite a lot of bird. He took a liking to me and Reggie, and to be truthful I found him a very likeable sort of a chap. He was rather short, wore glasses and his manner was mild and inoffensive but he certainly had a brain. He had built up a considerable fortune out of his criminal activities and took care to hang on to it. His wife, Gipsy, was a card, a very good-looking woman with raven-black hair, always dressed in the height of fashion and carrying on her fingers a King's ransom in jewellery.

Billy helped us to a great extent in those days. He had forgotten more about running clubs than most club-owners would ever know. He gave us advice very freely without looking for any return and we never had a cross word with him, which is just as well when one remembers what happened to Jack 'Spot' Comer. This merchant, a big, loudmouthed bully who had his origins in Whitechapel and was for a time associated with Billy in some of his enterprises, decided the time was ripe for him to take over as guv'nor of the West End. A ferocious striping at the hands (and razor) of 'Mad' Frankie Fraser did nothing to cool his ambitions. After the surgeons had sewed his face together he continued to prove that he was stupid as well as brainless by carrying on his attempts to topple Billy from his throne. His activities were brought to an abrupt conclusion by the attentions of one Albert Dimes (born Alberto Dimeo) who chased the luckless Spot down a Soho side-street and gave him a proper seeing-to before a crowd of witnesses who were later found to be both dumb and blind.

Whether the non-to-gentle dissuasion of Mr. Comer was performed at the instigation of Billy Hill I do not know, nor do I care to hazard a guess. Mr. Comer changed his name to Colmore and, according to my latest information, subject to confirmation, is utilising his inconsiderable talents in packing a well-known brand of sausages into suitable containers at a factory in Park Royal.

Billy, at the time we were acquainted with him, was quite involved in West End gambling clubs, where thousands of pounds changed hands nightly behind locked and well-guarded doors. The whole procedure was illegal, numerous assorted members of the Old Bill either conducted raids or took bribes depending on what was in season, but it was all sewn up because the game of cops and robbers was played according to the rules. Photographs of me and the twins occupied a prominent position on the notice board in the CID room at West End Central nick over an adjuration to all officers that they should report sightings of these characters together with reports on the people they met and where those meetings took place. At the same time we were being approached by certain high-ranking officers with offers of immunity in return for specified cash payments.

Don't be deceived, Mr. Member of the General Public, by the high sounding and pompous utterances of Commissioners and Superintendents of the police authority. I don't say they benefited in a pecuniary sense from the questionable antics of their junior officers. What I do say is that they knew enough about those antics to take action before a major scandal developed. Need I do more than mention the name of Detective-Sergeant Challoner and the official associates of Mr. Porn-Peddler Humphreys to make my point?

At this juncture I can hear the howls of protest. Here comes Charlie Kray working off a grudge against the Old Bill, trying to get his own back because his brothers were handed a massive dose of porridge. Let me make it clear that I will stand up and be counted on the basis of facts, and the facts are that a poorly paid police will not stand by and watch fortunes being made in defiance of the law (however stupid the law may be) without some of their number claiming a share of the loot. In making these statements I am not pleading justification for anything that me and my brothers may have done. I am asking the reader of this book to apportion blame where it lies, and to apportion it fairly. If the walls of the Mason's Arms in Maddox Street could speak (and there are people who know what I mean by that remark) then the general opinion of the impartiality of British justice would undergo a profound change.

Now that I have got this off my chest, let me use a few of the words at my disposal to sum up the position in which me and my brothers found ourselves in the summer of 1958. The balance sheet looked something like this. On the credit side were two active young fellows, Charlie aged thirty two and a bit, Reggie coming up to his twenty fifth birthday. Between them they controlled a small empire in the East End comprising one successful club and a number of money spinning spielers. They had cash in hand, money in the bank, a brace of handsome motor cars, wardrobes stocked with good clothes, many good friends and very few enemies. On the debit side was a brother on the run from the Old Bill, who had been at liberty long enough to prove his sanity and complete the rest of the prison sentence which was hanging over his head.

Reggie and I put this reasonable proposition to Ronnie, who would have none of it. In a way it was understandable for the following reason. While he was in Wandsworth Ronnie had spent some time in the company of Frank Mitchell, a simple giant capable of extreme brutality, who had been in and out of mental institutions for years. In the same way as Ronnie, he had been certified insane and was being detained in prison without a firm date for release. This was Ronnie's perpetual nightmare, that he might suffer the same fate. How to dispel this fear was the problem we had to solve.

We hit on an idea. Using an assumed name we made an appointment for Ronnie to see a Harley Street psychiatrist. He went along, told the psychiatrist a cock-and-bull story about his impending marriage and a touch of insanity way back in the family, and asked the head-shrinker to give an opinion on his (Ronnie's) mental condition. The head-shrinker who, like most men in his profession wasn't too good in the top storey, was highly amused, asked Ronnie a few questions and sent him on his way with a written statement to the effect that he (Ronnie, not the psychiatrist) was in possession of all his marbles.

We thought that would do the trick, but it didn't. Now that the shadow of insanity had been lifted Ronnie began to enjoy his freedom, taking risks by going out and about, having a few drinks here and there, visiting friends in broad daylight and so on. Once he strolled the length of Bethnal Green Road, returning the greetings of people who thought he was Reggie. Then he would change almost overnight and stay indoors, spending his time sleeping and reading. He also had bouts of heavy drinking. We were at our wit's end to know what to do for the best. I made a few enquiries in the right places and came to the conclusion that Ronnie was suffering from the after-effects of the considerable quantities of drugs which had been pumped into him both at Winchester and Long Grove. What was obvious was that he needed medical attention, but to take him somewhere to get it would mean disclosing his identity and giving details of his past treatment.

The problem was solved for us. The Old Bill knew the close ties between Ronnie and Reggie, and they also knew that the twins would be celebrating their twenty-fifth birthday on October 17th. It was a simple matter of putting two and two together. All the Old Bill had to do was to put a constant watch on Reggie from the morning of the 17th (which was a Friday) and wait for Ronnie to turn up or for Reggie to lead them to Ronnie's hide-out. As it happened, Ronnie came to Vallance Road after dark on the Saturday and we had a slightly delayed birthday party which went on until the early hours of Sunday morning.

Whether it was out of consideration for the feelings of Mum and Dad (who went to bed about midnight) or whether the Old Bill became bored with waiting for Ronnie outside the house I will never know. Anyhow, at three o'clock in the morning as the party was on its last legs, they got in the house as one of our friends opened the door to leave, two uniformed officers and a couple of male nurses from Long Grove, and Ronnie's period of freedom was at an end.

I had the feeling that Ronnie was relieved that the matter was taken out of his hands. He put up no resistance and didn't even try the old mistaken identity lark, which would have been no good in any case, because the twins were no longer identical. Ronnie had put on weight and his face was drawn and haggard as a result of the mental strain he had suffered while on the trot. He went out very quietly and was taken off to Bethnal Green nick where he was to spend the rest of the night. There was to be no sleep for Reggie and me. We spent early morning hours arranging for our solicitor and a doctor to accompany us to Bethnal Green nick at the crack of dawn to make sure that Ronnie was not being given treatment by Freeman, Hardy and Willis, the well-known boot manufacturers. It had happened before. We intended to make bloody sure that it didn't happen again or, if it did, there would be credible witnesses present as observers.

Let me make it quite clear that we didn't go to the nick to cause trouble or to make any attempt to help Ronnie to escape. That didn't seem to be the opinion of the officer in charge when we arrived and asked if we could see Ronnie. He was either an inspector or a superintendent, I forget which, but he behaved more like an obergruppenfuehrer in the SS. We were in the charge room, Reggie, Perkoff our solicitor, the doctor and myself, when this character stormed in yelling 'Out, out, get out the lot of you!' Perkoff made a formal protest, the doctor revealed his identity, Reggie and I stayed stum – but we went just the same.

The only thing we could do was to wait outside the nick until Ronnie came out, which he eventually did in, of all things, a taxi-cab, which set off at a fair old lick westwards down the Bethnal Green Road. We fell in smartly behind it, Reggie and me in his car and behind us a couple of pressmen in their own motors. It was like a scene out of the Keystone cops, and it became more so when a squad car, obviously called up by radio, joined us as we came to the Oval in Kennington. After that it was follow my leader all the way to Epsom, jockeying for position at traffic lights and weaving in and out of the lanes of traffic. At one point the squad car lost ground and came roaring up from behind, cutting sharply in front of Reggie and forcing him up on the pavement. It didn't frighten Reggie but it put the wind up me.

We were still right on the taxi's tail when it pulled into the gates of Long Grove. Reggie parked his car, we got out and walked up the drive to the reception with the squad car following us at walking pace. The Old Bill made no attempt to interfere with us in any way, probably because the reporters were close behind. We again made a request to see Ronnie, but found ourselves in the principal's office instead. He was a very reasonable sort of man who offered us a cup of tea and told us, among other things, that we had done our brother no favour by assisting him to escape. We put our point of view equally forcibly and maintained that our brother was certainly ill but wasn't, in our view, insane. I'll say this for the man, he listened to what we had to say and didn't tell us that we were talking rubbish, and the upshot was a promise from him that Ronnie's case would be given every consideration and permission was given for us to see Ronnie there and then.

Ronnie was not re-certified. Within a few days he was back at Wandsworth to serve out the remainder of his sentence, a matter of a few months. Though he didn't spend Christmas with the family he was back with us once more when Spring came to Bethnal Green. This was a bit of a puzzle to me. It doesn't need a mathematician to work out that Ronnie was in detention from November of 1956 to May of 1958, was at liberty until October of the same year and was released finally in May of 1959, making a total of twenty-four months imprisonment, two years by my (or anybody else's) reckoning. Now why was this? Ronnie had been sentenced to three years, he had broken every rule in the book, he had belted a screw, he had escaped from confinement and yet one third of his sentence was remitted. I'm not silly enough to think that the authorities feared a frontal attack on Wandsworth headed by the Kray brothers. What did occur to me was that, somewhere along the line, a grave mistake had been made in the diagnosis and treatment of my brother Ronnie's condition. Doctors and surgeons bury their mistakes. Could it be that psychiatrists just get rid of them as quickly as possible? Your guess is as good as mine. On balance I tend to agree with the humorist who said that anyone who consults a psychiatrist should have his head examined.

Prison is a good place to keep out of, but it's better than the looney-bin. Ronnie must have thought so, for he settled into the routine at Wandsworth and avoided serious trouble. All the same, the prison doctor put him on tranquillisers. I wasn't too pleased about this, nor was Reggie, but the time was not far distant when he would be out and we could then get him the best possible treatment. Meanwhile Reggie and I got on with the job of earning that little extra which makes the difference between a good living and comparative affluence.

This stage of my story is as good as any to comment on what have been described as the protection activities which we are supposed to have carried on. According to some of the professional scribes who reported the doings in what they sensationally (and sometimes romantically) called 'gangland', club owners, restaurant proprietors, small shopkeepers and suchlike would be approached one day by a tough-looking character who would hint at the many perils of conducting a business which could not be covered by insurance. This gent would then go on to say that, for a nominal weekly sum to be paid in cash, he and his associates would ensure that the aforesaid owner of the business would have no aggravation from any of the tea-leaves and rough-house merchants in the area. The trembling victim would then hand over a bit of money each week, the amount depending on the size of his business, and everybody would be happy. In the event that the trembling victim refused to comply with the polite request, mysterious attacks would be made on his premises, bricks would be thrown through his windows, villains would indulge in brawling in his club or restaurant to the consequent detriment of furnishings and fittings and so on.

It is a well-known fact that newspaper proprietors are in business to sell newspapers and sensational stories boost circulation, but this sort of childish twaddle is fit for comic papers. In the dog-eat-dog environment of the East End men have to be hard to survive and harder still to become successful. Hard men didn't play kid's games for pennies, nor did they operate on the level of juvenile tearaways.

These are the facts of the so-called protection racket as they applied to us. We owned a club, a billiard hall, a second-hand car business and operated a number of successful spielers. As I have explained before, we had no aggravation in these enterprises because anyone who interfered with us would be on a hiding to nothing. I personally wasn't a fighting man, although I had been a professional boxer, but I was a bloody expert at stopping those who fancied their chances. As a result, others engaged in similar projects to ours noted our freedom from trouble and actually came along to us with invitations to become associated with them. It was a practical proposition from everybody's point of view. After all, the owner of an illegal spieler could hardly go running to the Old

Bill if a couple of hooligans started a fight in his gaff. But once it became known that the Krays were involved in the management of the enterprise it would be a very bold villain indeed who would dare to put a foot wrong. I remember one occasion when Danny Green, the owner of a very nice club in Stoke Newington called The Grange, was having a lot of trouble with the local tearaways. He came to us with tears in his eyes, begging us to go into partnership with him, and was very upset when we refused. Stoke Newington wasn't our area and anyway we had enough on our plates with our existing commitments.

The big question is, on what level does one make the moral judgement? Of course, naughty people shouldn't operate spielers and nasty villains shouldn't go about making trouble, but these are the facts of life and we don't yet live in Utopia. In practical terms, we policed our own enterprises and you can bet your boots that the villains feared us far more than they feared the Old Bill. We didn't advertise ourselves with armoured vehicles and a crashhelmeted, baton-carrying private army as do others engaged in the 'protection racket', but in our own way we were just as effective.

In this area of argument I am not going to allow myself to be placed in a defensive position. Me and my brothers had built up a profitable little empire as hard men in a hard environment, and when we required hired help we didn't go to the female department of the Labour Exchange. Our employees were not asked to provide impeccable references or evidence of academic achievements, but they had to satisfy two essential requirements. The first was that they had to be honest in their dealings with us no matter how they dealt with others. The second was that they should be completely loyal. If they satisfied these conditions they were well paid and well looked after. If, on the other hand, they decided to improve their financial position at our expense the matter was not reported to the authorities as a criminal misdemeanour. They were dealt with in an unofficial fashion which didn't hurt us one little bit but which proved moderately painful for them.

This is what is known as rough justice, an occupational hazard in many professions, and one that perhaps occurred more frequently in the rough and tumble business affairs of the East End than in, say, the Stock Exchange. A 'hammering' in Throgmorton Street and a 'hammering' in a narrow street off the Bethnal Green Road are just different aspects of the punishment which befalls those who transgress. Believe me, I'm not being facetious. There's a definite parallel which the more philosophical reader will clearly see.

Let me give an example. We had a valuable and trusted chap at the Double R called Barry Clare, whom I have mentioned previously. He locked up the club one night, went home to Tooting where he lived with his mother, saw her safely to bed and then put his head in the gas oven. Now there had to be some reason for a happy guy like Barry to do such a thing, so we put the word about and discovered that he had been blackmailed over a long period of time. If he had only told me or Reggie about it we would have done something, but he kept it to himself.

We discovered the identity of the blackmailer by chance. I was standing in the doorway of the Club one evening when a car drew up at the kerb with a couple of fellows in it. I ought to explain that I was similar in height and build to Barry, and could be mistaken for him in a poor light and at a distance. The bloke on the passenger side got out of the car and called to me. 'Hello, Barry. Got it ready for me?'. There was no doubt in my mind that this was our man, the dirty bastard who had driven Barry to suicide. My first impulse was to stretch him out on the pavement, but that would have been no punishment. I said 'Sorry, mate, it's not Barry. You'll find him round the billiard hall.'

They drove off and I immediately got on the telephone to Reggie who I knew was at the hall and told him to expect a visitor who would be asking for Barry. I also told Reggie that I suspected that this fellow was the blackmailer. I learned afterwards that Reggie accused this man when he turned up, the fellow became truculent and told Reggie to mind his own business, whereupon Reggie proceeded to give him the beating of his life. According to reports Reggie was quite merciless. He kept the man on his feet and used him as a punchbag, propping him against one of the billiard tables and reducing his face to a bloody mask. He was then taken down to his mate waiting in the car, thrown into the passenger seat, and the driver was told in no uncertain terms to make himself scarce.

That is what I mean by rough justice. Some people may think we should have handed the fellow over to the police, but Barry couldn't give evidence from the grave.

To get back to the question once again of moral judgement and the exercise of this judgement in a society many of whose members live outside the law, there are certain conventions which must be understood. All law is not good law, and there are some acts dating back to ancient times that are so out of step in this modern age that they are held in ridicule. Legislation which is designed to prevent criminal activity is, on the whole, good law and of benefit to the community when properly administered. Legislation which creates criminals out of law-abiding people is bad law. Take a look at motoring legislation for example. It's a safe bet that the ordinary citizen who leaves home in his car in the morning will, in the first mile of his progress, have broken at least one and probably more of the numerous rules and regulations contained in the Vehicles (Excise) Act, the Road Transport Lighting Acts, the Petroleum Act, the Road Traffic Acts, the Road Safety Act and the Road Traffic Regulation Act, to name but a few. But the prize piece of legal buffoonery was the Betting and Gaming Act as it existed before the first day of May 1961. Its provisions were flouted, laughed at and universally defied by millions of ordinary people, aided and abetted by those 'criminals' who provided them with facilities for indulging in their dreadful vices, such as putting a couple of bob on a horse, playing cards for money, pulling the handles of one-armed bandits and similar anti-social and illegal pursuits.

Reading these words in 1976 you probably think I'm

kidding. Not a bit of it. It's all there on the Statute Book for anyone to read who cares to take the time and trouble.

In this farcical situation a large and profitable industry not only operated but flourished. From time to time the Old Bill, armed with axes, descended upon the dens of vice where hardened gamblers took their daily exercise by tugging away at the levers of one armed bandits. The machines were smashed to smithereens, thus giving the Old Bill a bit of exercise too, the proprietors were hauled before the courts and fined fairly heavily while the legal eagles debated very seriously and at great length whether, in these pursuits, the element of skill was greater than the element of chance!

The moral issue here is quite a simple one. If the majority of the members of any society look upon gambling as a social evil, then it should be ruthlessly stamped out. If, on the other hand, it is clearly shown that millions of people like to have a little flutter on the horses, speculate a few bob on the turn of a card or feed coins into a mechanical contrivance with the hope of getting back more than they put in, the legal authority which tries to put a stop to it is not only banging its head against a brick wall but making a bloody fool of itself in the process.

I know I'm going on a bit, but I don't want anybody to be under any delusion about the way in which me and my brothers made our very comfortable living. The Double R was a conventional club operated according to the laws that govern the conducting of such places. It had to be because, apart from any other consideration, it was situated only a couple of hundred yards from Bow nick. In any case, we had no reason to evade the licensing laws – the club made enough money without that. It was run in an orderly fashion. In fact the only punch-ups on the premises took place in the upper part which we had converted into a gym as part of the amenities of the club, where assault and battery was strictly according to the Marquis of Queensberry.

The Regal billiard hall and the car business were also quite legal, but the spielers were quite definitely not – at least before

May Day 1961. Mark you, it was all very gentlemanly when the Old Bill decided that one of our gaffs was next in the queue to be nicked. We pretty well knew beforehand, because there were no off-duty coppers among the punters on the appointed day. I remember particularly when the Regency Club was done, aptly enough in the pantomime season just before Christmas of 1960. The Regency was a really nice place on which we had spent a lot of money, rigging it out with television and a proper betting counter and a 'blower' for direct communication with the course. There were also card tables where the punters were able to fritter away whatever they had managed to win on the gee-gees.

I was on duty on the day of the raid, assisted by one of our men, Limehouse Willie, of whom more will be heard at a later stage. The Old Bill made their entry and went through the usual paraphernalia of checking identities and taking names and addresses and nicked everybody on the premises, down to the poor old bloke who did the cleaning. We duly appeared at North London magistrate's court where we were fined a total of about a hundred and fifty pounds (including costs) as principals. The punters, accused of the crime of being frequenters of a common gaming house, were bound over in the sum of £10 for a period of twelve months.

Examining the economics of this punitive expedition, the authorities couldn't have shown much of a profit. A hundred and fifty quid seems a poor return on the employment of a posse of the Old Bill and the expenditure of a considerable amount of the court's time. Had we run our businesses on these lines we would have soon been skint. Still, it was all down to the taxpayer.

What was most illuminating was the comment of the North London magistrate, Mr. Frank Milton, as he dished out the fines. I quote him in full.

He said: 'The law on what is and what is not permitted is not a very easy one and some people think not a very logical one. It is going to be changed in a way which might in time, if the law comes into effect, make some but not all of your

111

activities legal. Meanwhile you were conducting activities on quite a large scale which were illegal.'

His words may not have carried the weight of a pronouncement by ex-Lord Chief Justice Goddard (who, by way, had retired in September), but I am sure they found an echo in the thoughts of several thousands of people throughout the country. They certainly found an echo in mine. I paid the fines and left the court on the Saturday morning. On Monday the Regency was open for business as usual.

This period in the lives of me and my brothers has never received much publicity. After all, why should it? There's nothing sensational in the hard graft and attention to detail that goes to building up most profit-making enterprises. There is naturally a fundamental difference in operational methods between creating a chain of grocery stores in the London suburbs and setting up clubs and spielers in the East End. The main difference lies in the staffing, and in our business we were obliged to be very selective indeed.

I hope I have been successful in painting a clear picture of the background against which our struggle for the good life took place. In the East End the gentle, unassuming boy grew into a gentle, unassuming man and in due course went to his anonymous grave with little to mark the time he had spent on earth except for the sorrow of his relatives. The boy who has an ambition for money and power must, of necessity, be hard, ruthless and able to do more than hold his own in an area where polite discussion is rare and force is the only argument understood by all. Me and my brothers carved out positions of power, influence and (unfortunately) notoriety by the exercise of these enforced procedures. We looked for similar characteristics in the people we gathered around us, for the nature of our business demanded it.

Look at it this way. In the operation of clubs and spielers considerable amounts of cash money are always floating around. This was a constant temptation to those whose trade was relieving others of their possessions. It was necessary to demonstrate to these gentry that attempts to divert Kray money to their own use was tantamount to making an application to enter the intensive care unit of the local hospital.

There was no lack of applicants for the jobs we were able to offer. Men we had known since childhood, whom we could trust to put our interests first, came along to get their share of the generous rewards we provided. That they had spent part of their lives as guests of Her Majesty was no bar to their being accepted. What was good enough for the Queen was good enough for us.

It is interesting to note that, out of this very practicable arrangement, grew the legend of what was to be referred to at a later date as 'The Firm'.

FIVE

There are times in every man's life when he sits back and has a good think about his past, his present and his future. As Shakespeare – or Marlow or Bacon – said, there is a tide in the affairs of men which taken at the flood leads on to fortune.

There was certainly a fair old tide running towards the end of 1960 and the early part of 1961, and I knew all about it because I was caught up in it. In the way of business I had no complaints. Me and my brothers were making money and, so far as the material things were concerned, we wanted for nothing. In our part of the metropolis we were on the top and we intended to stay there, but we were young enough and sufficiently ambitious to want to go further.

I was thirty four, happily married with a ten year old son, all three of us in good health and with no financial problems. Mum and Dad were fine – we saw to that – and the only clouds in an otherwise blue sky were the troubles of the twins, which didn't interfere with business but made their social life a little tricky. Ronnie had completed his stretch at Wandsworth, but he was far from well. The prison doctor, the sort of comedian whose jokes created gales of tears, said he was suffering from the effects of confinement. Our own doctor got him into St. Clements' hospital where at least he could receive proper treatment. Reggie had landed himself in a spot of bother which was the result of a series of unfortunate incidents.

It came about like this. During the time Ronnie was on the trot Reggie had spent some time in the area of Finchley where Ronnie was staying with friends. A chap called Danny Shay, a gambler with a motor business and a shady past, had been very helpful during this period and Reggie didn't forget debts. Shay came to Reggie one day and asked his assistance in collecting a gambling debt from a Polish shyster by the name of Podro, who owned a small shop in the Finchley Road the profits of which would have kept a sparrow alive – but only just. Podro's real income was derived from backing the biggest certainty in the gambling world, which was simply collecting the cash when he won at cards and welshing on the debt when he lost. He had worked a flanker on Shay to the tune of a hundred quid.

Now this chap Shay was no strong-arm man and Mr. Podro was a very wily customer who was well aware that gambling debts could not be collected through the normal legal channels. When Shay and Reggie turned up one day in a car driven by Georgie Osborne, a friend of Reggie's, the intention was to frighten the wily Podro into paying up and looking as pleasant as he could in the process. Podro, however, had other ideas. With a couple of the Old Bill hiding in the back of the shop, planted there by previous arrangement, Podro could well afford to throw his weight about, which he proceeded to do, going on about demanding protection money and so on. Reggie, a man of few words in such situations, hung a right-hander on Podro's chops, the Old Bill emerged from hiding and Shay, Reggie and Osborne were nicked.

I will never understand the offical mind as long as I live. Reggie, who had blatantly assisted in Ronnie's escape from Long Grove without even getting his wrist slapped, was charged with demanding money with menaces. I ask you? At the time Reggie had more money than he knew what to do with. Is it feasible that he would stick his neck out for peanuts which, in any case, belonged to some other monkey? It just doesn't make sense, but it gave the press a field day, GANGSTERS IN FINCHLEY ROAD, CHICAGO-STYLE

METHODS ALLEGATION, so ran the banner headlines and this would have been a funny story were it not for the fact that Reggie copped eighteen months at the Old Bailey. Poor little Shay earned himself three years. Georgie Osborne, who had done nothing more serious than drive Shay and Reggie to the wily Podro's establishment, got eighteen months. The law didn't endorse his driving licence, but maybe they forgot that. Come to think of it, I don't think Georgie had a driving licence anyway.

All of this takes me back to my philosophical remarks at the beginning of this chapter. With Reggie away in Wandsworth and Ronnie definitely not in the best of health, the responsibility of keeping our affairs in good running order was fairly and squarely on my shoulders. I was chasing around like a blue-arsed fly between the Double R (which had been expanded to include a gymnasium) and the various gambling joints which we either owned or in which we had an interest. It was at this point that I had to ask myself if it was all worth it and to come back with the answer that I had no option, that it was my duty to my brothers to look after their interests. Luckily I had a few good lads around me in whom I had the utmost trust. They weren't the old family retainer type, far from it, they were hard men who put themselves about in the right places and at the right times so that nobody was under the delusion that the Kray enterprises were ripe for picking while Reggie was away and Ronnie in hospital. Of course there was trouble, because more than one greedy eye had been cast on our successful operations, but there was no question of seeking police protection. It was a matter of hitting first, hitting hard and continuing the process until the opposition was demoralised and completely defeated.

I know it's deplorable and shouldn't be permitted, but violence exists as one of the hard facts of life. Once caught in its vortex there is no way out except emigration. True, there is a small percentage of humanity which preaches that one should turn the other cheek, and I am sure that they find happiness and fulfilment in practising what they preach. If everybody was like them our prisons would be empty of men convicted of crimes of assault upon the person (a nice way of describing a couple of sharp hooks to the hooter) and, you know what, there would be no wars! Don't accuse me of splitting hairs. I've never started a war in my life. That can safely be left to the moralists who claim that God is on their side. Funny how He can manage to be on both sides at once.

Curiously enough, one of my most able helpers during this crucial period was a very tasty individual who had been a Commando during the war. He had been trained to maim and, if necessary, to kill with his bare hands. He was then let loose in Civvy Street to earn his living as best he could. I don't think I need to make the obvious point – and he wasn't the only one of his kind either.

While on the subject of violence I'd like to try and make it clear, to the best of my ability, what it all amounted to. There was what I would describe as the normal sort of violence, a punch-up at a street corner, an isolated brawl in a pub or a club where the maximum damage suffered by those involved was a few cuts and bruises, no serious matter in a district such as Bethnal Green where the time-honoured way of settling differences was with the fists. Such things are fairly rare in Berkeley Square but common east of the Strand. Then there was the superior and planned type of violence involving the use of 'tools' or 'weapons' such as knuckledusters, knives, razors and iron bars, usually indulged in by groups of youthful hooligans, where the injuries would need careful attention in the casualty department of the local hospital. Major violence, which often took the form of sophisticated torture and resulted in injuries of the most terrifying description, was rare. Rarer still was the extreme violence which ended in death.

If one is to believe sensational newspaper stories and evidence given in courts by villains-turned-informers, Charles and Edward Richardson were arch-practitioners of the cult of violence in its most bizarre forms. Having suffered myself from sensational publicity I reserve my opinion. Of course I knew the Richardsons, but had little to do with them. They kept to their province south of the river, and didn't interfere with us. When we met it was on neutral ground such as the Astor Club, just behind the South side of Berkeley Square where Sulky, the owner, and a good friend to me and my brothers, maintained a peace that was rarely breached by even the most hardened tearaway. I must make the point that is accepted by everyone who has had to fight hard in the process of achieving success in any area of life, which is that violence is bad for business and the last resort when all methods of peaceful persuasion have been tried and have failed.

My personal reaction to the practice of violence is to avoid it at all costs. During my career as a professional boxer I gained the decision in eighteen of my twenty one bouts by using skill and experience. I really had no wish to inflict damage on my opponents, because it wasn't necessary to go to those lengths, I just wasn't that sort of fighter. Later in my life, when I was engaged in an area where the prospect of violence was always round the corner, I still held to the belief that a punch-up is no solution to an argument. Physical aggression leads to retaliation which in turn invites further violence and at the end of it all nothing is settled and only antagonism remains.

Don't get the impression from all this that I am a pacifist. I have lived my life in close contact with reality, and hard reality at that. But it's a funny thing that, amongst people who live hard and sometimes die hard, there is somehow a soft core of gentleness and warmth, a sympathy expressed in action rather than words which is nothing to do with anything but the human love and understanding in all of us, no matter what we are or what we have done. It crops up from time to time, suddenly, surprisingly, warmth and emotion that defeats a cruel purpose before it is begun – but that is where hope starts.

Maybe if I hadn't spent nearly seven years in prison these thoughts might never have occurred to me.

What does occur to me now is that I have made little mention of the men we gathered around us in those early days when we dived head first into the drinking club and spieler business with lots of enthusiasm but little experience. They were not employees in the strict sense of the word, but were trusted allies who looked after us and in return expected that we should look after them. There was Alf Willey, a large man four years my senior and known throughout the East End as Limehouse Willie, an expert on all forms of gambling with the sort of brain that could work out odds faster than a computer. There was Big Pat Connolly, a huge and happy man whose presence at the door of the Double R spelt a big welcome to the members and a formidable danger sign to potential trouble-makers. It amused me to watch him dance, this massive figure weighing more than twenty stone tripping round the floor like a barrage balloon on castors. Ian Barrie, a lifetime close and loyal friend of the twins, was also very much around, never pushing himself forward but always there when required.

Another of our 'big-boys' was Tommy Brown, known as the Bear of Tottenham. He was enormously strong but by nature quiet and withdrawn, and one had to know him very well indeed before being accepted as a confidant and friend. Billy Donovan was another of the big guys and I think the hardest man I ever met – what we refer to in the East End as 'tasty'. Georgie Osborne, who collected eighteen months along with Reggie in the affair of the wily Podro, was the same age as the twins and had been connected with them in one way or another all their lives. He managed Le Monde, a club in Limerston Street, Chelsea, for us. In '61 or '62, I don't quite remember which year, he began to drink heavily and died very suddenly, a great loss because he was a very old and trusted friend.

There were others who came and went, some of them to marry and settle down to a nine to five job, some to Pentonville, Wandsworth or The Scrubs.

Now all of these men had criminal records, but they were not selected because of that. It was incidental to the life they led as hard men that they came into conflict with the Old Bill.

We had premises, clients and large sums of cash to protect, and we chose the men for the job. If, in the course of their work, they fell foul of the police and collected a bit of porridge, their spell in jail was made as comfortable as possible and their wives and dependants didn't suffer.

I want to clear up, here and now, the sinister implications of the use of that two word description The Firm. In the East End it was quite usual to refer to any group of persons who worked together in an enterprise which kept no books or records, dealt in cash (known as 'readies') and provided their own social security without sticking stamps on cardboard folders, as a Firm. The description was not a Kray copyright. The villains and thieves, the robbery-with-violence boys and so on were known as mobs, and there was a vast difference between a firm and a mob. You may take it from me that we were not the only firm operating in the Bethnal Green manor, but we were far and away the most successful and the best organised, which is why we were the best known.

As can be imagined, we were well acquainted with the Old Bill at both Bow and Bethnal Green. The Double R, as I have mentioned before, was a mere couple of hundred yards from Bow police station. In general, a truce was maintained between the Old Bill and ourselves and, apart from the occasion when the Regency was raided, they didn't interfere with our activities and we had no interest in interfering with theirs. However, just about the time Ronnie came out of St. Clement's and while Reggie was still in Wandsworth, I sensed that trouble with the Old Bill was on the cards.

It has never been any secret that a certain amount of corruption exists in the police force, and both Ronnie and Reggie had been the subject of approaches by one or two of the local bent officers. These approaches had been turned down flat, not on any moral grounds but because they both realised that, once bribes were handed over, the whole thing snowballed into a situation where the work of years could be destroyed in a matter of days. Ronnie, anyway, hated the Old Bill and Reggie hadn't much time for them either. As for me, I was quite happy to get on with the job and take my chances.

An indication of the way the wind was blowing happened early in 1961. Ronnie and I were at Vallance Road when Big Pat Connolly's wife telephoned to say that he had been taken ill very suddenly. A friend of ours by the name of Jimmy Kensit happened to be on the spot with his old banger and, since it was the nearest available transport, we hopped in and set off for Big Pat's place to see if there was anything we could do to help. When we got there we found that Connolly had been taken off to hospital with suspected polio. This was a pretty serious business. We had all been in recent contact with Connolly, but my first thought was for Dolly and Gary, to get in touch and tell them to go to the nearest hospital for an anti-polio injection.

I rang Dolly from a call-box in Queensbridge Road and we then decided to get back to Vallance Road on the double from where we could telephone everybody who had been in recent contact with Connolly. On the way Jimmy Kensit stopped outside his flat in Pritchard's Row. Then everything began to happen. A squad car roared up and stopped, out of it leapt the Old Bill, one in plain clothes and two in uniform, and it was plain that the object of their attention wasn't a murder or a robbery with violence but Jimmy Kensit, Ronnie and myself.

What was it all about? The plain-clothes man, a detective constable by the name of Bartlett, did all the talking while his uniformed colleagues prowled around Kensit's banger, inspecting tyres, testing brakes, looking for the Road Fund licence which wasn't there and making themselves generally useful in investigating serious crime. The bold Bartlett, smart, alert and straight out of a Dixon of Dock Green script, conducted an inquisition, whose car is this, it has been reported stolen, what's your name, where have you been, where are you going, so you're Charlie Kray and you're Ronnie Kray, where's the other one and so on. It was a pantomime. All we needed was a Fairy Godmother, who luckily turned up in the shape of a well-known local judo expert, black belt Billy Gipp, who trained at the gym over the Double R and was a highly respected citizen of Bethnal Green.

This was manna from Heaven. In front of the Old Bill and a gathering crowd of residents of Pritchard's Row, I asked Billy to carry out a search of the car and our persons. The bold Bartlett objected as a matter of form and Billy paid no attention as a matter of principle. The curtain came down on the first act as the three of us were ushered into the squad car and taken off to the nick.

In the interval, before the curtain went up on the second and final act of the panto, many things took place. The bold Bartlett strutted about in Dalston nick, told us we were the scum of the earth, prophesied that we would all be eating porridge shortly, organised searches of our respective homes without the benefit of warrants and finally disappeared (without a puff of smoke) before we were released, after having been charged with – wait for it – being suspected persons loitering with intent to commit a felony!

The curtain went up on the second act at Marylebone Police Court. The bold Bartlett, ably assisted by a uniformed officer, gave testimony from the witness box under oath to the effect that Ronnie and I had been seen trying the door handles of parked cars in Queensbridge Road at a certain hour in the forenoon (it was later proved that, at that time, I was talking to a telephone engineer at 178 Vallance Road) and that we fled in Kensit's car after being warned by him, via a blast on his car horn, that we were being watched. It must have come as a shock to the bold Bartlett when it later transpired in evidence that Kensit's car was equipped with a horn together with a button to operate the same – but there was no wiring in between. That's right. The horn just didn't work.

Of course the case was thrown out. The magistrate, Mr. John Aubrey-Fletcher, didn't call the bold Bartlett a bloody liar, nor did he direct that the papers be sent to the Director of Public Prosecutions to consider the question of giving false evidence under oath. Yet what bothered me was that the case was brought at all. The bold Bartlett (who was later convicted of interfering with small girls) was only a pawn in the game.

The prosecution was initiated at a higher level, but why?

I found an explanation in part in an incident which took place about the same time as Ronnie and I were hauled before the court. Reggie was walking down Vallance Road one day when a woman came up to him, accompanied by a policeman, and said 'That's the man. I recognise him. That's the man who robbed my father.' It turned out that the lady, a Mrs. Lilian Hertzberg, had some time previously walked into her father's flat at Arthur Deakin House in Stepney and into a pair of villains who were turning the place over. Some jewellery and other articles to a total value of five hundred and two pounds went out of the door, along with the villains of whom one, according to Mrs. Hertzberg, was Reggie. There were two hearings in the lower courts before Reggie appeared at the Inner London Session, and during this time Reggie was held in custody, the police having objected to bail on the grounds that witnesses might be intimidated.

Whether Mrs. Hertzberg genuinely believed that Reggie was one of the men she saw or was suffering from hallucinations is a matter for speculation. However, at the Sessions, she had a change of heart, mind or spectacles and admitted that she could not give a positive identification. The case was thrown out and Reggie was granted costs against the police (or out of public funds, which is another way of putting it).

I have dealt with these incidents at some length because they had great significance, in my opinion. At the time these prosecutions took place we were drawing substantial incomes from our various enterprises, which included the highly lucrative Esmeralda's Barn, a very posh gambling club in Knightsbridge. It wasn't commonsense that we should indulge in sneak-thieving, trying to open the doors of parked cars in one of the meanest districts in London, breaking into Stepney flats on the off-chance of hoisting near-worthless jewellery or a few quid in cash. What stood out a mile was that our cards had been marked for us, somewhere in the higher echelons of the Old Bill the order had gone out to lean on the

Krays. Why? The answer was obvious. We had bought ourselves a lot of things, cars, clothes, jewellery and so on, but we hadn't bought any policemen.

In that, I believe, lay the explanation for the tactics employed by the Old Bill. Reggie and Ronnie took it all in good part, didn't bother to take any action for false arrest or malicious prosecution, had a laugh and a drink and carried on with the job of making money. It was then that they first began to glory in that feeling of invulnerability that I mentioned earlier, the state of mind that comes to a fighter after a string of victories, the blithe belief that nothing can touch them, that they are the winners even before the bell sounds for the beginning of the first round.

In this breeding ground germinates the spirit of recklessness that may one day burst into terrible flower.

He was a big man with a bland, open face, great charm of manner and a quiet chuckling laugh that started at his mouth but somehow didn't get as far as his eyes. His name was Leslie Payne. Reggie met him at the premises of Johnny Hutton, a Leyton car-dealer with whom we had done some business. If I remember rightly the meeting took place in the early part of 1960 while Reggie was on bail awaiting trial in the case of the wily Podro.

This Payne was a very bright boy indeed. In his middle thirties, a year or so older than me, he had led a very full and extremely crooked life. According to what he told me, he had been an officer in the Army (I discovered later that he never rose above the rank of sergeant) and had successfully fiddled his way through the war and its aftermath acting as an unofficial agent for the disposal of surplus military stores usually before they had been classified as such. Most of these enterprising exploits had been carried out in Athens where, he explained, everyone was at it, flogging lorries, petrol, food and drink to the native Greeks and making small fortunes in the process.

He struck me as being a very talented and knowledgeable

man who could have made a lot of money in honest dealing, but he seemed to prefer to go about things in a devious way, bending the law as and when necessary. His confederate was a little fat man by the name of Freddie Gore, an accountant of sorts, well-educated and a wizard with figures. The two of them were engaged in some sort of dodgy car business at the expense of the finance companies who in those days would lend money on anything with four wheels and a log book. I thought it rather strange that this pair should be operating in the East End, where they stuck out like a sore thumb, but I suppose they had their reasons.

I always had a quiet giggle when I saw them together. They reminded me of a ventriloquist and his dummy. I could visualise little fat Freddie sitting on Payne's knee, one going through the motions and the other providing the chat. I never got around to deciding who worked the controls.

During the months following his meeting with Reggie, Payne was continually turning up with ideas and propositions. We did one or two deals with him through our car sales but his other projects rarely got beyond the discussion stage until he came up with the news that a first-class club in the West End was on the market. This was right up our street. There was every indication that the Betting and Gaming Act would become law in a short time, and this was an opportunity to be in on the ground floor of what promised (and turned out) to be the gambling bonanza of all time.

Payne and Gore worked out the financial details, we put up the money and Esmeralda's Barn in Wilton Place was ours. Reggie and Ronnie became directors, Payne was the secretary and Gore fiddled the books.

They say Fortune makes strange bedfellows, and at first sight the association between Payne and us seemed unusual, but it was quite a practical arrangement. He was a very able man, an expert at initiating all kinds of promising schemes, but he always had to have somebody up in front. Not that he was shy or retiring, far from it, but I think he liked to see himself as the power behind the throne.

A good example of this was when we had the meeting on the occasion of taking over a controlling interest in Esmeralda's Barn. It took place in the flat of a retired naval officer, Commander Drummond, who lived over the Scotch House at the junction of Knightsbridge and Brompton Road with an excellent view of Harrod's from the sitting room windows. The Commander was a real old sea-dog with bright blue eyes, a small moustache, a very courteous manner and the most amazing canine friend I have ever come across in the whole of my life. This animal, a cross-bred collie by the look of it, was almost human. A word, a glance or a snap of the fingers from the Commander brought instant obedience and Ronnie, who loved animals, was mad about it. I remember him saying that the sort of man who could win such trust from an animal could himself be trusted.

However, I am straying from the subject. Whether Payne had roped in the Commander or the other way round I couldn't be sure, but the Commander did most of the talking. There were seven of us all told, Payne and Gore, Ronnie, myself, de Faye and Burns (the major shareholders in the company that owned Esmeralda's Barn) and our naval friend. Payne sat and smiled, Gore scribbled figures on pieces of paper, de Faye showed no interest except when money was mentioned and the only disagreeable note in the proceedings was sounded by Burns, who made a rude remark or two on the subject of East is East and West is West and never the twain etc. I broke the news to him that Rudyard Kipling belonged to another era and that we weren't there to discuss class distinctions but to do business. We finally settled on a mutually agreeable figure and the deal was concluded.

I was to see much of the Commander in the ensuing years, and the more I saw of him the more I liked him. He was a bit of a mystery with his beautiful flat, expensive clothes, vintage Rolls and no visible means of support except his remarkable talent for bringing people together. For all I knew he might have had a substantial private income, but he never mentioned it.

Esmeralda's Barn turned out to be a gold mine and no trouble at all. Tony Mancini, a good friend of mine, joined us as manager, and his services were to prove invaluable. He was an expert on big-time gambling, a short, dark man always impeccably dressed and a heavy gambler with many friends of a similar disposition. It shook me sometimes when I saw thousands of pounds being staked on the turn of a single card at the chemmy tables. I had an occasional dabble myself, but not to that extent.

By May of 1961 the Betting and Gaming Act had become law, the Kray brothers had been cleared of trying the handles of parked cars and robbing working-class flats, the Old Bill had closed down the Double R (they had to do something) and we were really in business in the West End. But we didn't turn our backs on Bethnal Green altogether. It was there that we were born and brought up, and our real friends lived, people we had known all our lives. Our new acquaintances, lords and ladies, wealthy businessmen, stars of stage and screen, could never take their place.

Mum was, as always, the centre of our lives. We wanted to give her everything she wanted, yet she wanted very little. She steadfastly refused to budge from Vallance Road, where she was among relatives and friends, and was happy when, from time to time, the twins went back home to the small room they shared when they were children. When Reggie and Ronnie spoke of 'home', they didn't mean any of the several places in which they could live – 178 Vallance Road was home to them, and it was there that they took their closest associates to meet their mother and have a cup of tea in the upstairs sitting room. The twins made no attempt to conceal their humble origins, on the contrary they were proud, not in the boasting or inverted snobbery sense but simply because they saw no necessity to adopt manners and accents which, as T. S. Eliot said, would be as incongruous as 'a silk hat on the head of a Bradford millionaire'. People could accept them for what they were and on their own terms or they could piss off. As a social attitude it was not only honest but entirely successful.

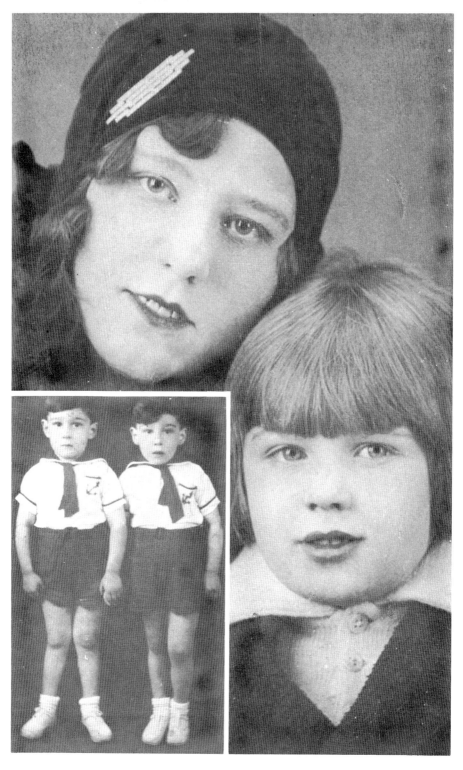

Young Charles with Mum, Violet Kray. *Inset* The twins.

Charles wins his first six-round professional fight.

Ronnie, Reggie and Charles: 'The Fighting Krays'.

Above (From left) Charles Kray Snr, Violet, Tommy Hall, Charles' ex-wife Dolly, and Charles.
Below (From left) The Mayor of Bethnal Green, Councillor Robert Hare, with Charles, Ronnie, and Charles' son Gary.

Above (From left) Leslie Payne, Reggie, Ronnie. *Below* (From left) 'Mad' Teddy Smith, Ronnie and Lord Boothby.

Above Reggie and Eddie Pucci, Shirley Bassey and Jimmy Clark are in the foreground on the right. Charles is on the far left. *Below* Fund-raising for the Mile End Hospital at the Krays' Kentucky Club. Front row (from left) Danny La Rue, Barbara Windsor, George Sewell, Sulky of the Astor Club, Terry Dene. At the back on the right are Queenie Watts, James Booth and Victor Spinetti.

Above (From left) Eddie Pucci, Ronnie, George Raft, Reggie, Rocky Marciano and Charles.
Below Fund-raising for the Peter Pan Society at the Krays' Cambridge Rooms: (from left) Charles, Dolly, Noel Harrison, Reggie, Micky Forsyte, Lita Rosa, Ronnie, Barbara Windsor, Ronald Fraser.

Above When Sonny Liston visited the Kentucky Club. In dark glasses is Lennie Peters, who became a pop star as half of Peters and Lee. *Below* At yet another charity do the Club re-ran Ted 'Kid' Lewis's fight films. (From left) Ronnie, Terry Spinks, Charles, Bobby Buckley, 'Staff', Ted Lewis and 'Kid' Berg.

Above Charles Snr and Violet with Larry Gaines (standing) and the raffled racehorse Solway Cross.
Below The Brooks at Bildeston, the mansion the twins bought. Mum and Dad moved into a cottage in the grounds.

Above Charles lands a right. *Below* The twins in boxing gear.

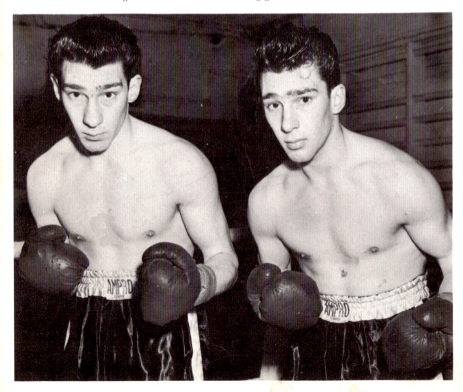

The Evening Standard's cartoonist Jak commented on the Krays' careers. *Above* The caption was 'Gang War Flares Up in London's East End'. *Below* At the Old Bailey Reggie called prosecutor Kenneth Jones, QC, a fat slob.

"Would you clarify that last point again, you fat slob!"

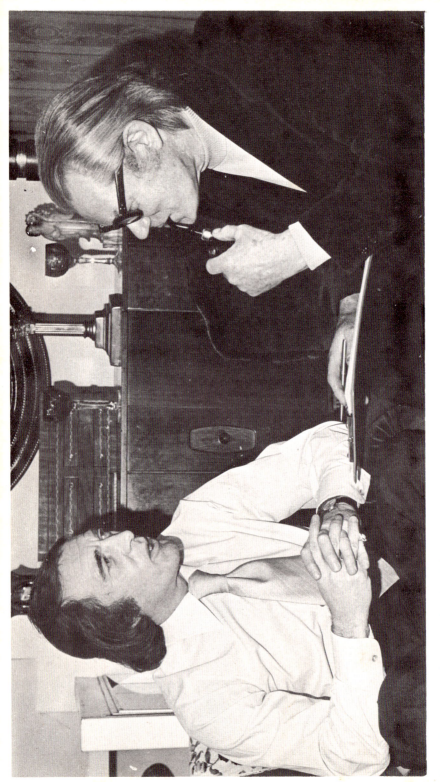

Charles Kray today, with co-writer Jonathan Sykes.

Looking back now on the picture of the three of us in those affluent days, it was not unsatisfactory. True, both Reggie and Ronnie had served prison sentences, but they made no secret of the fact. In our line of business it was nothing unusual – many of the well-dressed and suave gentlemen who greeted the members of their clubs with a big smile and a few welcoming words had eaten their ration of porridge and showed no signs of suffering adverse after-effects. In fact many of them were respected members of society with a stake in the community and homes in the stockbroker belt. In any case there was no great social stigma attached to having done a bit of 'bird'. Most sensible people adopted the attitude 'there but for the grace of God go I,' and left it at that. The thought occurs to me now that, if everybody were to be punished for the crimes they had committed, the prisons would have to be greatly enlarged. There would probably be more of the population inside than outside. Without going into detail, which would be pointless after this lapse of time, I confess that I pulled a few strokes which could have qualified me for the porridge stakes, but I was lucky. I only saw the inside of a prison from the visitor's viewpoint, and even that arm's-length acquaintance had its deterrent effect. I had no desire whatsoever to become an inmate.

To get back to the twins, there is no doubt that they were popular with the night club set, that happy band of pleasure-seekers who were to be seen in the smart restaurants and the fashionable clubs. As a consequence, there were few social and theatrical gatherings at which the twins were not present, not as curiosities to be observed from a distance, as some post-1968 commentators would have us believe, but as characters in their own right, rough and ready perhaps but none the less intelligent and amusing. In their identical well-cut, midnight blue dinner jackets they made a very presentable pair, their behaviour was correct – too correct on occasions in the presence of ladies – and, though they both were fond of a drink, it was only Ronnie who occasionally had one over the eight.

As for myself, I was naturally on the spot at all material

times but I was not a great socialiser. I liked to get home to Dolly and Gary and put my feet up in my own place like any family man. The many photographs taken at the time show Reggie and Ronnie very much to the fore along with the various notabilities in the boxing, show business and social worlds with whom they were friendly. I was rarely featured and then mainly in the backgrond, which suited me fine. Much of my work was done behind the scenes, where I kept a close eye on the day-to-day events in a business empire which was rapidly expanding.

It was during that time that I began to learn a lot, not only about business but about Leslie Payne. The man had a mania for money, he was like a bloodhound whose nose twitched only when there was cash in the offing. He was doing well out of the profits from Esmeralda's Barn, but that wasn't enough. Along with Freddie Gore and using capital put up by all of us, he took us into the long-firm fraud field, an illegal area where the risks were low, the profits high and the turnover speedy. No sooner was one venture abandoned than another was started. The whole procedure was like putting coins into a one-armed bandit and collecting the jackpot every time you pulled the handle. The mechanics were complicated and I didn't properly understand them even though Payne explained the set-up but, as in all enterprises of this nature somebody had to carry the can or, to use the slang phrase, end up with a paper hat. According to Payne's Law, the suppliers of goods were first in line for the paper hat treatment. I had my own ideas about that and stayed far enough out on the fringes of the operations to ensure that no paper hat fell on my head. Payne and Gore were too fly to be directly involved, and anyone who wanted to put a paper hat on the twins was welcome to try. They were nobody's mugs.

The long firm could have lasted a long time but Payne was ever the one to add complications. It seemed that his mind needed the extra stimulation of repairing the damage caused by throwing a spanner into a smoothly-working piece of machinery. He was like a chess player who would suggest changing the relative positions of the king and the queen to add a further dimension to the game. In fact I was sure that it was all a game to him. He was earning a huge income, but still maintained the modest house in Dulwich where he lived with his wife and baby daughter. He did allow himself the luxury of a bit on the side, a very beautiful middle-European girl who was known as Yutke and described herself as a model, but she didn't cost him much so far as I could see. Yet so long as Payne had enough money to pay his bills (which he always did, very promptly) then money ceased to matter and the power game took over.

I must admit I rather liked the man, and so did Ronnie, but Reggie couldn't stand him at any price. I had met with this sort of situation before so I didn't pay too much attention. It was unusual for both the twins to like the same person, but since I was the one who had the most contact with Payne it was easy for me to prevent matters coming to a head.

Just about this time, when our West End ventures were expanding rapidly, stories began to appear in the press on the menace of 'gangsterism' and the rise of the 'protection' racket. No names were mentioned, but obvious references were made to twins and ex-boxers, and the impression was created that West End clubland was a seething inferno of menace and extortion where timid club owners with soft hands and softer heads shook with terror as scar-faced villains muttered hoarse threats into their shell-like ears as they relieved them of the contents of their wallets. Bollocks! Editorial policy, like charity (to which it bears not the slightest resemblance in other respects), creates a multitude of sins – the misquotation is not mine but Oscar Wilde's – and certain newspapers jumped on this hobby-horse with an enthusiasm which was only matched by their lack of knowledge. West End club owners were not chickens. They were hard and practical men engaged in enterprises with a faint flavour of criminality and if Scarface Joe of Walworth came along one evening and threatened to smash a few glasses they gave him a few quid (which they could well afford) and sent him on his way. This was in the smaller establishments. In the more lavish places Scarface Joe wouldn't get past the doorman.

Let's get this into proper perspective. Running any lucrative business calls for a high degree of intelligence coupled with experience and ability in the particular field of operation. The gambling and drinking club operation is highly sophisticated, and success doesn't just happen but is brought about as a result of a lot of hard work, skill and a knowledge of human nature. Me and my brothers learned these things the hard way from the clubs we ran in the East End and also in the early days of Esmeralda's Barn. The club proprietor had to be an amalgam of practical businessman, genial host, first-class organiser, father confessor, general fixer and, in cases of staff shortage, relief barman. Between us the twins, Payne, Gore and myself fulfilled these essential qualifications. Scarface Joe of Walworth didn't bother us, nor did he bother the Meadows brothers, the Nash brothers, Freddie Irani, Paul Raymond, Gilbert France and old Uncle Tom Cobleigh and all.

Believe me, I'm not being facetious. Sensational stories about gangsters and protection rackets are properly the province of those who write newspapers for people who can't read, and I have no quarrel with that. They behave according to their lights. Equally, the organisation and management of drinking and gambling clubs is the province of the type of men I have mentioned. To draw the obvious parallel, no club owner has ever put himself in a position where he has had to pay a peer of the realm the sum of £40,000 agreed damages plus indemnification against costs plus a crawling and abject apology to that peer and the other person involved in what was the most shameful and ignoble campaign in the history of the British press. I refer, of course, to the scurrilous and completely unjustified attack on Lord Boothby and my brother Ronnie by the Sunday Mirror in 1964. Make your own judgement – I know what mine is.

Here are the facts. In our natural progression to the lush pastures of the West End, where the rewards were high and the risk small, we took our experience and reputation with us. We expanded not because we breathed threats down the necks of our fellow club proprietors but because we knew what we were about and employed the tactics of the board room to get what we wanted. Of course somebody had to suffer, but in the dog-eat-dog world of business that was inevitable. Consider the cost in terms of human tragedy when a stock market operator in Throgmorton Street, by a skilful series of share manipulations, destroys the livelihood of thousands of men in the industrial North. I wouldn't like to have that sort of crime on my conscience.

A final word. It is true that a protection racket flourished in West End clubland, but it wasn't operated by thugs, gangsters and criminals. It was in the hands of a few gentlemen with moderate salaries and expensive tastes who had no need of membership cards. Their right of entry to private clubs was guaranteed by a small and not very impressive card signed by no less a person than the Commissioner of Police for the Metropolis. I have reason to believe that several club owners co-operated with these gentlemen. We would have no truck with them at all, which in the light of later events may have been a mistake on our part. At the time we didn't think so.

To get back to the East End, from which in essence we had never been far away and with whose residents we maintained regular contact, we opened the Kentucky club, opposite the Empire Cinema in Mile End Road, in early 1962. This was as they say on the playbills, 'in response to popular request'. Since the Double R had been closed down, many of the old clients had asked us when we intended to open another place, so we did just that. Finance was no problem, thanks to Esmeralda's Barn, which was doing its best to compete with the Royal Mint in churning out the ackers, together with Payne's little larks which paid big dividends. In consequence the Kentucky was refurbished regardless of expense and looked it. Needless to say, it was packed every night.

What began to worry me about this time was the way

Reggie and Ronnie chucked money about. I suppose I was being rather conservative, but I was always one for the quiet life. Dolly, Gary and myself had moved into a nice flat in a council block in Poplar and lived in quite a modest style. The twins, however, were well into the social swim, mixing with the upper crust and wining and dining in Mayfair's exclusive restaurants and night spots. Naturally in their position they had to be seen about and it was all good for business, but I would have liked to see some of our profits invested in betting shops which, now that betting was legalised, had begun to spring up all over the place. Unfortunately I was in a minority of one.

What I did approve of was the charitable affairs in which we became involved. As has been mentioned, we were always available to help at church functions and suchlike in our younger days, and now that we had both the facilities and the money to do something about helping others we were approached by (and made approaches to) the various bodies who administered charities in the Bethnal Green area. I won't make any bones about it. Charitable activities were good for the image – and it wasn't all that unpleasant to lash out a few quid for the benefit of old people and kids and, in general, do something in a practical way to help those who had not been so fortunate as us.

To put it briefly and bluntly, me and my brothers were East End lads who had come up the hard way, accumulating a few quid on the climb up the ladder. It was publicly stated on more than one occasion that our charitable efforts were some sort of conscience money, that, in the words of the poet, we gave to pity what we owed to justice. Our association with Bob Hare, the mayor of Bethnal Green and a tireless worker for charity, came in for some less than complimentary comment. Bob himself, a really fine and warm-hearted man, was referred to in a slightly derogatory manner as a van driver for the local meals-on-wheels service. This I will say of him – he was a dedicated man who devoted his life to community service, and I'm sure he would have scrubbed floors if that had been necessary in the pursuance of his aims.

There was no adverse comment from the nurses at Mile End hospital, the Queen Elizabeth Hospital for Children, the Cancer Campaign appeals, the Repton Boys' Club and other organisations which benefited from our fund-raising efforts. They took the money thankfully and we gave it happily. It was also good, clean fun in which we were joined by local notabilities such as Ted Kid Lewis, Terry Spinks, Billy Walker and the management and cast of the Theatre Royal, Stratford-atte-Bow. During the time the film of Sparrows Can't Sing was being made, the Kentucky was used as part of the location, and we had regular visits there from Barbara Windsor, James Booth, Victor Spinetti, George Sewell and La Littlewood herself, a remarkably plain-spoken lady with enough charm to lure a bear from a barrel of honey.

We often made the Kentucky available for charity functions, and also hired local premises for other events. One of Reggie's promotions at the York Hall in Bethnal Green was unique. On an all-in wrestling bill he matched Bobby Ramsey, boxer and properly gloved for the bout, with Roy (Chopper) Levacq, a judo and karate man fighting under all-in rules. It was the same Ramsey who had been involved in the Martin affair where Ronnie was awarded three years in 1956. It was all a bit of a giggle which the capacity audience enjoyed. Sitting in ringside seats were the two Terrys, Downes and Spinks, Kid Lewis, Kid Berg, our old judo friend Billy Gipp and Bob Hare, mayor of Bethnal Green. The decision, in case anybody is interested, went to Ramsey who knocked out Levacq in the second round.

It was all happening in the East End during 1962 and the early part of 1963. Reggie and Ronnie's show-business connections in the West End resulted in a procession of international stars appearing at the Kentucky. Billy Daniels, the Old Black Magic man himself, came along after his stints at the Palladium. The Clark Brothers made guest appearances, and we gave a party for them at the Queen's Hall, Commerical Road, where Lennie Peters, the blind singer-pianist who later became famous as the male half of Peters and Lee, entertained the guests. It had become the smart thing to do, spending an evening at the Kentucky, rubbing shoulders with the cast of Oh What a Lovely War from the Theatre Royal, being entertained by the plentiful local talent including Colin Hicks (Tommy Steele's brother), Queenie Watts from the Iron Bridge pub Canning Town and others too numerous to mention. Daniel Farson, television interviewer and son of the famous Negley Farson, was a regular visitor in pursuit of his favourite hobby, which was drinking. One night, I remember, we closed the club and left him sleeping in a chair. He was still there the following day when the cleaners turned up.

The best party we ever had at the Kentucky was after the world premiere of Sparrows Can't Sing which took place at the Empire Cinema opposite the club. Royalty was present in the shape of Princess Margaret's husband, who had recently changed his status from plain Anthony Armstrong-Jones to Lord Snowdon. He didn't cross the road to join us, though I'm sure he would have loved to do just that – he was, and still is, not the conventional sort of Royal – but the whole of the cast turned up in force. Lord Effingham, who had joined Reggie and Ronnie on the board at Esmeralda's Barn, was there spreading his brand of aristocrat charm around. The party went on until the early hours of the morning.

One story that I must tell while on the subject of the Kentucky happened one night when we were featuring a midget entertainer by the name of Little Hank in cabaret. As the lights went down and the spots focussed on the stage, Little Hank emerged from the wings to start his act. Suddenly, from the other side of the stage, Ronnie made an entrance holding what seemed to be the end of a dog's leash. Whatever was on the other end of the leash was obviously reluctant to make its bow. Ronnie gave a few tugs, and there it was, a very small and extremely handsome donkey which stepped daintily to the footlights and waited for the applause, which wasn't long in coming. The audience roared as Little Hank gravely mounted the donkey's back and sang his opening number while Ronnie stood by with a very straight face. He saved the laughs until later, when he brought the animal down to the bar, where it stood patiently while Ronnie had a few drinks. The looks on the faces of the members as they came through the door and saw a real live donkey at the bar can well be imagined. Later Ronnie gave the donkey to a member as a present for one of his children.

For me the funniest part of the incident was that the chap who took the donkey home turned up at Vallance Road about three in the morning asking what he ought to do about his unsolicited gift. Little Jenny was keeping the whole neighbourhood awake with interminable hee-haws. 'Put its bloody head in a sack,' said Ronnie, and went back to bed.

Shortly after the party to celebrate the opening of Sparrows Can't Sing, the Kentucky Club closed its doors. The request for renewal of the club licence had been turned down by the local justices without any reason being given, nor were they obliged to give one. I found this action disturbing. There seemed to be no valid objection to the manner in which the club was conducted, the rules had been carried out to the letter, applications for the extension of hours when necessary had been made in the prescribed form and had been granted. Now why should an establishment which added to the amenities of the district and was well patronised by respectable people be closed down literally at a moment's notice? There was only one answer to that question, and I didn't like it very much. It was the same old business all over again, the faceless gentlemen with the warrant cards being denied what they considered to be their legitimate perks and hence taking what they considered the necessary action. They had failed to nail us on the ridiculous criminal charges of trying the handles of parked cars, being suspected persons loitering with intent to commit a felony, burgling a lousy council flat, but they had been successful in closing the Double R and they did the same with the Kentucky. Yes, the Old Bill was on the trail again, teaching the bloody upstart

Krays that the law's demands, however illegal, should be met. Well, you can bet your boots that the bloody upstart Krays were hardened in their determination not to hand over one single penny, so it was deadlock, wasn't it?

The closing of the Kentucky made not the slightest difference to us financially. Our operations had broadened to take in a number of clubs in the West End, the twins owned a small hotel, the Glenrae, in Seven Sisters Road and Payne was concluding successful negotiations for a controlling interest in the Cambridge Rooms on the Kingston by-pass. Esmeralda's Barn, where we had installed a discotheque in the basement, was more than earning its keep. Payne and Gore had reached the stage where they were able to set up a legitimate company which later took on the dignified name of the Carston Group with very posh offices in Great Portland Street. Payne had a financial connection with an obscure bank and the money was rolling in as the number of long firms went into – and out of – operation.

Now that the Kentucky had gone out of business I saw much less of the twins, who were spending much of their time between the Cambridge Rooms and the Glenrae. We still had our weekly meeting when, along with Payne and Gore, we went over the proceedings of the previous seven days, counted the considerable takings and had a share-out. At one of these weekly meetings Payne was absent. Gore told us that he had taken off for Nigeria and would be back in a few days.

This was very unlike Payne, who was always very punctual and dependable, and we couldn't help wondering what it was all about. Reggie was quite angry. He had never liked the man, and was convinced that he was up to some monkey-tricks which would leave us holding the baby. Ronnie and I soothed him down, Payne returned in due course and all was explained. He had paid an exploratory visit to Enugu in Eastern Nigeria and gone part of the way to committing us to the construction of a new township in the bush, a scheme which sounded hare-brained at first but, as he began to outline the possibilities, grew more attractive. We now realised why he had made a point of bringing young Ernest Shinwell, the son of Manny Shinwell MP, to the Kentucky on many occasions. It was this young man who had brought the scheme to Payne's doorstep.

That was the beginning of what I always thought of as the Great African Safari, called G.A.S. for short – and it certainly turned out to be a real gas, and no mistake. Looking back in the light of experience we were lunatics ever to become mixed up with the project. This was a job for large merchant banks with access to enormous funds. We discovered later that young Shinwell had hawked the proposition round for a long time without finding any takers and must have gone to Payne as a last resort. What I found surprising was that Payne should have fallen for it in the first place, because he had more actual commercial know-how than the three of us put together. All I can think is that success had gone to his head and he began to imagine himself as a Napoleon of finance. True he had amassed a tidy fortune both for himself and for us, but in the context of building a city from scratch our combined assets were peanuts. The way he put it to us, the development would be what is known as self-funding, meaning that we would pick up money in the shape of deposits which in turn would be used as capital for further stages in the construction work. It was, he explained, rather like building a pyramid, but what he didn't make clear was that the pyramid was standing on its point and not its base. It was a job for an expert juggler, but Payne had only progressed as far as parlour tricks. He hadn't reached the big league yet.

Still, all that was in the future, and it was the present we had to take care of, a present with a sinister background because the information filtered through the grapevine that the Old Bill was taking an even closer interest in our movements and doings than ever before. We weren't unduly worried – the Old Bill had not shown themselves to be very bright at fixing us up on past occasions – but it was an aggravation we could well do without at this particular time when the ability to get about freely was essential to our plans.

For example, G.A.S. once under way, there would be a good deal of shuttling to and fro between London and Nigeria, appointments to be kept and negotiations to be carried out which could well be jeopardised by some clumsy action on the part of the Old Bill, such as nicking us for trying the handles of parked aircraft at London Airport.

At this period in time we developed eyes in the backs of our heads. We needed them.

SIX

G.A.S. got off to a flying start, and when I say flying I mean exactly that. On and off we were engaged in this business for the best part of the year 1964, and something in the order of £12,000 went into the coffers of the various airlines plying between London and Lagos. The turbanned Asians who flew the interior journeys from Lagos to Enugu also had a fair slice of the bounty provided by the bunch of mad Englishmen who had embarked on the venture of providing a country on the brink of civil war with a new city.

I must hand it to Payne: for a man who hated flying he stood up to these journeys very well. Every time he stepped into an aircraft he went white, and his hands shook so much that he had difficulty in fastening his seat belt on take-off. It's a long way from London to Lagos, and the poor fellow was on tenterhooks every minute of the time. When it came to the flight from Lagos to Enugu in a small sixteen-seater plane with an Asian pilot he nearly had a baby. I felt rather sorry for him. As for me, I enjoyed the trips and it was quite an experience to be dropped into this black community with its very different habits and customs. The Presidential Hotel in Enugu was surprisingly comfortable. The first thing Payne did was to make a dive for the Safari bar and down a few stiff ones to calm his nerves.

Reggie and Ronnie made a couple of trips with Payne and Gore, who had a small team of architects and surveyors of varying colours trooping around with them. I understood that a company had been set up with a couple of local men on the board, but that sort of activity was down to Payne whose head became bigger and bigger as the scheme progressed. While negotiations were going on in Enugu efforts were being made in London to persuade influential and wealthy people to invest money or to lend their names to the project. Among those approached were Lord Boothby, a former Tory M.P., and Hew McCowan, son of a rich Scottish baronet and landowner. These names figure significantly in later stages of this story. Ernest Shinwell gradually dropped out of the picture, either because he saw the writing on the wall or was eased out by Payne, and went on to promote other ideas, finally ending up with a three year stretch for fraud. He was a sad example of the son of a famous father who just didn't have what it takes to live up to the family name.

For the Kray enterprises back in the old country it was a dodgy period. Although money was flowing in, G.A.S. was swallowing cash like an open drain. Payne kept on assuring us that everything was going fine and that soon we would hit the jackpot. We trusted him and took him at his word because there was little else we could do, and anyhow he had set up a number of highly profitable operations in the past. In retrospect, we were living in a fool's paradise – we should have cottoned on to the fact that the big money boys shied away from having anything to do with the business because they knew what was in the wind. So we shuttled back and forth between London and Enugu, meanwhile keeping the home fires burning as though we were feeding them on fivers.

In the middle of all the kerfuffle came the notorious Boothby case. It all started off simply enough with Ronnie, having obtained an introduction to Lord Boothby, going round to see him about G.A.S. They had a couple of meetings at Boothby's flat, which also doubled as his office, at the second of which Ronnie had a few photographs taken, quite a normal thing which Ronnie loved and to which Boothby made no objection. In the course of these meetings Boothby said he thought that the proposition was viable but ultimately Ronnie had a letter from him in which he said that he did not have the time to devote to such a large-scale project and there the matter ended – or so we thought.

The pictures were duly developed and printed, destined for Ronnie's scrapbook. One of them was particularly good. It showed Ronnie and Boothby sitting side by side on a settee looking fairly serious (they had, after all, been discussing a multi-million-pound deal). By some devious means not unconnected with a photographer wanting to make a bit on the side a print of this picture found its way into the offices of the Sunday Mirror. No blame for the subsequent happenings rests on the photographer, who was only making himself a few bob by selling his work. There can be no comment too scathing, however, for the behaviour of the editorial board of a responsible organ of the press in building up a vile and scurrilous campaign in which thugs, peers, clergymen and prominent public figures were alleged to have indulged in homosexual practices on a widespread scale in London and Brighton. All this was based on the evidence of a photograph which has since been published innumerable times and couldn't be more innocent.

The first few blasts of hot air went into the balloon on the 12th of July. The Sunday Mirror carried a story by our old mate (?) Norman Lucas under a banner headline PEER AND A GANGSTER: YARD PROBE. Amid a mass of hysterical speculation which credited Sir Joseph Simpson, the Metropolitan Police Commissioner, with issuing instructions to Detective Chief Superintendent Fred Gerrard to mount a top level investigation into 'the alleged homosexual relationship between a prominent peer and a leading thug in the London underworld', four points were clearly labelled as being of importance. They were allegations that Mayfair parties had been attended by the peer and the East End thug, that the peer and a number of prominent public men had indulged in questionable activities during weekends in Brighton, that the peer was involved in relationships with clergymen and that people who could give evidence on these matters had been threatened.

The affair blew up into a major scandal. Despite the denials issued by the Home Secretary, Mr. Henry Brooke, and Sir Joseph Simpson, practically the whole of Fleet Street joined in the hunt. To a reading public whose appetite had been whetted by the Profumo scandal of 1963 this was an extra ration of titillation. More hot air was pumped into the balloon which by now had assumed monstrous proportions. The balloon burst on the 1st of August, after a few pinpricks had been administered by Private Eye, who happily took the piss out of the Sunday Mirror and named Reggie and Ronnie as the two so-called thugs. On that August day Boothby, with typical bluntness, and ignoring legal advice, wrote a letter to the Times in which he referrred to the Sunday Mirror campaign as a tissue of atrocious lies.

On the 4th of August the Daily Express, with the joint and kind permission of Boothby and my brother Ronnie, published 'that picture' and put an end to speculation.

On the 5th of August Mr. Cecil King, chairman of the International Publishing Corporation, made an unqualified apology to Boothby, paid him £40,000 by way of compensation and also paid his legal costs. The noble peer donated £5,000 to the King Edward VII Hospital.

On the 19th and 20th of September the Daily Mirror and the Sunday Mirror respectively gave four column inches of their valuable space to apologise to my brother Ronnie. He received nothing by way of compensation, which he donated in full to the Home for Fallen Newspaper Editors, in the hope that Mr. Reginald Payne (no relation to our Les), ex-editor of the Sunday Mirror as of August 14th, might receive a share.

As a happy footnote to one of the most discreditable blots on the history of British journalism, my brother Ronnie threw a party at the Crown public house in Cheshire Street, Bethnal Green. Boothby was not among those present, but among the many well-known personalities who showed no fear of being photographed with the so-called thug Ronnie Kray was Judy

Garland.

At this point I would like to make a personal comment. If my brothers had been the thugs and gangsters which certain sections of the press made them out to be, Fleet Street would have been full of cripples. It is a matter of fact and history that not one of the men who were responsible for what Boothby referred to as a 'tissue of atrocious lies' received so much as a slap on the wrist.

Now back to G.A.S., which at this crucial stage in its progress was beginning to assume the aspect of an excerpt from the Black and White Minstrel Show. A lot of time, effort and money had been poured into a seemingly bottomless pit, but when in October of 1964 we left on the final visit to Enugu (though we were not to know it then), Payne assured us that this was pay-off time and we would shortly be rolling in money and on that note we departed.

There were four of us: Payne, Gore, myself and a chap called Gordon Anderson, a Canadian with wealthy and influential contacts in his own country. We duly arrived in Enugu and moved into the Presidential Hotel. Payne downed a couple of stiff drinks to assist his recovery from the rigours of the flight and then started the round of meetings with contractors, visits to the site and all the paraphernalia which had always seemed to me a waste of time but which Payne enjoyed to the full. He strutted about, the Great White Chief among his loyal but savage subjects, a Victorian coloniser, with Freddie Gore at his heels like a faithful spaniel.

After we had been there a few days I sensed that all was not going well. One of the native building contractors, who had paid over an introductory fee of £5,000 some time before, wanted to get on with the job but for some reason or other Payne kept fobbing him off in what I thought was a pretty off-hand way. He was quite a nice fellow – in fact they all were – and, apart from the colour of their skins, they behaved very much like their counterparts in England. I didn't know the ins-and-outs of the project, but it seemed to me at the time that something ought to be happening, and I felt a bit sorry for this particular fellow who probably had a gang of pick and shovel merchants standing by waiting to start on the foundations of the new city. This contractor was eternally hanging about in the lobby of the hotel trying to get hold of Payne, who in turn spent his time dodging him. I tried to have a word with Payne, but all I got was a remark to the effect that these fellows had to be kept in their places, a kind of 'we white chaps must stick together' argument which didn't appeal to me at all. However, my feeling was that Payne and Gore knew what they were doing so the best thing to do was let them get on with it.

Unhappily, Payne and Gore did *not* know what they were doing, because the next thing that happened was that the contractor opted out of the scheme and asked for his five grand to be handed back to him. Of course his money, together with much more, had long ago vanished into the voracious maw of G.A.S. He and Payne had a blazing row, the upshot of which was that the contractor went to the police and filed charges against Payne and Gore, who were promptly arrested and thrown into jail.

Now the whole atmosphere changed. Gone were the polite smiles and the bows and the handshakes. Gone also were the Government officials who had previously been so much to the fore in the negotiations. I went down to the jail to see Payne and Gore, which had its funny side because Payne, in the stinking surroundings of a black felons' compound, was still behaving as the Great White Chief. Gore was terrified, but that was a normal condition with him. I had a few words with Payne, who suggested that Anderson and I should pack up and get out to the airport where he would join us as soon as he had put the local chief of police in his place.

Payne was wrong again. Anderson and I packed our bags, went out to the airport but there was no sign of Payne. I realised then that it was all down to me and that I'd better get cracking and do something about springing Payne and Gore from jail, because they could do nothing about it themselves. I got hold of a Nigerian solicitor whom I had met on previous visits. His advice was simple. The only way to get Payne and Gore out of jail was to produce the £5,000 as quickly as possible.

It was Saturday in Enugu – it was also Saturday in dear old England. I put in a call from the hotel to Reggie and Ronnie and sat over the telephone through the rest of the day and well on into Sunday afternoon before I had absolute confirmation that the money was on the way. With this established, I went back to the solicitor.

This was where the comedy really began. Of all the high-up Government officials who had previously met us in official cars with flags flying and motor-cycle escorts, not one was to be found. It was apparent that they had washed their hands of the whole business and so far as they were concerned Payne and Gore could rot in jail forever. As for me, I was desperate. Anderson had already left for Lagos and I was really on my own.

Desperate situations call for desperate remedies. I got hold of one of the hotel servants, a very obliging coloured boy whom I had helped out of a spot of trouble when he was mugged for his wages by giving him a fiver. He promised that, if the worst came to the worst, he would arrange for a car to take me to Port Harcourt, the nearest place on the coast, from where I could get out of Nigeria. Fortunately this wasn't necessary. A call came through from the solicitor to say that he had found a judge who would sign the necessary bail forms on production of my passport and the £5,000 which was the bone of contention.

The nightmare wasn't over yet. I had no idea what had been going on behind the scenes when I was picked up at the hotel by this solicitor and another coloured chap. I got in the car and we drove off into the jungle along a narrow road that looked as if it led to nowhere. According to the solicitor we were on our way to this judge's private house, but by now I was suspicious of everybody, not being quite sure what capers Payne had been up to. I had visions of being knocked off and left in the jungle, just another mysterious disappearance, and I wasn't too happy about the prospect. However, it all turned out right in the end. We came to a clearing after about quarter of an hour's drive and there was the judge's house, a fairly large bungalow set in a nice garden, all very peaceful and quiet apart from the jungle noises. The door was opened to us by a woman in native dress, we went in and saw the judge who inspected my passport and granted bail on the sureties of the solicitor and myself and back we went to Enugu to get Payne and Gore out of the nick.

It wasn't before time. They had been cooped up in a small room ever since their arrest, and they were filthy dirty, thirsty, hungry and very tired. Gore was demoralised, and Payne on the brink of breakdown. They both were unable to understand the seriousness of their predicament. This was no time for kid gloves or politeness. I spelled it out for Payne in a few simple words which he couldn't fail to understand, and we were on our way to Enugu airport. We encountered no trouble there, in fact I had the impression that the officials were glad to see our backs. At Lagos there was some delay due to the fact that Payne's passport had been impounded by the police, but that was cleared up even though the plane had to be delayed on the tarmac waiting for us to board. When the landing wheels released contact with Nigeria I sat back and breathed freely for the first time in three days.

So the Great African Safari came to an end, leaving me and my brothers poorer but wiser. The irrepressible Payne was no sooner back in London than he began dabbling in stolen bearer bonds in which we took a brief but unenthusiastic interest. I made a trip to Montreal with Payne and we also paid visits to Geneva and Paris, but the sort of cloak and dagger stuff that went on was outside my experience, all these mysterious meetings with people who talked in riddles and telephone numbers and so on, waiting in hotel rooms for men who never arrived or who turned up in another place with a load of excuses instead of the gear they were supposed to deliver. It was all meat and drink to Payne but I found it very wearing. So far as the twins were concerned they had scrubbed Payne after the Nigerian business, and it wasn't very long before I followed their example and gave Payne the old heave-ho. While he had not exactly shown us the road to wealth, and was at times an embarrassment we took bloody good care that he had no chance to show us the way to the poorhouse, There was also another disturbing factor in the Payne situation. He was beginning to make references to the Syndicate and the Mafia in his conversations, and I for one wanted no part of a set-up which, from what I had heard, dealt with their affairs on the basis that a million dollars equals ten corpses.

The end of 1964 marked a turning point in the careers of me and my brothers. Looking back over the past few years, we had come a long way in a fairly short time. The billiard hall, the Double R, the little gambling clubs in the East End, then Esmeralda's Barn and the Kentucky, all of them were stepping stones to a position where we were on first name terms with those who had also made their mark in their own spheres. We had had our ups and downs, there were times when we had to deal with opposition in the terms in which it was presented to us, times when we cut corners and regarded the law as something to be circumvented rather than obeyed, but we had made it from comparative poverty to affluence by sticking to the job in hand and allowing nothing and nobody to stand in our way. I can clearly see the moral objection to some of the tactics we used, but we don't live in a very moral society. In the jungle of business the weakest go to the wall, and only the strong survive and are successful.

We had made many friends along the way, men and women from all walks of life who took us at face value and were not deterred by our lack of education and, in the case of Reggie and Ronnie, the fact that they had done time. The legend, fostered by the press, that we were a trio of scar-faced thugs, is a long way from the truth. At the age of thirty-one the twins were a very presentable pair of young men who could hold their own in any gathering. As for myself, I took people as I found them, often went out of my way to be pleasant and agreeable in any ticklish situations that arose, and I think I can safely say that I made a good job of whatever I turned my hand to.

Of course life is never one long sweet song for any of us. There had been times when things looked black, but we faced up to the problems as they presented themselves and, win a few lose a few, we managed to come out on top in the end. It's not very difficult to put a foot wrong when dealing with punters who find pleasure in drinking and gambling, but we'd been at the game long enough to recognise the signs of trouble and put a stop to it in a diplomatic way before things got out of hand.

On the lighter side there were comic moments. Shortly after we had taken over Esmeralda's Barn I tried my hand at the chemmy table and came out winning about £350. When I told Reggie about my bit of good luck, he decided to have a go himself. I wasn't there at the time, but when I saw him later he was falling about laughing. He had done some heavy betting and lost £750 in the space of an hour, which didn't please me very much even though he found it amusing. Reggie was very casual with money. When it was there he spent it as though there was no tomorrow. Then there was the time when Ronnie decided to buy a racehorse and took a thousand pounds to acquire a nag called Solway Cross, which never did any good and finally injured a leg, which was repaired by an operation known as 'firing'. That was the end of its racing days, but its subsequent fate makes a very amusing story.

At the end of the summer of 1963 we threw a big party at the Cambridge Rooms. It was just after a number of enterprising gentlemen had got away with two and a half million from the Glasgow to London mail train, but the party was in no way intended to celebrate that piece of skullduggery but to raise money for an East End charity, the Peter Pan Society for Handicapped Children. It was a fine day and we had put up a marquee in the gardens for those who wished to enjoy the fresh air. The guest of honour was world heavyweight champion Sonny Liston; Lord Effingham was there as was Vice-Admiral Sir Charles Evans (Evans of the Broke); and there was a fine turnout from the bookmakers and publicans of Bethnal Green. Our old mates from the Theatre Royal at Stratford (atte Bow) also came along: Barbara Windsor, George Sewell, Victor Spinetti, Murray Melvin, in fact almost the whole company including La Littlewood herself. About four hundred guests in all enjoyed the late summer weather, ate, drank and joined in the fun.

The highspot of the day was the raffling of Solway Cross. The tickets at a pound each went like wildfire, the horse went to a lady publican from Stepney, who immediately put it back for auction, Lord Effingham mounted the improvised rostrum and the animal was knocked down to Ronald Fraser the actor who cheerfully paid two hundred guineas for the pleasure of owning an animated grass cutter. The Peter Pan Society benefited to the tune of some twelve hundred pounds, and everyone was happy. Sonny Liston, a large and amiable man, chatted to Kid Lewis, Terry Downes and Terry Spinks, all champions in their day, and our show business friends took care of the entertainments side of things free, gratis and for nothing. It was one of those days that should have gone on for ever. It didn't, more's the pity.

A few thoughts occur to me at this stage in my story which should be expressed. What sort of people were me and my brothers? What was the private face behind the public figure? What was the motivation that drove us to achieve the fame (or notoriety) and the affluence we enjoyed? In replying to these questions I mean to be as objective as possible and to write what seems to me to be the truth.

I have given facts about our early life and struggles which should enable the reader to draw certain conclusions. In the case of the twins, their clashes with the Old Bill have been set down factually, and there was no doubt in my mind that they were conditioned to a deep distrust of the law and the men who administered it. Even so, not every copper was their enemy. The three of us were on friendly terms with certain officers of the law who had known us for many years, men who never asked for or received a penny from us. They were conscientious men doing their job as guardians of the law who knew when and where to draw the line and who refused to become emotionally or financially involved in the game of cops and robbers. From them came unsolicited information, often accompanied by friendly advice, of the sort of trouble we might be stirring up if we did this, that or the other. We liked them and I believe that they didn't dislike us.

The public image? Well, the twins attracted publicity because they were flamboyant, spent money as though they were printing it (they weren't – that was a specialist job) and didn't give a bugger what anyone thought of them. They were a gift to the sensational press to whom the distortion of fact was more a question of habit than achievement. The New Statesman, a journal not given to immoderate comment, called the Mirror reports on the Boothby affair 'a classic example of gutter journalism conducted with almost incomprehensible incompetence'. Not that the twins gave a damn about press comment, in fact they had a sneaking admiration for chaps such as Norman Lucas of the Mirror. Fearless themselves, they respected fearlessness in others. So the legend grew, fed by slanted press reports, that the twins were thugs and gangsters spreading bloodshed and terror wherever they went, and growing fat on the proceeds of extortion. I personally received little mention apart from the occasional reference to 'their elder brother Charlie'.

In public life there is much that goes on behind the scenes that never reaches the ears of the masses due to such things as editorial policy, censorship, the curious laws of libel and considerations of the public interest (whatever that may mean). In every section of our society from Royalty downwards there are intrigues, secret meetings, passing of privileged information and so on, stories that will never be told in even the most sensational memoirs. This is especially true of the twilight world of clubland where 'bent' coppers, wealthy thieves, high society and the aristocracy of the entertainment world are fused into a mixture almost as dangerous as high explosive. Add to that mixture a few con men and a sprinkling of educated felons, who are always to be found in the vicinity of large sums of cash money, and it is not hard to understand the nature of the problems that were bound to crop up. One of these problems centred around the arrest of the twins in January of 1965 on a charge of demanding with menaces. The true story behind this highly-publicised (and ultimately abortive) prosecution is a good example of the distortion of fact and behind-the-scenes intrigue that I have referred to.

During 1964, when much time and money was being spent on the Great African Safari, news filtered through to us that the Old Bill were showing a good deal of interest in our movements. Some of this information was supplied by friends in the force and was reliable in the sense that it came from 'straight' men who had nothing to gain by spreading rumours. In essence what we learned was that a certain Detective Inspector Leonard Read, known as 'Nipper' in criminal circles, was making fairly widespread enquiries about us, and making no secret of it either. This 'Nipper' Read (funny how these nicknames persist – Capstick of the Yard was never known as anything but Charlie Artful) was a young and ambitious officer who, so far as we knew, was dead straight. The news of his activities didn't worry Reggie and Ronnie overmuch until one day in January of 1965 he walked into the basement bar at the Glenrae Hotel and nicked them both.

During the next three months the twins were kept in custody pending trial at the Old Bailey. The prosecution case was that the twins had been concerned with another person in demanding money with menaces from a certain club owner who was referred to in the lower court proceedings as Mr. M. A lurid tale was unfolded of meetings in the Grave Maurice public house and the Glenrae Hotel where veiled threats were made by the twins that something nasty would happen if Mr.

M. failed to avail himself of the service of a doorman and a receptionist provided by them. In return for these services, it was alleged that the twins demanded a percentage of the club takings. The club owner refused the offer, so the prosecution story went, and at a later date a drunken writer created a scene at the club causing twenty quid's worth of damage. Those were the allegations – now for the facts.

Hew Cargill McCowan, the mysterious Mr. M., who was later to put Sir before his name and Bt. after it on the death of his father, was a wealthy habitué of West End night clubs who lived in a flat in Portland Place and kept a boa constrictor which he fed on live mice. Ronnie and he had met in 1964 when there was a possibility that he might invest cash in the Great African Safari, but the negotiations came to nothing. Some time later he created a scene at the Cambridge Rooms and Ronnie not only threw him out (discreetly) but also told him to stay out.

The club in question was the Hideaway in Soho's Gerrard Steet in premises owned by Gilbert France. McCowan had a fairly substantial stake in the operation.

The drunken writer was 'Mad' Teddy Smith, a man with a criminal record who had spent some time in Broadmoor and was, like McCowan, a fully paid-up member of the Association of Homosexuals.

The disturbance at the club, involving damage to the extent of twenty pounds, was a private and personal dispute between Smith and McCowan. The twins were acquainted with Smith but had not seen him for six months prior to their arrest.

One last but very cogent point. Protection racketeers whose demands are refused don't send drunken writers along to smash a few bottles and glasses. They put in a mob who give the place a thorough going-over.

I have provided the fact and the fiction and you may take your choice. To me the outstanding feature of this farrago was that Detective Chief Superintendent Fred Gerrard and Detective Inspector Leonard 'Nipper' Read had any part of it. That these highly experienced police officers should permit themselves to be used as pawns in the gratification of a private grudge was beyond belief. The only alternative explanation was, as I have said before, that orders had gone out from higher up that the Kray twins were to be subjected to as much aggravation as possible as part of some ingenious plan the purpose of which was to put them out of business or persuade them to emigrate. It may even have been possible that public money was spent only with the purpose of keeping the twins in custody for three months pending the trial, a matter which was raised in the House of Lords by Lord Boothby. I have red-hot news for the authorities. The twins owned a hotel, and would have been quite happy to stay there. What is more, they would have been delighted to accommodate a police guard as their guests. That would have saved taxpayer's money.

Joking apart, I am not attempting to present the twins as two poor struggling East End lads who were under constant persecution by the Old Bill, nor do I think that this was the twins' attitude. In all our operations we were advised by legal experts who were aware of everything we were doing. They were smart, it's true, and took advantage of loopholes in the law – but show me any business man who doesn't do that and I'll show you a potential bankrupt.

Before I leave the McCowan business I must mention one highlight in those six dreary days of low-key drama at the Old Bailey. This, by the way, was the second trial. The first one lasted nine days after which the jury failed to agree on a verdict. For what the entertainment must have cost it was a very poor return for the money. The principals, Mr. John Mathew for the prosecution and Petre Crowder and Paul Wrightson (both Q.C.s) for the defence put on performances which would have been described by a theatre critic as very professional. The supporting roles played by 'Nipper' Read and 'Freddie' Gerrard were adequate but not startling – perhaps they knew that nothing much was expected of them. The star of the show was the incumbent of St James the Great in Bethnal Green, the Reverend Edward Foster.

The events which led to the appearance of the reverend

gentleman in the witness box at the Old Bailey were as follows. One of the principal witnesses for the prosecution, a handsome twenty-one-year-old by the name of Sidney Vaughan who was referred to in the proceedings as McCowan's 'partner', came to see me at my home. He was a worried young man. On the one hand he was being pressed by McCowan to give false evidence against the twins. On the other hand he was understandably reluctant to commit perjury. His problem was resolved for him by divine intervention in the person of the Rev. Edward Foster, who turned up in the middle of our conversation quite unexpectedly. Vaughan discussed his problem with the priest and decided to change his testimony, as a result of which the Old Bailey was treated to the unusual sight of a minister of the Lord in the witness box.

Prosecuting counsel, who by now had realised that he was on a very sticky wicket, subjected the priest to a searching cross-examination. Finally, in desperation, he asked the Reverend Foster why he had not reported the whole matter to the police, to which he replied that he thought it proper to report it to his superior – no, not God, but the Archbishop of Canterbury. Shortly after this point in the trial the jury decided they had heard enough. The case was stopped and the twins went free.

A final footnote to the affair. Gilbert France, the real owner of the Hideaway, offered the club to the twins. They accepted the offer, re-named it the El Morocco, and held a party there to celebrate their freedom. Surprisingly, 'Nipper' Read turned up, impelled by some obscure motive known only to himself, and on the basis of the old adage 'let bygones be bygones' accepted Ronnie's invitation to have a glass of champagne. One of the many photographers present captured the moment for posterity, which didn't do Ronnie any harm. By the same token it didn't do Nipper much good.

The public lives of me and my brothers have been the subject of acres of coverage in the press. I now propose to comment on our private lives, because I believe it is essential to this story that the reader should not only know what we did but why.

To start with myself, I had had some problems in my domestic life in the years between 1960 and 1965 with which I had to cope as best I could having regard to the demands on my time. It was inevitable that my periods of absence from home should cause my wife Dolly to feel neglected to some extent, and I must admit that I did tend to take her for granted, a common failing in the Bethnal Green male. She was a good wife and mother and she gave our son Gary all the love and care he needed, but nevertheless there must have been times when she felt bored and frustrated, which I could well understand.

I remember vividly that evening in the Green Dragon when things came to a head. Dolly and I were there along with the twins and a few others, including a young, good-looking chap called George Ince. I was standing at the bar talking to a couple of friends and Dolly was sitting at a table with Ince. Dolly's two brothers were also in the club. Suddenly Reggie came over to me and told me to get Ince out of the place or there would be trouble. I didn't know what it was all about, but I saw the look in Reggie's eyes and realised that this was no time for argument, so I got young Ince on one side and told him to scarper, which he promptly did. I then went back into the club to find out what the trouble was.

It all came out, the story that everyone knew except me. The twins gave me the broad outline and Dolly's brother filled in the detail. George Ince and my wife had been meeting frequently for some time and it was pretty evident that they were having an affair. Naturally my first reaction was to dash out of the club and have a word with Ince, but he was nowhere to be found, and in fact I have not seen him from that day to this. Later, and in a calmer frame of mind, I had it out with Dolly very quietly and without any shouting or recriminations, because I didn't want to take the final step of breaking up the family. My son was at a very impressionable age, and to be quite fair to Dolly she had never involved him in any way with her affair with Ince, so I took the decision, rightly or wrongly, to let sleeping dogs lie. In any case, I was now able to spend more time at home, due to the fact that I had been granted a licence to operate a theatrical agency. This was a practical matter which fitted in with our club interests. All the cabaret acts which had been formerly booked through various agencies were now booked through mine, which had many advantages, not the least being that agency fees now were paid to me. I enjoyed the work and the income was not to be sneezed at. The Clark Brothers, the famous American dancing act, who were old friends, handed over their European affairs to me, and I took on the management of a group called The Shots with whom I had a fairly successful run.

All this meant that I saw less of the twins but more of my wife and son. Since that evening in the Green Dragon, Dolly had the dead needle to both of them, which wasn't surprising. As for Reggie and Ronnie, they made no secret of the fact that they thought I was out of my mind, but I had made my decision and that was that. So it became like old times in our flat in Poplar, and we were even more a united family when our daughter was born in June of 1965.

From what I have said of Reggie there will be no doubt in anyone's mind that he was a man of considerable passion with very fixed ideas about right and wrong according to his own code. He possessed in a marked degree what I would call a quality of apprehension, an ability to see what people were getting at before the words were out of their mouths. Above all, he was remarkably quick to act, not in an impulsive or unthinking way but because his faculties were unusually sharp. I remember one occasion when we threw a party at The Horns in Kennington. David Bailey, the photographer, and Francis Wyndham of the Sunday Times came along ostensibly as guests but really to collect material and pictures for an article which Francis had in mind for the colour supplement.

The huge room was full, and they were a very mixed crowd.

David Bailey was darting around using up film as though it was toilet paper when one of the guests, a bit of a villain who had had one over the eight, decided that he wanted his picture taken and grabbed Bailey by the neckerchief which he wore loose at his throat. Reggie was some distance away. He seemed to sense the disturbance, was on the spot in a flash, planted a right hook on the offender's chin and had him out of the way literally in a matter of seconds. Even close bystanders didn't realise that there was anything amiss. Probably one of Reggie's main faults was to hit first and not bother to ask questions after.

When Reggie fell in love he did so whole-heartedly, and brought to the affair much of the passion and intensity he showed in the battle of life. The object of his affections was not a society beauty on the club scene or a starlet of stage and television (which could have been possible). She was, like us, an East Ender, the daughter of Frank Shea who had known the twins since they were youngsters. Her name was Frances and Reggie had been courting her since she was sixteen. That old-fashioned word courting entirely describes his behaviour towards her for, although there were other women in his life, Frances was the one who would become Mrs. Reginald Kray.

At the age of twenty-one, Frances was a very beautiful and vivacious young woman, full of the enjoyment of life and yet, as I saw her, there was an element of tragedy about her. One had the feeling that, behind the bright smile and the gay conversation, there was a dark shadow of doubt and uncertainty which showed in her quieter moments when she thought no-one was looking at her. But she was a radiant bride when she and Reggie were married at St. James the Great in Bethnal Green Road on that April day in 1965. The Reverend Edward Foster tied the knot, David Bailey took the pictures and Bethnal Green turned out in force to watch the proceedings. The two Mums, Violet Kray and Elsie Shea, shed a few conventional tears, the guests guzzled the champagne, the newlyweds departed for a honeymoon in Athens and we all went off to our respective homes. I watched

Ronnie as he climbed into his car. I felt I knew then what loneliness was all about.

A wedding brings together a lot of people who may not have seen each other for years, and many of the Bethnal Greeners who had not seen the twins in each other's company for a long time commented on the marked difference that now existed between them. Reggie weighed little more than he did in his boxing days, but Ronnie had put on weight and his movements were now more ponderous. What these people did not know was that Ronnie, ever since his experiences in the psychiatric ward of Winchester prison and Long Grove mental hospital, had been taking powerful tranquillising drugs in increasing doses as his body built up a resistance to them. This process had begun in Wandsworth, continued on his release from prison and, so I was told by doctors, would probably go on for the rest of his life.

These drugs were derivatives of phenothiazine, in the chlorpromazine group, and were known variously as Stemetil, Largactil and Reserpine. Beyond the fact that they were effective in the treatment of vertigo and vomiting and induced lethargy without interfering with the state of consciousness, little was known of the side effects. I had this on the authority of a specialist in mental disorders who was sufficiently cynical in his profession to tell me the story of the wonder drug which could cure all known diseases but wasn't used because only someone as fit as a fiddle was able to withstand the side effects. I am convinced that it was the side effects of these potent drugs which brought about the marked change in Ronnie's physical appearance. What it was doing to his mental state, God alone knows.

I had ample opportunity to observe Ronnie's behaviour while he was taking these drugs, and it followed an invariable pattern. If for some reason or another he missed taking his tablets, and this coincided with a time when he was under emotional pressure, he would indulge in some form of violence, hurling a chair across the room or smashing his fist through a door panel. What added a further hazard to an already dangerous situation was Ronnie's obsession with swords, knives and guns. Over the years he had acquired a collection of all types of weapons, including antique and modern firearms, some of which decorated the walls of his flat in Cedra Court. He kept them oiled and polished, and would occasionally demonstrate to his cronies the speed with which he could take them apart and re-assemble them. Both Reggie and I advised him to get rid of these things more than once, but we might just as well have spoken to a brick wall. Ronnie was a grown man, and what he did was his own business.

The famous educationist A. S. Neill once said that there is no such thing as a problem child – there are only problem parents. I will swear to it that no child in the world has had more love, devotion and care than we three received from our mother. She was, and is, an incredible person by any standards. Don't take my word for it. Look back over these pages and ask yourself what kind of a woman it was who coped with every situation presented to her, who took comparative poverty and riches in her stride and remained unchanged, who preserved her family against misfortune and retained throughout all her trials and troubles a calmness and patience which would have done credit to a saint. She is today, with her fifty-year-old marriage still intact, a serene and lovely lady whose warmth and understanding and sympathy command the respect of all who come in contact with her. So where did it all go wrong with Ronnie?

Never mind the high-flown theories of so-called experts who claim to be able to see into the inmost recesses of the mind. The dark and violent world of fantasy into which Ronnie retreated on occasion was created when a prison doctor first prescribed that he should be given Stemetil, not to cure a condition but to control a rebellious mind.

Where do I find the words to express my feelings about my brother Ronnie, to whom I am still bound by ties of blood and affection? How can I, who knew him well, describe his thoughts and emotions when he went armed into the haunts of men who lived by violence and, in some cases, died of it? All I am able to do is to present the facts as they were known to me: to say that behind the rough-diamond tycoon image that Ronnie showed to the world was a desperate man whose drug-induced state caused him to see hatred and enmity all around him; and to thank God that the only men who suffered were those who themselves lived beyond the boundaries of decency and civilised behaviour and who, given the opportunity, would have handed Ronnie the same treatment that he dished out to them.

I have never condoned violence, whether committed by my brothers or anyone else. Yet I have to accept the fact, as we all must, that we are living in the most violent century in our history, surrounded by wars and the threats of wars on an unprecedented scale. Dead men littering a far-off battlefield are just as much part of man's brutal inhumanity to man as the affray in a club or a dark side-street which ends in bloody injury and death. Violence as an expression of some deep feeling is present in all of us. It can be controlled – and some day, please God, it will.

SEVEN

After the public uproar of the McCowan trial and the private excitement of Reggie's wedding, life developed a slower tempo. The Old Bill had burned their fingers badly in their abortive attempt to fit up the twins on extortion charges, and it was obvious that they would think twice before having another go. Whether it was coincidence or a glass of champagne in the El Morocco that led to 'Nipper' Read's transfer to the team investigating the Great Train robbery is anyone's guess – or perhaps the powers-that-be decided that it was more important to chase two and a half million quid than waste manpower and public money on chivvying a couple of men who would never acquire that sort of money in a lifetime.

Reggie and Frances duly returned from their honeymoon in Greece, and Reggie was at once plunged into the business of building up the new club, a job which he tackled with his usual enthusiasm. It wasn't long before El Morocco became one of the 'in' places on the night club round, crowded nightly with stars of stage, screen and radio and those who liked to be seen with them. Through my agency, which was doing very nicely thank you, I supplied the cabaret acts on the usual ten per cent basis. It looked as though we were about to embark on a lengthy period of peace and prosperity, which pleased me very much. I began to think in terms of broadening my own field of action, and started a little business manufacturing ladies' coats in premises over Bloom's Kosher restaurant in Aldgate.

This was so successful that I moved to a larger place in Hackney where I employed twenty full-time machinists and a designer who wasn't much to look at but knew more about ladies fashions than the ladies knew themselves.

It was all most convenient. I would call in at the factory on my way to the office in Tottenham Court Road, pick up a load of coats which I would drop off in the West End, and pay another call as I made my way back to Poplar in the evening to see how things had gone during the day. I was quite the little capitalist.

Life, of course, is never one long, sweet song. Though I was seeing less of the twins, a few things came to my ears which were rather disturbing. Victory over the Old Bill in the McCowan case appeared to have gone to their heads, and, instead of letting sleeping dogs lie, they were going out of their way to make laughing stocks out of such people as Fred Gerrard and 'Nipper' Read. It was understandable that they should do this – it's only human to get your own back, and the three months in Brixton still rankled. What the twins had done up to this time was to sit back and let the Old Bill come at them, but now they were carrying the war into the enemy's camp. Good military tactics, true, but not the sort to be used against a highly organised police force with its network of informers backed by the most sophisticated techniques that public money could buy.

Mention of informers brings me to Alan Bruce Cooper, who came on to the scene about the time the El Morocco opened. He was a small man with a little moustache and a stutter who lived in style in Kensington, drove a Rolls and was never without money. He impressed the twins, particularly Ronnie, but I had my reservations. I had a tendency to suspect fellows who talked in telephone numbers after my experiences with Payne. Tommy Cowley, an old friend and a shrewd judge of character, swore that Cooper was a police spy and 'agent provocateur'. To my mind he was anything but straight, everything he did and said reeked of large-scale larceny, but it was none of my business and I kept my opinions to myself.

164

One thing struck me as being rather peculiar. His initials were the first three letters of the alphabet, but maybe that was just coincidence.

It was clear that Cooper was attempting to involve the twins in a web of international intrigue. He arranged for Ronnie to accompany him to New York, a happening which mystified me, because the United States Consulate in London doesn't hand out visas as though they were trading stamps and anyone with a criminal record might just as well save the taxi fare to Grosvenor Square. According to Ronnie it was easy. He and Cooper (who travelled on a U.S. passport) merely flew to Paris, obtained a visa from the U.S. Embassy there and then continued onwards to New York. It all sounded too simple to me, but to Ronnie it was a huge joke and another victory chalked up against the Old Bill. He had spent a pleasant week in New York, touring the night spots, meeting a few notables and renewing old acquaintances, while the Old Bill in London were going quietly round the bend wondering where he was and what he was up to. I've no doubt there were a few explosions at the Yard when they discovered the facts.

At this juncture a few words about the reputed connection we had with the American Mafia wouldn't come amiss. I have had no personal experience of the workings of this mysterious organisation, though like practically everyone else in this country I have read books and news items and watched very sensational films which have claimed to give the inside story on this intricate network of crime sometimes referred to as The Syndicate. Common gossip – which I have learned to discount in favour of credible information – linked the Mafia and its feudal Sicilian rules of loyalty with almost all areas of business in the United States both legitimate and otherwise. If these stories were to be believed, the whole of the United States democratic process from the President down through Senate and Congress spent their time making laws while the Mafia ran the country, making mockery of those laws and substituting their own rules. It all sounded a bit far-fetched to me.

Rumour had it that George Raft. ex-film actor and host at the Colony Club in Berkeley Square, was the London Representative of the Mafia. Now I knew George well, spent a lot of time in his company, and took Dolly, Mum and Dad to dine with him on more than one occasion; and if he was the front man for the Mafia then I'm the Shah of Persia. George was just a nice fellow, a good host with an attractive manner and personality, doing a job of work and glad of the money. To the Colony Club he was one of their more important assets. For reasons which were not disclosed, and probably would not have been understood by most people if they had been published, George Raft was deported as an undesirable alien in 1967.

The same sort of rumour circulated about what were known as 'junkets', organised trips by parties of Americans who thought London might be a better place for losing money than Las Vegas. After the Betting and Gaming Act became law, hundreds of these junkets were organised to the great delight of the owners of London casinos and clubs and, incidentally, the British Tourist Board, for the gambling Americans didn't spend all their money at the tables. Naturally, we came in for a share of this business and, after meeting scores of these visiting firemen, I found nothing to suggest that the trips were anything more than a good idea thought up by a bunch of enterprising travel agents. Of course, it was quite possible that the travel agents were members of the Mafia, but like most sensible persons I would like to have proof of that before I believed it.

I am not attempting to prove that the Mafia or Syndicate doesn't exist. I did once meet one of the known heads of the Mafia, a very smooth gentleman by the name of Angelo Bruno, who stopped off in London for a few days in the course of a tour of Europe. He showed a small interest in the gambling operation in the Metropolis, talked to many people in the business including the twins and myself, and went on his way. My impression was that he considered British gambling very small beer in comparison with the American scene, as indeed it was. In the casinos of Las Vegas more money changes hands in a week than the London gaming clubs handle in a year.

Whether Cooper was involved with the Syndicate or not has always been a mystery. In fact the man was a mystery altogether. There were rumours that he was one of the organisers of an international arms smuggling ring supplying, amongst others, the I.R.A., Palestinian terrorists and groups of mercenaries. It was also said that he had a finger in gold and narcotics smuggling. Looking at this small and inoffensive American, it was hard to believe that he was engaged in any form of dangerous enterprise. Apart from his wealth, or at least the outward and visible signs of it, he could have been an insurance salesman or any sort of fairly successful white collar worker. But behind that nondescript exterior there must have been a very clever man because, as far as I could discover, he had no criminal record, at least in the name of Alan Bruce Cooper, aged thirty five or thereabouts, United States citizen resident in London, Brussels and Geneva. There was always the possibility, of course, that somewhere along the line a change of identity had taken place. That A.B.C. initial somehow was just a bit too good to be true. Stranger things have happened.

Sufficient information about gambling clubs and the way in which they are organised has been provided earlier to leave the reader in no doubt that the chance of getting something for nothing attracts a wide and varied range of characters, most of them honest and respectable but some of them anything but that. The temptation is enormous. A crooked croupier, in league with one or two punters, can clear several thousand pounds before the inevitable discovery of his dishonesty. A good con man, having built up a reputation for prompt settlement, passes a succession of worthless cheques in a lightning tour of the casinos and is heard of no more. Then there is the 'laundry merchant', a gentleman who has amassed large sums of cash by dubious means and wishes to turn it into 'clean' money. He goes along to the casino, buys a large quantity of chips for cash, has a few drinks and a mild flutter, then exchanges the chips for a cheque ('I don't want to carry a lot of money at this time in the morning') and hey presto! his tax-free gaming profit goes into his bank account and no questions asked. It is in this atmosphere with its vague odour of criminality that the snide remark, the careless hint that so-and-so intends to do this-and-that to such-and-such engenders suspicion that becomes a feud and finally erupts in bloody violence. A classic example of this occurred in March of 1966, when a pitched battle between armed men in a gambling club ended in one death and five cases of serious wounding. I mention this particular event only to give weight to the fact that running a gambling club is not all champagne and canapés.

The scene of the battle was Mr Smith's Club in Catford, on the main A21 route from London to the south east and some ten miles from the West End. This plush and well-managed place with its cosy bar, excellent restaurant and expensively furnished gaming rooms was financed by a group of Northern businessmen and opened its doors in October of 1965. Right from the start it was an enormous success, packed with clients until the early hours of the morning. This happy state of affairs lasted until shortly before dawn on the 8th of March 1966. Then the shooting began.

Eye witnesses who later gave evidence at the Old Bailey described the horror of the scene. According to their stories, several men stayed in the club after the legal closing time of 2 a.m. Most of the staff had gone to their homes and only the manager, the doorman and a receptionist remained behind to close the premises after the men had gone. But the men did not go – at least, they did not leave the club in the usual way via the front door. At about 3 a.m. fighting broke out accompanied by the shouting of oaths and insults and the smashing of glass. Then, suddenly, came the roar of a shotgun and the crackling of small arms fire, and the battle spread into the street at the rear of the club. It was all over very quickly. A dying man with a bullet wound in his back was found in the yard behind the club. Another man, with a bullet in his leg, was discovered in the garden of a house nearby. Four others turned up in the two local hospitals, Lewisham and Dulwich, suffering from gunshot wounds. It was quite a night.

Who were these men and what was it all about? The answer to the first question can be found in police files. Richard Hart, the man who unfortunately died that night, was liked by everyone, and it will always be a mystery that he became involved. Of the five wounded, the names of two of them were significant. One was Frankie Fraser, a formidable tearaway with a long record of violence including attacks on prison officers. The other was Eddie Richardson, younger brother of Charles Richardson. Both the Richardson brothers and Fraser were to appear at the Old Bailey in April of 1967 on charges of extortion, causing grievous bodily harm and robbery with violence.

What was it all about, this little war in Catford? The probable cause was only briefly mentioned at the subsequent trial by the officer in charge of the case, Detective Superintendent Cummings, who said, 'This affray was gang warfare arising from the protection rackets in clubs.' It was a loose and general explanation which broadly fitted the facts, but it was far from being complete. Do men commit murder for a few quid a week? In my opinion the answer is in the negative. Murders are committed and in the majority of cases there are corpses to bear witness to the fact, but there are deep and often-concealed motives for the taking of human life which are not to be explained away by greed for money in small (though regular) amounts.

An incident in Fraser's early life as a young tearaway in the Elephant and Castle manor is worth telling. In those days there was a well-known local feud between the Carters and the Brindles. Fraser's sister was married to a Brindle. In order that nobody should be in any doubt as to where his loyalty lay, Fraser chose the first available opportunity to sort out Johnny Carter, the clan leader, and chase him through the back streets behind the Old Kent Road. Carter ran because Fraser was not only carrying a gun – he was using it. Carter got away, but if he had been shot and killed it wouldn't have been a killing for money, just old-fashioned feuding finding expression via the muzzle of a gun.

The average citizen, with his ingrained respect for law, will find it difficult to understand the code by which men like Fraser lived. The small world in which they practised their brutalities was an enclosed world and very much outside the law. I have seen that world at close quarters, witnessed the displays of primitive passion and often heard the phrase that was the forerunner of a bloody skirmish 'It was either him or me for it.' The death of Richard Hart had its roots in a very deep and personal antagonism which was wiped out in blood.

It was in precisely that sort of 'him or me' situation that my brother Ronnie put a bullet through George Cornell's head on the evening of the 9th of March 1966.

The scene of the shooting was the bar of the Blind Beggar, a public house in the Whitechapel Road immediately opposite the London Hospital and almost on the corner where Vallance Road joins the main thoroughfare. The victim was a man known as George Cornell, whose real name was Myers, an associate of Frankie Fraser and a very tough character indeed. On this particular night he was out of his usual haunts, which were normally south of the river. He was also frequently to be seen in West End clubs, including the Astor in Berkeley Square.

He was well known to the twins as flash and loud-mouthed, but up to this time he had not interfered with them and, on that basis, they tolerated him. However, word had come through to Ronnie that Cornell was putting it about that he intended to usher that 'fat poof' Kray into the next world as soon as a suitable opportunity presented itself. His reason for making the threat was not very clear, but Ronnie was not one for enquiring into reasons. The fact that Cornell had made the threat was enough for him.

The encounter in the Blind Beggar was, I believe,

accidental. It was a most unusual place in which to find Cornell, only a stone's throw from our parents' home in Vallance Road, Had he deliberately gone there looking for Ronnie? It was a question that would never be answered by Cornell. Ronnie was carrying one of his guns, a 9 mm. Luger and, no doubt believing that Cornell was also armed, fired at him and left the pub at full speed.

Those were the bare facts, but what were the circumstances behind this bizarre event. At the Old Bailey, when Ronnie stood accused of the murder, the only evidence called was that of the barmaid at the Blind Beggar, who testified that Cornell was at the bar drinking in the company of another man when two others walked in. According to her story, both of them produced guns, one of them fired two shots into the air and the other, whom she positively identified as my brother Ronnie, fired one shot at Cornell. Then, she went on, Ronnie and his companion ran out into the street and she rapidly made herself scarce in the cellar.

At the inquest on Cornell at Westminster Coroner's Court evidence was given by two men who were drinking with him. They were Albert Wood, a Walworth bookmaker, and John Dale, who described himself as an interior decorator, from Stepney. Wood said he saw the shooting but did not know the two men involved. Dale said he was on the way to the toilet when he heard shots, but saw nothing of the actual incident. The coroner, Mr. Gavin Thurston, returned a verdict of 'murder by persons unknown'.

Where did I stand in all this? I have never condoned violence in any shape or form, and the guilty knowledge that my brother had killed was something I had to live with. The bullet that shattered Cornell's skull also shattered any dreams that Reggie and myself had of a quiet, peaceful and prosperous future. Though the world lost nothing – and probably gained a lot – by the removal of this useless villain from the scene of his activities, the irretrievable deed had been done. That the Old Bill made only the most perfunctory enquiries was to be expected, but it did not lessen our anxieties to know that they were no doubt happy to have one less villain to occupy their time and energy. Some five months after the killing, the Old Bill went through the motions of requesting Ronnie, Reggie and Tommy Cowley to 'assist them with their enquiries', but nothing came of this and the case went into the official files as one more unsolved murder.

In examining my own conscience there were several factors I had to take into account. An important one was my loyalty to my brother. I could no sooner have gone to the Old Bill and informed against him than fly in the air. On the contrary, I make no bones about saying that I would have done anything in the world to protect him against the consequences of his actions. Again, though I was sorry for Cornell's family, I could not find it in my heart to feel pity for a man who had himself been responsible for crimes of unbelieveable violence. But the major and over-riding consideration was that knowledge of this affair should be kept from our mother. Rightly or wrongly, Reggie and I took every precaution against such a happening. There was gossip, true, and some of it must have reached Mum's ears, but gossip is one thing and outright proof another.

One thing that will always puzzle me is one aspect that was never explained to me by my brother. Did Ronnie intend to kill Cornell? I am told by experts that the 9 mm. Luger is a tricky weapon with which to put a bullet into a small area even at close range. Ronnie was no marksman. Most of his Army service was spent in the glasshouse, where instruction in the use of small arms is not encouraged. Also, his eyesight was not all that good. It is an academic question which will probably never be answered; not that the answer would benefit either Cornell or Ronnie.

One final comment. At the Old Bailey in 1969 a lurid picture was painted of the whole of the East End knowing who had shot Cornell but being terrified to testify. There was no public terror here, only public indifference. For all the ripple it made in the Whitechapel ponds, Cornell could have died peacefully in his bed. Only four people could have said what happened that night in the bar of the Blind Beggar. One was Ronnie, who has always refused to discuss the matter in detail. Another two were Wood and Dale, the witnesses at the coroner's inquest. The fourth was the man who was said to have fired two shots in the air and disappeared into the night before Cornell's body hit the floor.

There had been quite a few bullets flying around in the London area in the early part of 1966. The twins, who had no intention of becoming targets for some trigger-happy villain, decided they were due for a holiday and went off to Tangier, leaving me and Tommy Cowley to look after the shop. Tommy has not received much mention so far, but he was a friend of long standing who could be relied on. He wasn't a very big chap but, as the old saying goes, they don't make diamonds as big as bricks, and what Tommy lacked in inches he made up for in alertness. Like me and my brothers he had been born and bred in the East End and like us had missed out on the old education lark, yet if degrees were awarded in the University of Life Tommy would have rated an M.A. at least.

We didn't have to mind the store for long. The twins were back inside three weeks. They had had a good time, painted the town red with the help of a few old mates who were over there (including Billy Hill), and then came to the conclusion that cous-cous was all right but a home-cooked meal was better. They returned to a London that was more quiet and peaceful than when they left, and soon settled back into the normal routine as if George Cornell had never existed and the happenings at the Blind Beggar were only an unpleasant dream.

At this point in my story I think I should make some comment on the increase in the use of firearms that had been so noticeable over the space of few years. There was a time when no screwsman would think of carrying a gun, and even the 'blag' mobs were content with pickaxe handles. The general argument was that the man who carried a gun would have to use it one day because, no matter how much he waved it about as a frightener, there would come a time when somebody would refuse to be frightened. Again, the use of shooters as a habit would lead to the Old Bill following suit and using guns themselves, which wasn't a pleasant prospect.

That sort of morality went by the board during and after the war. Men who had been trained in the use of arms and the taking of human life had few scruples about carrying a gun and using it if necessary. The practice was not so widespread in this country as it was in the United States, where firearms were more readily available and the men who used them were gangsters in the strict sense of the word, men who killed as part of their trade, mercilessly and without remorse. Our lot were very pale imitations. The great majority of the shootings that took place within my experience were the result of some personal disagreement, a dispute over a woman or the publishing of a grave insult which, so far as the insulted person was concerned, could only be wiped out in blood. There was also the odd accident because bullets are apt to fly in unexpected directions and are no respectors of persons.

A shooting which aroused widespread interest at the time was that of Thomas 'Ginger' Marks, who was, according to reports, fired on by men in a car outside the Carpenter's Arms in Cheshire Street. This pub was owned by the twins and managed for them by the daughter and son-in-law of a man called Harry Hopwood, who was to figure prominently as a prosecution witness at the Old Bailey in 1969. The incident took place around midnight on the 2nd of January 1965, at which time the twins were safely tucked up in their beds. They were not, in any case suspected of complicity in this incident.

Apart from the gunman (or gunmen) in the car, whose identities, like the whereabouts of Marks, have remained a secret until this day, the one man who knew most about the matter was James Evans, who had admitted being Marks' companion on that fateful night. Now a strange story begins to unfold which had its beginnings one night in December of the previous year, when a man called George Foreman opened the door of his flat in response to a knock and was immediately on the receiving end of a shotgun blast directed at his genitals. It was alleged at the Old Bailey in April of 1965 that the finger on the trigger of the shotgun was that of James Evans, but the jury didn't agree with the allegation and Evans was acquitted. What did transpire during the course of the trial was that Evans' wife had been associating with Foreman, that Foreman had been convicted in January of being in possession of a gun and ammunition and that Foreman was an associate of men who had been convicted in connected with the Great Train Robbery. Add to these facts the mysterious fire that broke out at Evans' home (the House of Peacocks at Beulah Hill) and the pieces begin to fit together to form a picture.

But that picture is incomplete. It was known that George Cornell had threatened the life of Ginger Marks. Also Marks' wife, Anne, laid the blame for the events that led to her husband's death directly at Evans' door. Furthermore the acquittal (in October of 1975) of four men charged with the murder (one of them the brother of George Foreman) casts doubt on Evans' conflicting descriptions of the events of that night in Cheshire Street. One thing is certain. The public has not heard the last of the late Thomas Marks.

During this period in the middle sixties there were several occasions on which guns were used which did not come to the notice of the Old Bill, mainly because those involved came to no great harm and were, in any case, not the sort of people to go running to the law for protection. So far as I was concerned, though I found it disturbing to think that I might one day be at the receiving end of a bullet, I had a distaste for firearms. To put the whole business into perspective, it is fair to say that guns were used by only a small minority of men who were well known and who were given a wide berth by those who wished to stay out of trouble.

The most widely publicised shootings at that period of time were the affray at Mr. Smith's Club and the killing of George Cornell at the Blind Beggar. Though they were closely linked in time, that was the only connection. It has been suggested that they were part of a gang feud between my brothers and the Richardsons, but nothing could be further from the truth. The elder Richardson, Charles, had spent some time in the military prison at Shepton Mallet where he met the twins and was accepted by them as a fellow rebel against Army authority. When, at a later stage, Charles and his brother Eddie were engaged in their operations from their scrap-metal yard in Camberwell, they confined their activities to a well-defined area south of the river Thames. They kept out of our business and we kept out of theirs, and the only common meeting ground was the Astor Club in the West End. I don't say that my brothers and the Richardsons were bosom friends, but there was a mutual respect coupled with a knowledge of what was bad for business that precluded any notion of either side interfering with the other.

What did unite us with the Richardsons, to some extent at least, was recognition of the common enemy. I have made previous reference to the gentlemen with Savile Row tastes and Lambeth Cut incomes whose right of entry to members' clubs was guaranteed by no less a person than the Commissioner of Police for the Metropolis. They were a minority movement, as were the gun-carrying tearaways on the opposing side, but both made a substantial contribution to the erosion of the rule of law and did, at times, make a mockery of the administration of justice.

An example of this occurred, in August of 1966, some little time after the twins had returned from Tangier. A certain Detective Sergeant Townsend (not to be confused with Detective Superintendent Ronald Townsend, who was connected with enquiries into the shooting of Ginger Marks and George Cornell), who was stationed at Hackney, was said by my brother Ronnie to have approached him and asked him for money in return for some unspecified favours. My brother's allegations were supported by tape recordings of conversations which took place in the bar of the Baker's Arms pub in Northiam Street, Hackney, between Ronnie and Townsend, which Ronnie handed over to the Old Bill together with an official complaint. It was, on the face of it, a cast-iron case. Townsend had demanded money, the conversations had been recorded, Eric Marshall the licensee of the Baker's Arms had testified to their authenticity, and Townsend was in the shit up to his neck – or so it seemed. In the event it was not all that simple.

To be quite fair to the Old Bill, they are concerned to stamp out corruption in their ranks for obvious reasons. A trap was set for Townsend with a bundle of identifiable notes which were collected by him and almost immediately thrown away when some of his colleagues came on the scene. The evidence was sufficient for the Director of Public Prosecutions to initiate proceedings against the officer. It was not sufficient for the Old Street magistrate, who issued a summons requiring Ronnie to attend the court as a witness.

Ronnie's reaction to this was characteristic. 'Fuck 'em. I've given them the lot. I'm not going to go into a witness box to put anybody away – not even a bent copper,' he said, and promptly went into hiding. The Detective Sergeant was remanded, on bail naturally, and the affair dragged on until April of '67, when Townsend appeared at the Old Bailey, full of fight after his extended holiday. Ronnie was still on the missing list. At the first trial the jury failed to agree, and at a second trial Townsend was acquitted. Though there was a considerable weight of evidence against him, he was fortunate in having Mr. John Mathew as counsel for the prosecution.

This learned gentleman, whose job it was to prove Townsend guilty as charged, made his opening speech to the jury with an astonishing attack on the twins. He said, 'It may well be that some of you have heard of two persons known as the Kray brothers, Ronald and Reginald Kray. They are notorious characters. They are persons of the worst possible character. They have convictions between them for violence, blackmail and bribery. Their activities were always of interest to the police.' The jury must have been surprised that the twins were not standing in the dock.

It should be mentioned that Mr. John Mathew was the counsel for the prosecution when my brothers were accused of demanding with menaces from Hew McCowan and were acquitted. This may have had some bearing on what, in my opinion, was an unjustified attack on Reggie, who was not concerned in the case. It was Ronnie who evaded the witness summons.

Harking back a few years to 1960, when Reggie was in Wandsworth, he met up with a fellow called Frank Mitchell, a rather simple-minded giant who had spent most of his life in one institution or another. He was about four years older than Reggie, but from an entirely different background, a deprived child who had received a sketchy education at a school for the sub-normal, began stealing at an early age and progressed from remand home to Borstal to prison by predictable stages.

Over six feet tall, spectacularly muscled and as strong as a bull, but with the mentality of a child, he was a target for the 'hard-case' screw. He was unofficially beaten-up and officially flogged, soaked up the punishments and came back for more. He fought his persecutors with the ferocity of an animal and yet there was something in him that was responsive to a kind word or a gentle gesture. In Wandsworth he developed an obsessive hero-worship for Reggie, the sort of thing not uncommon in the all-male society of prison, and Reggie went out of his way to make existence more tolerable for this unfortunate man who was serving a sentence of life imprisonment with no fixed date for release.

After leaving Wandsworth, Reggie still took an interest in Mitchell, taking steps through the usual channels to ensure that he did not go short of 'comforts'. I paid a visit on one occasion and found it hard to believe that this shy and inarticulate man could have committed the brutalities for which he had been sentenced.

Some time after Reggie's release from Wandsworth, Mitchell was accused of causing grievous bodily harm to another prisoner by stabbing him with a knife, an uncharacteristic offence which could not be dealt with as an internal matter under prison rules. When he appeared at Marylebone Court, handcuffed to a screw and surrounded by police, we had arranged for him to be defended by Nemone Lethbridge, the young woman barrister who was the leading figure in obtaining the release of convicted murderer Jimmy O'Connor from jail, and who subsequently married him. Mitchell was acquitted and went back to Wandsworth, but was later transferred to Dartmoor, where we visited him on a few occasions.

I shall never forget my first impression of that grim, grey pile plumped in the middle of the huge expanse of wild country known as Dartmoor. The name of the institution is not Dartmoor but Her Majesty's Prison, Princetown, Devon, and it was built in the reign of George the Third to house French prisoners of war. We came to it from the Exeter Road on a fairly fine spring day, but there was no sunshine in the hollow of Princetown, where even the trees looked sad. Bold notices along the roadside ordered motorists to keep moving. The main building, when we came to it, was like an ogre's castle from a Disney fantasy, dark, forbidding and somehow threatening. I remember thinking to myself, God help the poor sods who have to spend time here. Once on the inside, it was even more terrifying, massive stone walls ravaged by time and moisture, an overall odour of damp and decay which even defeated the smell of disinfectant, the nearest thing to hell on earth I have ever experienced. I was told, even in the height of summer, the walls of some of the cells dripped with water.

According to newspaper stories published at the time of Mitchell's escape from the Moor, he led the life of Riley, scouring the countryside on the backs of wild ponies, drinking in remote pubs, guzzling Scotch in his cell and having it off with a local schoolmistress in a barn. I have had first-hand experience of the imaginative powers of reporters, but this beat cockfighting. It's true that he was permitted some relaxation of the rigorous discipline of the country's hardest nick, but this was solely because the usual forms of punishment were a waste of time in his case. Romantic stories on one side, Frank Mitchell wanted one thing, and that was to be out.

It all happened in the most casual way. Scotch Jack Dickson came along to see Reggie with a story that Mitchell was threatening to kill one of the screws to draw attention to the fact that he was serving an indefinite sentence with no fixed date of release. Reggie, who had done what he could to help Mitchell by causing letters to be sent to the Home Office by various influential friends, came to one of his quick decisions, handed over a couple of hundred pounds to Dickson and told him to arrange the escape and have Mitchell out for Christmas. At this time Ronnie was on the trot with a witness summons out for him in connection with the Townsend corruption case. Dickson enlisted the help of Albert Donaghue and ex-boxer Bill Exley, a couple of his mates, and the next thing we heard was a report on television on Monday the 12th of December that Frank Mitchell had escaped from a working party engaged on building fences at a military range at Bagga Tor. So much for the life of Riley, by the way. Building fences on exposed moorland in the depths of winter doesn't quite fit in with riding ponies, carousing in pubs and poking passionate schoolmistresses.

According to the three musketeers Dickson, Donaghue and Exley, it was a piece of cake. They turned up in a car at a pre-arranged time and place and Mitchell, who was there waiting for them, hopped in and they were away. Mitchell changed his clothes in the car and, by the time his absence had been noticed and reported, he was well on the way to London.

The newspapers made a meal of it with banner headlines about the 'Mad Axeman', commandos and helicopters scouring the moors, the public warned not to approach Mitchell if he were seen, every word of which was read by Mitchell, who was safely tucked away in a council flat in Barking. The tenant of the flat was a sad little man by the name of Lennie Dunn known to all and sundry as Lennie Books because he ran a bookshop in the Commercial Road. Although sub-letting was frowned on by Lennie's landlords a bit of ready cash soon smoothed over that difficulty (the cash being paid to Lennie and not the local authority). With

Dickson, Donaghue and Exley taking turns in keeping him company, Frank Mitchell settled into his new and temporary home.

At the time of the escape and for some days afterwards I was confined to my bed with a throat infection, a fact which was confirmed in court at a later date by the doctor who treated me. However, as soon as I was up and about again, I had to take a hand in the situation. Ronnie couldn't show his face in the East End and Reggie was deeply involved in domestic troubles with his wife and in-laws. It didn't take me long to reach the conclusion, after talking to the three musketeers, that Jack Dickson had over-dramatised the matter, and that Mitchell had no more intention of actually killing a screw than flying in the air. Why had Dickson done this? It stands out a mile. Here were three hard nuts, the sort of men who would roar their heads off if someone copped a bullet in the belly, being given the opportunity of springing a prisoner from the Moor and keeping him in hiding with all the bills paid by the twins. To them it was a huge joke, and they did not have the intelligence to realise that they had a tiger by the tail.

For a time Mitchell was occupied with framing letters to the Press and the Home Secretary, Mr. Roy Jenkins, but once these had been written and sent off he had time on his hands. He wanted to get out and find himself a woman, but this was patently impossible. The problem was resolved by Tommy Cowley, who recruited the services of a hostess at Winston's. She was a good-looking and business-like blonde named Lisa Prescott who could be relied on to do a good professional job in any circumstances. Only someone as naive and unworldly as Mitchell could have mistaken professional competence for real affection. During their private hours together he fell in love with her. Then one evening, after a session of card-playing, drinking and trips to the bedroom with Lisa, Mitchell managed to get hold of Exley's gun. Now the joke was beginning to misfire. Here was a real life situation that was stranger than gangster fiction, an armed madman with the fresh taste of freedom and what he believed to be a loving woman at his side, holed up in a small flat in Barking and wanting to be away to enjoy his love in peace and tranquillity.

The answer, you say, is simple. Tip off the Old Bill and leave it to them to recapture the escaped man. But who was going to take the responsibility of precipitating what would inevitably turn out to be a gun battle in the Barking Road? Not me, and that's a racing certainty. It was decided that Frank Mitchell should be smuggled out of the country, more money was provided and Donaghue was given the job of transporting Mitchell on the first leg of the journey to a remote place in Kent. The completion of the trip would be in the safe hands of experts in such matters.

Whoever said that the best laid plans of mice and men often come unstuck was dead right, even though there were no mice about when Donaghue turned up at the Barking flat the night before Christmas Eve 1966. It has never been disputed that Donaghue and Mitchell left the flat together. A further undisputed fact is that, from the moment they stepped out into the night, Mitchell disappeared from the face of the earth and was never seen again.

Where did Mitchell go? Only one man knew, the man who closed the door of Lennie Dunn's flat behind himself and Mitchell on that fateful night of the 23rd of December 1966, the man who was later charged with the murder of Mitchell and had that charge withdrawn when he elected to give evidence for the Crown against me and my brothers, the man whose uncorroborated evidence was rejected by Mr. Justice Lawton at the Old Bailey in March of 1969, the man who had most to gain by shifting the burden of guilt on to others. His name was Albert Donaghue.

Here are the main points of the story he told on oath before a judge and jury. He left the flat with Mitchell and went with him to where a van was parked in Ladysmith Avenue nearby. Mitchell climbed into the back of the van, Donaghue followed him and immediately a fusillade of shots rang out. Mitchell died instantly, his body riddled with bullets. The men who fired the shots, said Donaghue, were Frederick Foreman and another man not on trial. The van was driven off and, after covering a short distance, stopped to allow Donaghue to alight, then contined to an unknown destination.

This story is, on the face of it, unadulterated poppycock. Frederick Foreman, the landlord of the Prince of Wales in Lant Street, Southwark, hated the very sight of Donaghue, and the brutal and violent Irishman returned that hatred with interest. Nobody in their right mind would put the two of them in the same building, let alone the confined space of a van. Then there was the absence of a hue and cry. To say that nobody noticed the goings-on in the back of a van on a Friday evening near the Barking High Road when, according to Donaghue, twelve shots were fired, is straining credulity to its limits. Yet there is no record that an alarm was raised or that anything out of the ordinary was reported to the police.

Many theories have been aired regarding Mitchell's fate, one of them being that he is alive and well in some remote and foreign clime. I doubt that very much. The most tenable theory, which happens to be the simplest explanation of the mystery, was advanced at the Old Bailey. It was that, when the two men came to the van that was to transport Mitchell to Kent, he suddenly decided that he wanted to go back for his lady-love. Donaghue attempted to prevent him, there was a struggle and, in the course of that struggle, Mitchell was shot and killed.

Theories apart, one undeniable fact remains. Donaghue is the one man who knows the truth and, unless he chooses to tell it, the fate of Frank Mitchell will remain a mystery for ever.

In the course of writing this book I have waded through masses of material written about the twins and their activities, checking a date here and a place-name there. It has been a fascinating business and has brought many things only half-remembered into sharper focus. In a book written by a well-known journalist I came across a minor item, a paragraph which referred to the twins' liking for ostentatious jewellery and to the fact that they both carried small reproductions of a scorpion fashioned in diamonds.

The twins were born on the 24th of October which, according to those who dabble in the realms of astrology, brought them under the influence of Scorpio, one of the twelve Signs of the Zodiac. There are some who believe that the movements of the sun, moon and stars have a great bearing on our day-to-day lives, and I'm willing to bet that there are literally thousands who take a self-conscious peek at their daily horoscope in the popular press. The twins consulted an East End fortune-teller from time to time who, so they said, made some very accurate predictions. Whether there is anything in this business of soothsaying is open to question, but the practitioners in that area don't seem to lack employment. I am told the late R. H. Naylor made a fortune out of casting horoscopes.

What did interest me as I ploughed through reams of transcripts and newspaper cuttings was the coincidence of names which cropped up in pairs at about the same point in time and in connection with the same incidents. When me and my brothers were accused of the murder of Frank Mitchell it was a statement made by Charlie Mitchell, a villain from Fulham, which helped to land me in the dock. At about the same time as Det. Superintendent Ronald Townsend was making his enquiries into the shooting of Ginger Marks, Det. Sergeant Leonard Townsend was making his debut on my brother Ronnie's tape recorder in the bar of the Baker's Arms. Ronnie once scared the living daylights out of George Dickson in the Green Dragon by sticking an unloaded gun into his ribs and pulling the trigger. The other Dickson, 'Scotch' Jack, played a principal part in Frank Mitchell's escape from the Moor. Then there was Richard Hart, shot dead in Mr. Smith's Club, and Ronnie Hart, an associate of Albert Donaghue. None of these men with identical surnames were related.

To continue with this dissertation on pairs, I have already mentioned Frederick Foreman, the landlord of the Prince of

Wales pub, whose brother George (no relation to the ex-heavyweight champion of the world) got himself shot in the genitals on the doorstep of his Vauxhall flat. Then there were the brothers Richardson, Charles and Eddie, to whom I have made earlier reference, and John and Tony Barry of the Regency Club, who will figure in a later stage of my story.

I mention these things only to show what part is played in the lives of some of us by coincidence, that strange trick of fate which cannot be explained in any rational or logical manner. As Hamlet said to an old mate on the battlements of Elsinore, 'There are more things in heaven and earth, Horatio, than are dreamt of in your philosophy.'

EIGHT

Whoever said that 'stone walls do not a prison make, nor iron bars a cage' was talking through the back of his neck. To be handed a substantial dose of porridge as a first experience at the age of forty-two is not the sort of thing about which I would write poems, and the stone walls and iron bars were very real things to me. On the 9th of May 1968 I was taken out of circulation and was to spend the best part of the next seven years until my release from Maidstone in January of 1975 as a not particularly willing guest of Her Majesty the Queen, God bless her. Before you get the wrong idea, let me inform you that I was not given the free run of Buckingham Palace with its extensive back garden. I was locked up in a variety of cells in a number of penal establishments ranging from excessively repressive to very easy. To someone who loved the open-air life, the week-ends in a caravan at Steeple Bay in Essex, the holidays in the South of France, swimming in the blue Mediterranean and basking in the sun, this was punishment indeed. Not that I'm complaining. In life one takes the rough with the smooth, and there's no point in howling about injustice unless and until you can prove that injustice has been done.

As soon as I knew for certain that I was going to spend several years in prison I accepted it as one of the facts of life and made up my mind to derive as much benefit as I could from whatever facilities the penal system provided. The first discovery I made was the world of books. I had never been a great reader but now, with time on my hands and the libraries of various prisons at my disposal, I developed an appetite for literature that surprised both the prison librarians and myself. I read anything and everything I could lay my hands on: the classics, historical works, modern novels – poetry you name it, I read it. While I was detained under maximum security rules it wasn't always easy to ensure a steady supply of reading matter, but once these rules were relaxed I had no difficulty at all. I didn't become an intellectual giant overnight but I learned a lot about the use of words, and I shall always look back on the time I spent with the great figures in English literature as time not exactly wasted.

One thing that struck me during the course of my reading was how much use is made of quotations (or misquotations) in general conversation. I cannot count how many times I have heard the phrase 'coming events cast their shadows before them'. The complete and accurate quotation comes from Thomas Campbell's poem 'Lochiel's Warning' and runs 'Tis the sunset of life gives me mystical lore, and coming events cast their shadows before'. This quotation comes to mind because it was apposite in the early months of 1967, when a considerable number of characters who seemed to have nothing better to do than wander around asking questions appeared in Bethnal Green and surrounding areas. That they were the Old Bill was obvious. What was equally obvious was that somebody up there, and I don't mean in Heaven, had decided the time was ripe to have another go at the Kray twins. Mark you, Ronnie had cocked a snook at the Old Bill by refusing to come forward and give evidence in the case of Detective Sergeant Townsend, which must have been a source of some displeasure to certain people. Ronnie, however, made a point of keeping out of the way and not visiting his usual haunts. He didn't cower in some remote hideout like a hunted animal, as has been suggested in some quarters. He just wasn't available except to those he wanted to see.

Another cause for anxiety about the future was the

ubiquitous American Alan Bruce Cooper, who was floating around like a fart in a colander – you never knew which hole he would come out of. He would suddenly appear in his office in Albemarle Street, where he had installed his girl-friend as his secretary, then away he would go to the States, ostensibly to visit his daughter suffering from meningitis. Then there would be telephone calls from Geneva, Brussels, Paris, Madrid and so on. He turned up one day in the Carpenter's Arms with a mild-mannered chap with glasses who looked like a schoolmaster. He introduced this man to me as Paul Elvey, and in a whispered aside informed me that he was a hit man for the Mafia. I formed the view that Cooper was a Walter Mitty type who lived in another world, but Tommy Cowley stuck to his opinion that the American was a police spy.

Reggie treated Cooper with caution, no doubt remembering the wily Payne and his extravagant schemes, but Ronnie's imagination seemed to be captured by this little man and his involvement in international intrigue, his claims to have been responsible for several assassinations in which he used highly sophisticated devices for the removal of his victims. One of these gadgets, which was demonstrated to Tommy Cowley, was a lethal brief case containing a hypodermic syringe full of potassium cyanide, a deadly poison which, when injected into the bloodstream, causes almost instant death. The needle of the syringe projected from the bottom corner of the case and the technique of operation was to get next to the intended victim, swing the case against his leg and quietly walk away. Death would occur within a matter of seconds but only a post-mortem examination would establish the cause, by which time it would be almost impossible to find witnesses who remembered the man with the briefcase – if he had even been noticed at all.

Another of Cooper's toys was a hunting crossbow which, according to Cooper, could kill at fifty yards without noise. As it was described to me it was an unwieldy weapon whose shape would be difficult to conceal. Anyway, I didn't treat Cooper all that seriously, and these stories about him and his grandiose plans I took with a pinch of salt. How wrong I was to dismiss this dangerous little man so lightly, but it's easy to be wise after the event.

There was one curious coincidence involving Cooper in which I figured personally. One day in the spring of 1967 I had a telephone call from Joe Kaufman, an American with gambling connections and an antique shop in New York who was well-known to me and my brothers. He was in Barcelona on a buying trip, and he invited me to come out to Spain for a few days with Dolly and the children, all expenses paid. My son Gary, who had just started a job with the Evening Standard on the distribution side, was reluctant to start his working life by going on holiday, so it was Dolly, baby Nancy and myself who arrived at the Avenida Palace hotel where Joe and his wife were waiting to welcome us.

The first curious happening was related to me by Joe, a keen amateur photographer. He had been taking a few shots of the city from the balcony of his suite, using a telephoto lens. Lining up a shot on the other side of the avenue Jose Antonio he found that he was looking directly into another telephoto lens which was aimed straight at him from an opposite balcony. I was rather amused, and informed Joe that he was probably not the only photographer in Barcelona, but the incident had more sinister implications, as I was to discover at a later date.

Joe had arranged that we should all go on and spend a week at Sitges, a very nice resort a few miles down the coast. We stayed at the Miramar hotel. About a couple of days after our arrival I was sitting by the swimming pool having a drink before lunch when who should stroll up but Cooper and his wife. He said he was in Spain on business and, knowing that I was spending a few days in Sitges, decided to drop in and say hello. I presumed that he had heard this from Joe, and thought no more about it, at least not at the time, but it all became crystal clear more than a year later. The Old Bill had a fully documented account of my trip to Spain, photographs of the party, Joe Kaufman, his wife, Dolly, my little girl Nancy and myself. They knew how much the holiday had cost, who had footed the bill – they even told me that I had made three telephone calls to London. I told them something they didn't know. The telephone calls had been made to my boy, Gary, who had arranged to be at home (he was staying with his grandparents during our absence) to take these calls.

The information could only have come from Cooper. If his lavish way of life was supported by the payments he received as an informer, then somebody somewhere had been paying him an awful lot of money. I wonder if it was worth it; but spending public money is just taking from a bottomless purse, so the question doesn't arise. I remember sitting in my cell one day and making an estimate of how much public money had been spent in putting away the so-called Kray Firm, coming up with a figure well in excess of a million pounds. As to whether the expense justified the result, this raises a delicate moral issue which I do not think I am qualified to answer. Perhaps the British taxpayer might have some views on how such a sum could have been spent to better effect.

In April of 1967 there were definite signs that there was something in the wind other than the threat of rain. The Old Bill were putting themselves about in a very active way, and among the trials taking place at the Old Bailey were those of Det. Sergeant Townsend, accused of corruption, and Charles and Eddie Richardson and several of their associates, charged with crimes that were much more serious.

Townsend was acquitted after a second trial, despite the weight of evidence against him. Whether the fact that Ronnie steadfastly refused to go into the witness box and give evidence against the man affected the result one way or the other was anybody's guess. What stood out a mile was that Mr. John Mathew, prosecuting for the Crown, left Townsend's counsel with little to do except twiddle his thumbs, watch his work being done for him, congratulate his client and pocket his fee. The only good thing about it was that Ronnie was now able to emerge from the shadows, which he did in pretty quick time. Nor surprisingly the Old Bill took no action against him for evading the witness summons. It is sometimes better to let sleeping dogs lie.

The Richardson trial was a larger and more important affair. At the end of July of the previous year the Old Bill had nicked Charles Richardson, his common-law wife Jean, mother of six children, and several other men associated with the Richardson enterprises. They were kept in custody without benefit of bail until their appearance at the Old Bailey in the following April, where they were joined in the dock by Charles' brother Eddie, and Frankie Fraser, who were serving sentences for their part in the shooting at Mr. Smith's Club. They faced a long list of charges including robbery with violence, demanding money with menaces, causing grievous bodily harm and so on.

There is no point in describing the trial in detail. It dragged on for over a month. In the early stages Jean Richardson was dismissed from the case and went home to look after her six children, who were going to be fatherless for a very long time. Then a procession of witnesses, many of them very doubtful characters indeed, testified to the orgies of torture presided over by the Richardson brothers, prosecuting counsel Mr. Sebag Shaw put in his two-penn'orth from time to time and his Lordship, Mr. Justice Lawton, dished out the porridge in very large portions. After sentences had been pronounced, the judge called into court the team of detectives who had been engaged on the case and publicly thanked them.

The trial of the Richardsons and the events leading up to it was important in one respect. It was the blueprint of the plan which was later put into operation against me and my brothers: sudden arrest, lengthy detention without bail, witnesses of doubtful character granted immunity and financial support as a condition of turning Queen's evidence and an enormous expenditure of public money as part of the process. Ronnie and Reggie weren't stupid. They followed the case as it was reported daily and saw the danger ahead, but they were not made of the stuff that is deterred by fear of consequences. Ronnie, always the more reckless of the two, went out of his way to let the Old Bill know that he was aware of their increasing interest in his comings and goings and didn't give a monkey's. Detectives keeping watch on his flat were often surprised by Ronnie's appearance with cups of tea, the offer of cigarettes and an apology for keeping them waiting. In the Grave Maurice pub in the Whitechapel Road he would wave a mocking greeting to the unobtrusive men who stood watching him from a remote corner of the bar and invite them over for a drink. Reggie was more circumspect, but a deep and personal tragedy was to occur which would affect him to such an extent as to change his personality literally overnight and turn him into a morose and anti-social shadow of his former self.

In the close and intimate relationships of a united family, tragedy can be seen for what it is, a heartbreaking business of tears and deep distress and private agony. Made public through the printed word, it becomes another statistic, one more digit added to the existing thousands. A man dies in the wreckage of a motorway pile-up and passes into the records of motoring fatalities as a number. Grief is left to the woman who loved him and the children who called him Daddy.

My brother Reggie loved pretty little Frances Shea with a passion that was almost beyond belief and understanding. He had seen her grow from a child to a young woman, they married when she was twenty-one and he thirty-three, he cherished and adored her as the one beautiful thing in his life – and at the age of twenty-three, two years after her wedding day, in the home of her brother and his wife but tragically alone, she died by her own hand. The popular press did its best to rob her death of dignity and detectives mingled with the mourners at her funeral. Her parents set stories afoot which were seized on by the gossips and scandalmongers, stories which grew wilder and more extravagant with each retelling, and in the middle of it all Reggie quietly did his nut.

I knew Frances well and was fond of her, and I think she liked me. We often had little chats, sometimes in a restaurant while Reggie was involved in some business discussion or other, sometimes at the flat in Cedra Court. Yet, though for most of the time she was gay and lively, there was always a hint of sadness behind the smile. She didn't want for any of the material things; Reggie gave her anything she asked for and much more besides. I don't think I'm exaggerating when I say that Reggie would have died for her, but that sort of passionate emotion isn't the rock on which successful marriages are built. It's the calm and quiet things that last.

Whatever Reggie might have been or was eventually to become, no-one seeing him at that time could have felt anything but a deep and abiding pity. I remember reading somewhere that marriage doesn't add two people together but just subtracts one from the other, the kind of clever remark which is misleading because there is a germ of truth in it. One thing I can say with absolute conviction and some knowledge of the facts. The death of Frances subtracted something from Reggie which will never be replaced as long as he lives.

In that summer of 1967 the exploits of my brothers were marked by an air of desperation. I was kept occupied by my agency, the coat factory and another little business I had started, the packing and distribution of potatoes, which sounds a bit comical but was a real money-spinner. It didn't surprise me to find, when I came out of prison, that this humble end of the vegetable trade had become big business in supermarkets and grocery shops. But that is by the way. Although I was not so deeply involved in their affairs as I had been in the days of Esmeralda's Barn, I saw Reggie and Ronnie fairly frequently and couldn't avoid the feeling, when in their company, that there was always somebody in the background watching points, noting all that went on and waiting for the moment to strike. I remember thinking that his was how the Jews must have felt when Hitler came to power in Germany, either looking round corners before they came to them or glancing over their shoulders to see who was following.

The only way in which this atmosphere affected the twins was in spurring them on to show an even greater defiance of authority. More than once I tried to point out to them that they were heading for serious trouble, but it was a waste of breath. Reggie, who had always been abstemious, began to drink heavily and behaved with a recklessness which was completely out of character. After Frances' tragic death he didn't seem to care what happened to him. Ronnie had never been cautious anyway, but he began to embark on some very dodgy projects with the aid and encouragement of Alan Bruce Cooper, the stuttering American, who now occupied a permanent place on the scene. Wild and extravagant plans for making vast fortunes were put forward by this dangerous man, plans which, like those of Payne the Brain, came to nothing. His credibility was finally destroyed when it was discovered that he was party to a clumsy plot to trap the twins into convicting themselves out of their own mouths in an amateurish set-up that involved the Old Bill, a Harley Street nursing home and a hidden tape recorder. I will come to that later.

Out of the welter of rumours, hair-raising stories and sensational speculation that was rife in this our last summer of freedom, three clear facts emerged. One was that the name Kray became synonymous with practically every act of violence committed in the Metropolitan area. A couple of villains carved each other up in a sleazy Fulham club and the word went round that the Krays were concerned in the bloodbath. Shootings in which both the aggressor and the victim joined in keeping the facts of the incidents from the Old Bill were down to the Krays. If all these stories were to be believed, the only acts of violence in which the Krays were not active participants were the Negro riots in Newark and Detroit and the Middle East war. It would be stupid of me to say that the twins were entirely blameless and, though they didn't make me a party to these matters, I was well aware that both Reggie and Ronnie at times dealt with their enemies in the only language these people understood, the language of armed violence. Take it from me, if the twins hadn't done it to them, they would have done it to the twins. It was all a question of who got there first.

Another fact became apparent during this time. I have made mention earlier of the belief in his invulnerability that comes to a fighter after a string of victories in the ring. Both Reggie and Ronnie had reached a point when they firmly believed that nobody and nothing could touch them, which is a dangerous state of mind. Caution goes out of the window and consequences are left in the uncertain hands of Providence – a sure way to eventual disaster. I saw it coming, and there was nothing I could do to prevent it.

The most important fact, and one of which we all had some knowledge, was that somewhere in the vast warren of buildings that houses the police arm of the administration of justice a spider was spinning a web. The name of the spider was 'Nipper' Read and the filaments that made up his web were the piles of damning documents that grew steadily from day to day, detailed reports on movements and activities, sworn statements from ex-associates more intent on saving their own skins than serving justice, all the minutiae of a thorough investigation building up into a dossier that would eventually find its way to the office of the Director of Public Prosecutions.

Against this background of constant surveillance by the Old Bill it was obvious that my brothers regarded everyone save their closest friends with suspicion. It was no secret to them that the Old Bill relied heavily on information supplied by 'grasses', men who provided that information for money or for the promise of immunity in respect of their criminal activities. Almost everyone in contact with the twins was regarded as a potential informer unless (or until) they had proved their loyalty beyond question. That they had to commit murder to prove that loyalty, as has been suggested by some far from impartial people, was a load of eyewash, the same sort of sensational rubbish that attributed to Ronnie, in conversation with Reggie, the remark 'I've done mine – now you go and do yours'. We all lived under the shadow of George Cornell's death. Both Reggie and myself were appalled when it happened, and would have done everything we could to prevent it had we had some foreknowledge of the event. So far as Ronnie was concerned the subject was taboo, but I am convinced that even he regretted that moment of bravado in the Blind Beggar. The odd carve-up, in the course of which some villain gets what he has been asking for, is accepted by him as an occupational hazard. He goes off to hospital, gets himself stitched up, the wounds heal and, apart from revenge, that is the end of the matter. But death is very final and the corpse that cannot talk is the most important witness to the deed.

Now I come to a point in my story where I have to set down on paper what I know of a happening which has been described as the most brutal and cold-blooded murder since Richard the Third was knifed to death on Bosworth Field almost five hundred years ago. It was a murder with little apparent motive which was presumed to have taken place on the testimony of an eye witness who described the scene in horrific detail. The whereabouts of the corpse has remained a mystery to this day, but the corpse had a name. It was Jack McVitie.

Who was Jack McVitie? He was a nothing man, a small-time villain with a high forehead – due to shortage of hair, not surplus of brain – and was used by the twins as an errand boy. He was in the same class as Henry 'Buller' Ward, and like him he also was widely known by a nickname, 'The Hat'. He was known to be very thin on the top, but this pathetic creature always wore a hat so that people would believe that there was hair under it.

It was alleged that he was done to death by my brother Reggie in a basement room in Evering Road, Stoke Newington, on a night in October of 1967. According to the story of the eye witness, McVitie was repeatedly stabbed in the face, the body and finally the neck, and died in a welter of blood which sprayed out over the walls, the furnishings and those present with dreadful impartiality. The body was then loaded into a car and dumped somewhere south of the

Thames.

Who was this eye witness? He was a villain and a man of violence; a close friend of Albert Donaghue, who was the last person to see Frank Mitchell before he departed on his last journey. He was a distant relative of me and my brothers and his name was Ronnie Hart. At the Old Bailey in April of 1969 his uncorroborated evidence was accepted by the judge and jury when a verdict of guilty of the charge of murder was returned against my brother Reggie. Found guilty of complicity in the murder were my brother Ronnie, Cornelius Whitehead, Albert Donaghue, the Lambrianou brothers Chris and Tony, Ronnie Bender, Freddie Foreman and myself. Ronnie Hart who, on his own admission, was present at the scene and actually assisted in holding McVitie while the stabbing took place, walked out of the Old Bailey a free man after having 'eased his conscience'. It was no doubt the workings of that same conscience which led to his attempted suicide about twelve months after the trial.

Before anything further is said I want to make one thing quite plain. I had nothing to do with the events leading up to the alleged murder or the later disposal of the corpse. The cynic will say that the prisons of this country are full of people who are victims of the miscarriage of justice, and that is as maybe. What I do say right here and now is that I spent almost seven years in jail for a crime I did not commit. I do not ask for sympathy or condolence. In my own good time and in my own way I shall prove my innocence. Hanratty and Timothy Evans are dead. I am very much alive, and intend to clear my name by due legal process and you can bank on that.

Now that I have, as they say in the House of Commons, declared my interest, I can get on with the story. I don't think there is any man alive better qualified than myself to make an inspired guess about what happened on that October night in the basement of the house in Evering Road. I had an intimate knowledge of the characters of all the men involved and was aware of the background against which the action took place. There is no point, after this lapse of time, in supporting the story that any of the accused were not there. So why didn't they plead guilty? There's a simple answer to that. You, sir, Mr. Managing Director, driving home pissed from the office party, stopped by the police, go for trial, hire counsel, lie yourself blue in the face after pleading not guilty, I only had two small whiskies . . . Any further questions?

There is no doubt in my mind that McVitie was lured to the scene of the crime for the purpose of being given a bloody good hiding. For what? Stories have been told that McVitie, said to be a man of courage, had stalked the streets of the East End armed with a shotgun and looking for the twins in order to settle some grudge against them. Cobblers. He was a drunken bum who had lost his bottle years ago, a poor wretch who hung around on the fringes of crime picking up the crumbs, a creature whose violence was reserved for the women who were foolish enough to become infatuated with him. He was a fetcher-and-carrier who rated nothing more than a mixture of pity and contempt. It was said that my brothers paid him to assassinate Payne the Brain. That was the joke of the century. Had they wished to see Payne out of the way they would certainly not have entrusted the task to this specimen of homo-not-very-sapiens. Let me make this quite clear. McVitie was due for a beating because he had challenged the authority of the twins. Drunk and boastful, he had put it about that he would relish the opportunity of sticking it on them, and there was only one answer to that. McVitie had to be taught a lesson in a language he understood.

When the man with the hat stumbled drunkenly down the steps to the basement of the house in Evering Road carolling 'Where's the birds and the booze?' he found neither. Instead there was a welcoming committee comprising my brothers and the two Ronnies, Bender and Hart. McVitie entered the room followed closely by Chris and Tony Lambrianou (who had brought him from the Regency Club) and the scene was set for what was intended to be a brief enquiry into McVitie's actions followed by the sort of beating that would effectively deter the recipient from repeating the offence.

To digress for a moment, Hart gave evidence at the Old Bailey that Reggie put an automatic pistol to McVitie's head as soon as the man entered the room, but the gun jammed. I doubt that very much. If there was a gun (and only Hart said there was) I would bet my bottom dollar that it was unloaded and used as a frightener. However, McVitie was not shot – so where do we go from there?

Here was a small room crowded with seven men, all of whom had been drinking heavily. That violence was about to be done to one of them was beyond question. From what I have been told by my brothers, the Lambrianous and Bender, who would have no reason to lie to me, this was the sequence of events. Ronnie taxed McVitie with putting the word around that he was out to get the Krays, and the frightened man made a dive for the window, a desperate and useless gesture that served to spark off the violence. He was dragged back into the room, and there began a systematic beating-up, fists and feet flying, a concerted attack against which McVitie had no defence whatever. Then, suddenly, there was the glint of steel as a knife was drawn and McVitie's face opened up like a red and terrible flower. The knife was in the hand of Ronnie Hart, who plunged it repeatedly into McVitie's face and body. Jack the Hat died as he had lived, in a welter of blood and violence.

It is common knowledge that my brother Reggie was convicted of the murder of Jack McVitie, and it is true that, by virtue of his presence at the scene, he was party to murder and as guilty as the others. That Hart wielded the knife that put an end to McVitie's life is an academic point which in no way lessens the guilt of any member of the group that stood around the corpse.

It is cogent that, at this point, I should give my reasons for believing that Ronnie Hart killed McVitie. It is simply a process of elimination. The Lambrianous were paper villains, concerned only to take whatever glory attached to their connection with the twins. They were not capable of killing. Nor was Bender. I must admit that the twins were perfectly capable of killing, indeed Ronnie had proved that in the case of George Cornell, but there would have to be an important reason, and I cannot think that McVitie was anything more than a minor irritant. In my opinion, supported by the facts as told to me and personal knowledge of the men concerned, it stands out a mile that the man who actually sent McVitie to his Maker was the man who had everything to gain by turning Queen's evidence, the close associate of that other perjurer Albert Donaghue, the man who walked out of the Old Bailey to freedom, the man known as Ronald Hart. Always eager to demonstrate to the twins that he was a hard man and ready to play his part in any enterprise, his zeal on this occasion had carried him too far.

To say that Ronnie and Reggie were furious is to put it mildly. It was no secret that McVitie had gone to Evering Road and it would not be long before he would be missed from his usual haunts. Some quick thinking and rapid organising was obviously called for. Delaying only long enough to clean up and change their clothes, Reggie and Ronnie, taking Hart with them, set off for Lavenham in Suffolk. The task of clearing up the flat and disposing of the mortal remains of the late Jack 'The Hat' MacVitie was left to the Lambrianous and Bender.

My brothers have been credited (if that is the right word to use) with responsibility for the disappearance of several persons from their spheres of action. One Johnny Frost, who for a time acted as Ronnie's driver, took it into his head one day to transfer his talents to new pastures. It was not long before it was being whispered around that Mr. Frost would never more be seen. In fact, Johnny Frost appeared at the Old Bailey on charges of fraud as recently as 1972. 'Mad' Teddy Smith, who stood trial alongside the twins in the McCowan case, was said to have been ushered into the Great Beyond on instructions from my bothers that he should be put out of the way. As recently as the spring of 1975, Teddy Smith was working as a chauffeur in London. Although there is only the most nebulous evidence to connect the twins with the disappearance of Frank Mitchell, it has been said that it was through their agency that the so-called 'Mad Axeman' was consigned to a watery (or earthy) grave.

The files on missing persons stored away in the records of the police forces of this country are crammed with the names and last known addresses of thousands of persons who, for a variety of reasons, have either disappeared or been made to vanish. I mentioned earlier that I was of the opinion that Mitchell was dead – yet I cannot rid myself of the feeling that somewhere in Europe or some other foreign land a large and simple-minded man has become part of the daily life of a small town or village. Stranger things have happened.

I can be quite certain about one disappearance. When the twins left London on that momentous Sunday morning in late October and sped through the morning mist to Lavenham, they knew that the body of Jack 'The Hat' McVitie would shortly be beyond recovery. There are experts in all trades and every walk of life whose names are well known even though they do not advertise. Among these experts are men who specialise in the removal of incriminating evidence whose services, though expensive, are guaranteed to be efficient and, above all, confidential. You may discount the theories that the bones of the late Mr. McVitie are shoring up a motorway, that he provided fodder for a herd of pigs, that he was incinerated, chopped up or slipped into a coffin made for two. The remains of Jack McVitie, confined in a stout weighted sack, were dropped from an aircraft over the middle of the English Channel, and his lonely funeral cost more than he had ever earned in his life. The job was carried out by the aforementioned experts whose names, for obvious reasons, will not be disclosed.

The twins were away for about a week, during which time they moved about in the small hamlets of Norfolk and Suffolk with Ronnie Hart in tow. They kept in touch with me by telephone, and I was able to assure them that the disappearance of the man with the hat had not occasioned any undue activity on the part of the Old Bill. This was surprising in itself since, as I have mentioned before, police surveillance over my brothers had been stepped up during the latter part of 1967. By rights the Old Bill should have been keeping watch outside the house in Evering Road. They must have kicked themselves when they realised later what a fine catch they had missed.

My brothers came back to London like kids with a new toy. Ever since they had been evacuated to Hadleigh in Suffolk they had developed an affinity for that rural section of England. It seemed to draw them like a magnet. Now they had found a house in the pretty village of Bildeston, only a few miles from Hadleigh, a large Victorian edifice in its own grounds of about eight acres with stables and a paddock and a stream running along one boundary. It was on the market for about £12,000, it was known as The Brooks, the twins had to have it – and they got it. Mum and Dad, who had left Vallance Road for a ninth floor flat in a tower block in Bunhill Row (not far from the Bank of England and Mansion House), moved into the cottage. For the next few months The Brooks was the centre of the twins' lives. They spent a small fortune on renovating the place, and began to talk about plans for retiring from the London scene.

Before I go any further I must correct some of the wild and sensational stories that circulated about the work that was done in and around the house. Rumours that machine-gun nests were established in the upper rooms, electrified fences set up on the boundaries of the grounds and guard dogs roaming the estate were just so much eyewash. In fact the only barrier ever erected was a wire fence alongside the stream designed to prevent the village children from taking an accidental bath. These children were allowed the run of the paddock where Ronnie had installed a donkey which they were permitted to ride.

So much for that highly-coloured piece of fiction. For the short time that The Brooks remained in the twins' possession it was used to the full. Christmas was celebrated in true East End style with lashings of food and drink and Mum as happy as she had ever been, surrounded by family and friends in a house that surpassed her wildest dreams. The ghosts of Cornell and McVitie were forgotten, the scarred and ugly face of villainy was a million miles away. A brief glimpse of a strange face in the village or a car moving slowly past the main entrance to the house were the only reminders that the Old Bill still maintained a watchful interest in our comings and goings. Though it could not properly be described as pastoral or idyllic, the atmosphere was nevertheless quiet and peaceful – the calm before the storm.

Back in London events moved steadily and inexorably towards the climax of the 9th of May 1968. Though I did not intend to, I must make one brief and final mention of John Pearson who was a background figure during this period. He was engaged in collecting material for a projected book about the twins and their exploits. Ronnie, his sometimes cruel sense of humour well to the fore, housed this well-educated and cultured man in a dismal basement flat in Bethnal Green, he was taken around and introduced to a large number of notorious and notable characters and, to use East End phraseology, the twins gee'd him up something rotten. Poor John. I hope the proceeds of his book of fiction masquerading as fact compensated for his sufferings.

The early part of 1968 also witnessed the departure of the stuttering American, Alan Bruce Cooper, whose standing with the twins was finally destroyed when he collaborated with the Old Bill in an attempt to obtain incriminating evidence against them. The plan that was set on foot was a typical Cooper strategem, a James Bond set-up almost infantile in its conception and execution. The ubiquitous Cooper set the scheme in motion with the usual spate of telephone calls and telegrams culminating in a frantic appeal from a Harley Street nursing home that the twins should visit him. He was, so he said, suffering from a burst duodenal ulcer, but whether he wanted the twins to perform the last rites or the operation wasn't quite clear. Joking apart, there was a nasty smell in the Cooper department. Tommy Cowley took on the role of hospital visitor.

It was, as I remember, about the beginning of March when Tommy made the journey to Harley Street. It sticks in my memory because it was around the time that George Brown resigned from the Foreign Secretaryship. The weather was cold, and Tommy wore his best vicuna overcoat. He reported back to the twins and I can do no better than relate the story he told in his own words. Here, to the best of my recollection, is what he said.

Tommy Cowley talking: 'It was obviously some sort of trap. There's Cooper lying in bed with a bust duodenal ulcer. It was like a comedy. If this is the way our Special Branch performs we must be the laughing stock of the whole world of espionage. Anyone with any sense at all realises what a bust duodenal ulcer is. He's lying there white as a ghost with one hand on his belly, because they couldn't hear in the next room the nurse comes bursting in. There's Old Bill written all over her and she says are you all right, here's the menu, what do you want for dinner. That was it. That was the plot, the cue to turn up the volume. She went out of the room so I said to Cooper you want to be careful, my old man had an ulcer and he died of cancer after. I looked out of the window and I thought where can they be. I couldn't see next door, but the Old Bill had to be there. Cooper asked me about the gelignite and I said what gelignite and he said the gelignite Elvey went to get in Scotland. To blow up Caruana. I said blow up Caruana, what are you talking about, you delirious or something, what's he gone to Scotland to get gelignite for, we're supposed to be the guv'nors in London, you want any gelignite I'll get you some today. They must have thought I was fucking mad, coming a stroke like that. So anyway I said ta-ta to Cooper and had it away.'

That was the end of Cooper as far as the twins were concerned. They had nothing more to do with him, but it transpired that Tommy Cowley's suspicions were well-founded. Exactly what role Cooper played officially will always be a bit of a mystery, but he certainly played the stool pigeon and conspired with the police in manufacturing evidence.

This brings me to something that I have been wanting to get off my chest, a point that I would make very forcibly. I have said all along that I never agreed with the use of knives and guns for the settling of disputes, and my most serious quarrels with my brothers were on that score. I'm not making excuses, because once Ronnie and Reggie had made up their minds to do something then it was as good as done. But in all fairness, the only characters who suffered bodily harm at the hands of the twins were villains whose stock-in-trade was violence – and armed violence at that. I defy anyone to say that my brothers ever raised a hand against non-violent persons. If that had been their policy, then Payne and Cooper and several others who conspired to put them away would by now be pushing up the daisies or, at best, carrying a few scars as mementos to their temerity.

During the early months of 1968 there was considerable tension in the air. It was now quite certain that the Old Bill were cooking up a fine old stew in which the Krays and their associates were to figure as the meat content. We were aware that a towering office block on the south side of the river, known as Tintagel House, saw the comings and goings of some of the top brass in the C.I.D., Commander John du Rose, the old Grey Fox himself, Inspector Frank Cater, Superintendent Harry Mooney and, last but not least, our own, our very own Leonard 'Nipper' Read, now a Detective-Superintendent and a more important light in the hierarchy of New Scotland Yard than the mere Detective-Inspector who drank a glass of champagne with Ronnie after the McCowan case. This was formidable opposition. The twins adopted the sensible policy of laying low, saying as little as possible and watching points.

Mum and Dad were now permanently resident at The Brooks, and the twins made full use of the flat in Bunhill Row. They must have felt some sense of security there, high up on the ninth floor which could only be reached by a sometimes unreliable lift or an arduous climb up eighteen flights of stairs.

It was actually quite a nice place for a council flat, constructed on two floors and quite commodious. There was a small car park adjacent to the block. Needless to say, my brothers never had any parking problems.

I wasn't particularly worried about my personal position. Within certain broad limits I had acted as properly as was possible in the circumstances of my involvement in my brothers' affairs, but I must confess that my conscience wasn't as clear as it might have been. Although by this time I was financially independent with the agency, the coat factory and the potato packaging projects returning a very good income, it would be foolish of me to pretend that I hadn't taken the easy money when it was available without enquiring too deeply into the source from which it came. I will go so far as to say that, had it not been for my brothers, I might still have been an East End dealer like my father before me, and maybe that wouldn't have been a bad thing. I don't know. Fate or Destiny or whatever you like to call it plays some queer tricks on us fallible mortals. As the poet said, there is a divinity that shapes our ends, rough-hew them as we will.

There was no Divine hand in the events of the early morning of the 9th of May 1968 when the rough-hewing came to an end and the shaping began. In a concerted and meticulously organised swoop the Old Bill, under the leadership of Nipper Read, took up the Kray brothers and everyone who had ever been associated with them. Nipper himself led the posse of armed men who went to arrest the twins. I have often had a mental picture of the scene, the arrival of the cars in the morning quiet of Bunhill Row, the large men filing into the lift (climb eighteen flights of stairs – not bloody likely), and the finger pressing the button for the ninth floor.

What would have happened, I wonder, if the ascending lift had broken down between floors.

NINE

It was rather a tight fit in the back of the Rover. There was a large copper on my right and another one on my left, and I had to indulge in some restricted acrobatics to look through the rear window at the home I was not to see again for almost seven years. Then the car swung round the corner and I settled myself for the short drive to Bow nick.

It wasn't until the car was cracking along Narrow Street that I began to realise that Bow was not to be our destination. I asked where we were going, and the copper on my left said I would know soon enough. The way he said it effectively put a stop to further conversation, and there was silence as we sped through the deserted City into High Holborn. I had plenty on my mind so the lack of chat didn't bother me too much. I now knew that there was something serious in the wind, and I was very worried. The Old Bill don't send out armed men equipped with handcuffs to pick up somebody for a parking offence.

West End Central Police Station is the headquarters of F division of the Metropolitan Police. It is handily situated in the posh purlieus of Savile Row, a modern chrome and plate glass building through whose portals have passed the elite of the criminal world. It was here that I ended up on this May morning, hustled through the door into a bedlam of noise and organised confusion, a sudden and disturbing contrast to the quiet ride through the deserted streets of early-morning

London. I had little time to look around as my captors closed in on me and took me through the lobby at express speed, but I did get a fleeting glimpse of some familiar faces before I was put into a waiting room. Limehouse Willie, who was easily spotted because of his height, was standing there in the lobby, so was Harry Hopwood and a few other merchants from the East End whom I knew by sight.

I wasn't in the waiting room very long, only long enough in fact for a sergeant to read out the charge against me and administer the formal caution, you are not obliged to say anything, but anything you say will be taken down in writing and may be given as evidence. I asked to be allowed to phone my solicitor, a request which was listened to very politely and just as politely refused, I was searched even though all my possessions had been taken from me when I was arrested, and finally I was locked up in a cell with only my few cigarettes (and no means of lighting them) for company. After the events of the past couple of hours it was a relief to sit down and begin to unscramble my thoughts.

It was as clear as daylight that the balloon had gone up, that the Old Bill had carried out a carefully planned scheme to round up and put under lock and key anyone who had ever been associated with the Krays in any way whatsoever. The cells adjacent to mine were beginning to be occupied. Over the rattle of keys and the crashing of doors I heard the unmistakeable voice of Tommy Cowley raising merry hell and through the small barred grating in the door of my cell I had momentary glimpses of men being escorted to their temporary resting places, men I knew well. The procession was almost endless and very significant. The fat was well and truly in the fire.

During the next couple of days the pieces of the jig-saw fell neatly into place. The Old Bill had brought off a real coup. Not even the smallest fish had escaped the dragnet put out by those redoubtable fishers in troubled waters, the team of dedicated felon-takers headed by Commander John du Rose ably assisted by his lieutenants, Superintendents Leonard Read and Harry Mooney. They'd got us and they meant to keep us. Like animals in cages, we were fed and watered and kept away from human contact. We were not allowed to shave, the washing facilities were limited and the only bright spot in the desert of discomfort was the attitude of the women cleaners, the Mrs. Mops who came in the early morning and brought us cigarettes and did what they could to make conditions more tolerable. Not that they could do much, but I would like to put my appreciation on record.

I saw my brothers for the first time since my arrest after two days had passed. I was taken from my cell into a room and there they were, dirty, scruffy and unshaven, bleary-eyed from lack of sleep. I don't suppose I looked any better, but I hadn't seen a mirror for a couple of days so I couldn't be sure. I was a bit surprised to see a fellow from Fulham, a well-known character by the name of Charlie Mitchell (no relation to the Axe-Man), but even more surprised to see, sitting behind a desk and wearing an inspector's uniform, a police officer whom I had met in the South of France, a very nice man indeed, and a fanatical Rugby player. He had roped me into a game against a French naval team in the St. Raphel Stadium, me who had never played Rugby football in my life – and the British team won. However, that's by the way, but this inspector had been plain Sergeant Vic Streeter when I first met him.

We had been brought up, along with this Charlie Mitchell, to hear the further charges in connection with American bonds which were being brought against the four of us. So far as I was concerned it was all double Dutch, but I was to grow accustomed to this sort of thing in the months ahead. After the mumbo-jumbo had been gone through I was returned to my cell in double quick time without being given an opportunity to have a word with my brothers, but shortly afterwards Vic Streeter came to see me. He was really first-class, said how sorry he was to see me in trouble, and told me that Dolly was in the station and I could see her for a short while. I wasn't too anxious for her to see me because I looked terrible, two days growth of beard, unwashed and quite smelly, but I did want to know how she and the kids were getting on.

When I heard what had happened after I was taken from my home I went spare. Dolly told me that the Old Bill had turned the place over, refused to allow Gary to go to work, wouldn't let her call in one of the neighbours and there wasn't even a policewoman on the scene. Now this was a serious matter, because it's against the rules governing police procedure to deal with women or young children unless a policewoman is present. I was hopping mad, and what made me more furious was that I was unable to do anything about it. Sure, the Old Bill had a job to do, and if they had to nick me then that was okay, but to subject a highly-strung woman and a couple of kids to that sort of harassing experience, by bloody Jesus Christ it was coming it a bit strong. Anyway Dolly had to leave and I calmed down a bit. This was no time to be losing my temper.

After Dolly had gone there was some activity outside my cell. Peering through the grating in the door I saw Limehouse Willie and a chap called Kennedy along with two other fellows I knew, Nobby Clark and Dave Simmons. I heard somebody mention bail. This cheered me up. After all, I had no criminal record and was a family man with business interests to look after. There seemed every reason to suppose that I would shortly be released. I waited and waited, but nobody came near me until the evening when a meal was brought by a constable, who cocked a deaf ear to my questions as to what was going on. It was now Thursday evening, and I had been in custody thirty-six hours.

Early on the Friday morning things began to happen. There was no confusion now, it was all orderly and very purposeful. The door of my cell was unlocked and, closely guarded by two coppers, I was taken down to the back entrance of the nick and ushered into a Black Maria. I had seen these vehicles before, but from the outside. Now I had the doubtful pleasure of my first introduction to the interior, and I didn't like it too much. There was a narrow passageway that ran along the centre of what was a converted large van, and on either side of the passageway were small cubicles which allowed the occupant to stand up or sit down but little else. Once inside the cubicle one was cut off from the outside world except for a restricted view from a tiny and semi-obscured window. It was a good job I didn't suffer from claustrophobia.

Now started the pantomime which was to be repeated often during the coming months. As the Black Maria moved out of the yard there was a sudden howling of sirens as the van picked up speed and literally flew through the streets. Through the little window I caught glimpses of the startled faces of pedestrians as they scattered before the onrush of the large blue van and its clamorous escort of cars and motorcycle. As a precaution it was hardly necessary. What could we do, locked up in our little dog-kennels without even a box of matches between us? As an exhibition of police efficiency, the pantomime was a howling success.

The journey was non-stop and brief, the destination Bow Street Magistrates Court. I had a sight of the Opera house (the only cultural centre in Europe where the audience waded ankle-deep in piles of rotting vegetables to see a performance of La Traviata) as, without stopping, the Black Maria swept under the archway leading to the rear of the court and disgorged its bruised and shaken cargo. Under armed guard, the Dirty Dozen were escorted to the comparative peace of the cells.

There is little point in describing the proceedings in the lower court. On this May morning, and on many mornings to come, me and my brothers and several others were charged with a variety of offences ranging from petty larceny to conspiracy, all of which were jettisoned when we appeared at the Old Bailey ten months later. It was quite clear that the Old Bill were merely concerned in keeping us in custody while they built up a cast-iron case. To my brothers, who knew all about remands in custody, this came as no surprise. To me, who had never before been in prison, it was a shocking experience.

The Black Maria which had brought us from West End Central to Bow Street also conveyed us to Brixton. It was a similar performance, sirens screaming, blue lights flashing, tyres screeching protest as bends were taken at high speed while the unfortunate occupants of the mobile dog-kennels were tossed about like so many peas in a drum. I never thought I would be glad to get into a prison, but the arrival at Brixton was a relief. It was a short-lived pleasure. My brothers had given me some idea what to expect on my introduction to jail as a remand prisoner. The reality, when it came, was degrading and very humiliating.

A prison is a prison, and the inmate is not allowed to forget it, no matter whether he is on remand or serving a sentence. Everything is done by the book. Under the watchful eyes of a couple of screws I had to strip down to the buff, and was then subjected to an extremely personal search. I asked one of the screws if he thought I had a gun stuck up my arse, but he appreciated the joke about as much as I relished his intimate attentions. I learned later the old con who knows he is going to get a stretch makes provision for his first few days in prison by packing some tobacco, cigarette papers and a few Treasury notes into a condom which he then inserts into his rectum. All very enterprising, but I had nothing up my sleeve as the conjuror said, so I was passed on to the regulation bath in nine inches of tepid water, for which I was duly thankful since I hadn't seen soap and water for three days.

I was then permitted to put on my clothes and was shown into a room where Reggie and Ronnie were waiting for me, just the two of them. The purpose was quite obvious. I didn't see the microphone, but there must have been one somewhere around. We confined our conversation to trivialities. Ronnie was in one of his more humorous moods as he described what took place on the morning of the arrests. He said they were both fast asleep when there was this enormous crash as the door of the flat was shattered and the Old Bill swarmed in with guns at the ready. The Nipper was in the forefront. Ronnie was told to get up. 'What'll you do if I don't get up?'

he said. 'Shoot me? You blokes have been seeing too many gangster films. You ought to be more careful with those guns. One of 'em might go off.' I saw the funny side of it. Ronnie was the last man in the world to be frightened by a gun pointed at his head.

My brothers seemed to be in good spirits, which was more than could be said for me. One thing we were all glad about was that Mum and Dad had been safely tucked away in Bildeston, though they came back to London on the double as soon as the news of our arrest reached them.

We were not left together very long. Whoever was at the other end of the listening apparatus soon realised that they were not going to overhear anything of importance. We were taken out and put in separate cells, on the same landing as far as I could judge, and I was left alone once more. I thought I heard in the distance the voice of Gordon Anderson, the Canadian chap who had been involved in the Great African Safari, and I remember wondering what he was doing in the nick. I sat down on the primitive bed and looked around me, taking in the details of this dreary place which was to be the centre of my existence for some time to come.

A prison cell is not an attractive pied-a-terre nor does it contain the accoutrements for gracious living. As I stood with my back to the door I faced an expanse of painted brick wall, the only break in it being the sole source of light, a small and heavily barred window set high up. On my right was the bed, a stout tubular steel and wire contraption hinged to the wall, and over in the far corner a triangular table bearing an enamelled bowl and jug and beneath it, on the floor, that relic of Victorian bedrooms, a pisspot. Against the left-hand wall stood a small but sturdy wooden table with a matching chair, and that was the lot. The decor was Home Office green and light brown, embellished with graffiti some of which, when I got round to studying it, was highly erudite. But it was the door that was the monster, a massive barrier with a peephole covered from the outside, a steel and wood Cyclops that came to life when a large key was thrust into its ancient innards.

That door was my enemy. On the other side of it was freedom, fresh air and sunshine, golden sands and a warm blue sea, woods and green fields and the open sky. On my side was the breeding ground of despair and hopelessness. Fuck it, I thought, now is the time to make the best of a bad job.

Man is an adaptable animal, and I soon learned to adapt. I won't go into the wearisome details of prison life. More than enough has been said and written about that. In any case, we had certain compensations in that, as remand prisoners, we were allowed to wear our own clothes and have meals sent in from the outside. Then there were the visits from Mum and Dad, Dolly and my children and those of our friends who refused to heed the attempts of authority to turn them back at the prison gates – and there was plenty of that. Many of the people we knew, actors and actresses, show business personalities, respectable businessmen and so on, were interviewed by the Old Bill and told in no uncertain terms that they would be well advised to keep away from Brixton.

I was now seeing the twins every day. We were allowed to exercise together (if walking round a small yard for half an hour a day can be called exercise), and naturally we discussed the situation. My brothers were reconciled to the prospect of a long remand in custody, an appearance at the Old Bailey and a substantial dose of porridge but, as I pointed out to them, I didn't see where I came into the picture. They were both quite uncompromising on that score, Ronnie particularly emphasising that I would have to take my chance with the rest. I had to be content with the knowledge that, at the very worst, I would have to face some minor charges. Both Ronnie and Reggie were sure that nothing could be proved against them in the cases of Cornell, Mitchell and McVitie. I had my doubts about that, but I kept them to myself.

The days became weeks, the weeks became months as the slow, relentless machinery of the Law took its course. The prison monotony was relieved by interviews with solicitors and counsel, appearances at magistrates' courts with the usual hair-raising journeys to and from Brixton in our old friend the Black Maria surrounded by its escort of police vehicles and motor-cycles, lights flashing and sirens screaming. I remember vividly one of these appearances at Bow Street magistrate's court about two months after we were arrested, because it provided the first indication of the tactics the Old Bill were to use subsequently, both in the lower courts and at the Old Bailey.

On this occasion we were all in the dock in front of the Metropolitan Chief Magistrate. After the preliminaries and a ration of legal mumbo-jumbo, the prosecution called its witnesses. One of them was Billy Exley, whom I had fought against in an amateur tournament – he gained a points decision – and who had been one of the organisers of Frank Mitchell's escape from the Moor. Now this Exley was a very hard man indeed, as tough as old boots, but he shuffled into the courtroom like an old man, collapsed into a chair and replied to questions in a whisper. Prosecuting counsel explained that Exley was suffering from a heart condition and might drop dead at any moment, but he wanted to clear his conscience before that event. What the purpose was behind this elaborate pantomime I have never been able to determine. What I do know is that Exley was as fit as a fiddle only a few months prior to his dramatic appearance at Bow Street and is now alive and well and working in a pub in the East End.

What got up my nose about Exley and others like him was this attitude of snivelling hypocrisy. Fair enough, let a man get up in the witness box and say that he wants to get his own back or that he is giving evidence because by doing so he hopes to get a lighter punishment for his own crimes. But for conscienceless villains like Exley and his kind to prattle about their duty as citizens and their devotion to the public weal was laughable. They didn't give a monkey's for morality, decency or the rule of law. All they were concerned about was saving their own skins. I can respect a man who is a man and stands up for what he believes in – but I have no time at all for smarmy, arse-licking toadies who will betray their friends in order to gain some small advantage for themselves.

About the time of the Bow Street hearing and Billy Exley's stunning performance as 'L'Homme aux Camelias' under the direction of Nipper Read and before a small and select audience, the special security cage at Brixton was completed. It wasn't all for the benefit of the Krays and their associates. As I remember, the lower floor of this prison within a prison was reserved for us. On the upper floor a couple of the cells were occupied by 'Mad' Frank Fraser and a chap called Stafford, both of whom were doing time.

The transfer to the cage made a change. For one thing, the beds were more comfortable, for another the doors of the cells were equipped with lift-up flaps instead of the eerie spy-hole. There was also a television room into which we were allowed in batches of two or three at a time. The security precautions were elaborate and efficient, and no contact with other prisoners was permitted. We were not even granted the privilege of attending the church services on Sundays. Presumably the authorities had decided that God, who helps those who help themselves, had assisted us enough already. Just the same, and in spite of the stringent security, we knew quite a lot of what was going on. One of the items of news that came through to us was that the Nipper, in various disguises, was visiting Brixton regularly in order to interview inmates who could provide him with information. On one occasion he came along in the guise of a parson, dog collar and all, to see his flock of stool-pigeons! A dedicated man indeed.

The weeks and months rolled on, summer turned to autumn as du Rose, Nipper Read and Harry Mooney worked on the Kray dossier. Leslie Payne contributed a novel length statement which had much in common with a work of fiction, and indeed little of this narrative was used at the Old Bailey. Alan Bruce Cooper and the comedian Elvey added their quota. So far as me and my brothers were concerned, we spent our time in consultations with solicitors and counsel, saw our visitors, ate, read books and newspapers and kept our ears to the ground to pick up the odd items of information that came through from time to time despite the security measures.

From my standpoint things looked pretty grim. Ronnie and Reggie, a very durable and optimistic pair as always, took a philosophic view of events and placed little significance on the fact that Albert Donaghue, 'Scotch Jack' Dickson and Ronnie Hart were not confined with us in the cage. I viewed this with a suspicion that was later to be justified when the three of them and many others appeared at the Old Bailey to give evidence for the prosecution.

Christmas of 1968 came along in due course, my twentieth wedding anniversary when, by tradition, the couple should receive gifts of china from their friends and relatives. Needless to say, the tradition was not observed, though I wouldn't have said no to a nice china pisspot for my cell. The old tin affair was showing signs of wear and tear. However we wished each other the compliments of the season, Mum sent in as much food and drink as was permitted even though money was beginning to get a bit short, and thus fortified we girded our loins for the coming battle. On the morning of Tuesday the 7th of January 1969 me and my brothers along with seven others appeared in the dock of the famous No. 1 Court at the Old Bailey variously charged with murder and complicity in murder. The Old Bill had ditched all the lesser charges, the mucking about was over, and now the real business was to begin.

Probably the most gripping entertainment in London is provided at the Old Bailey when an important trial is in progress. The show is put on regardless of expense, the brightest stars in the forensic firmament make their entrances and it's all free, gratis and for nothing. Smoking, cheering, clapping and booing are strictly prohibited, but then you can't have everything.

The Old Bailey – London's Central Criminal Court – is a huge and forbidding-looking building which occupies the whole corner site at the junction of Newgate Street and Old Bailey. It was built some seventy-odd years ago on the site of the old Newgate prison, which I suppose is one way of keeping up ancient associations. The main entrance is imposing with massive double doors solid enough to withstand attack by an army. Almost opposite the entrance is a pub called the Magpie and Stump, a favourite resort of the legal gentry when the courts are in session.

Talking about the Old Bailey, I believe that the origin of the term 'Old Bill' as a nickname for the police was a combination of Bill Bailey (won't you come home) and Old Bailey, which was shortened to Old Bill. I prefer it to The Fuzz or The Filth, descriptions with which the televiewer is familiar. Old Bill denotes a certain mateyness which isn't altogether absent from the relations between cops and robbers. Mind you, I'm not saying that I would kiss the Nipper on both cheeks if I met him in the street, and I have good cause for more than a touch of resentment against a few others. Just the same, not all coppers are bastards – but those who are make a very good job of it.

We came to the Old Bailey on the first day of the trial in our old friend the Black Maria with the usual escort and the fanfares of sirens. It was the first of thirty-nine similar trips we were to make before the trial ended on the 5th of March. Sid, the driver (I never got to know his surname), was a very nice chap who did his best to give us a comfortable ride in the circumstances. I had a chance to have a word with him one day, and asked him what would happen if we went over the side while crossing Waterloo Bridge. He assured me that he had an escape lever which released the whole roof. But, I said, suppose you are knocked out? He thought a moment, then said 'Well, that would be it – wouldn't it?'

When we arrived at the Old Bailey the procedure was always the same. The van was driven into the lower regions, a heavy steel shutter came down with a clang behind us and the van was then revolved on a turntable. One by one, we were led out between lines of uniformed police into the cells which give direct access to the dock. I must say it was all very friendly on the surface. There were 'good-mornings' all round as we were banged up to await the opening of the proceedings.

There's a distinctive smell about cells, whether they are part of a prison, a police station or a court. It's an odour I associate with despair, an unpleasant animal smell against which crude disinfectants daily fight a losing battle. At first I hated it, then learned to live with it, but I never got rid of the feeling that I was dirty. Even when I left prison behind me at the end of my sentence and was able to take as many baths as I wished, I still imagined that the smell was there. In the cells below the Old Bailey the builders had left a bit of the Old Newgate prison, or so it seemed. It was as though the ghosts of long-dead felons still polluted the air. But when I mounted the stairway and emerged into the dock all was sweetness and light. Here in this court, where the pomp, might and splendour of the administration of British justice is displayed to its best effect, I savoured the odours of deodorant and aftershave, the perfumes of the females in the public gallery and the aroma of best Ministry of Works beeswax which arose from the highly-polished woodwork.

I had been in this court before, but only as a spectator, free to come and go as I wished. Now I had a dock's-eye view, an entirely different matter. It took me some time to absorb the spectacle, the sombre background of black-robed barristers and court officials against which the colourful garb of the judge and the reds and golds of the huge coat-of-arms over his throne-like chair made startling splashes of colour. As the blur of faces came into focus I made out some that I knew, my counsel Desmond Vowden, John Platts Mills who was appearing for Ronnie and Reggie's counsel, Paul Wrightson. They were just three members of a very distinguished cast. I caught sight of Mum and Dad who were sitting with my wife in the public seats, but the dominating figure in the scene was that of Mr. Justice Melford Stevenson in full paraphernalia of robes and full wig, sitting high up in the seat of judgement.

All told there were ten of us crowded into the dock, together with a couple of prison warders which made it an even tighter squeeze. Along with me and my brothers were the two

Lambrianous, Ronnie Bender, Freddie Foreman, Ian Barrie, Cornelius Whitehead and Tony Barry, who had been granted bail at Old Street and was later acquitted. Some bright spark had had the idea that we should all be identified by numbered placards hung round our necks. We thought differently. Ronnie, in good voice, wanted to know if this was a cattle market. Mr. Justice Melford Stevenson, in much better voice and from a more commanding position, settled the matter by clearing the dock, and we all trooped down to the cells leaving the torn-up placards to be disposed of by court officials. In due course we were led back into court, the bright idea having been shelved, and the proceedings began.

Looking back on those thirty-nine days, those thirty-nine steps to incarceration, there are certain incidents that stand out in my recollection, some of them small and unrelated to anything, others highly significant. There was Kenneth Jones, counsel for the prosecution, making his opening address in a mellifluous Richard Burton-type voice which was very much at odds with his insignificant appearance. He made a real meal of the description of the way in which Cornell and McVitie met their respective ends. As a theatrical performance it could have been rated on a par with that of the ghost of Hamlet's father. As a statement of fact it was simple and straightforward. Ronnie stood accused of the murder of George Cornell with Reggie and Ian Barrie named as accessories. Both Ronnie and Reggie, along with the Lambrianous, Ronnie Bender and Tony Barry were charged with the murder of Jack McVitie. Neither Hart nor Donaghue were named in the indictment though Hart, on his own admission, was present at the scene. Donaghue had already pleaded guilty to being an accessory to the murder of McVitie and was duly awarded a sentence of two years imprisonment. Also named as accessories were Cornelius Whitehead, Freddie Foreman and myself.

These were the facts, as presented by Mr. Jones, that were to be considered over thirty-nine working days of costly legal argument.

To go into the trial in detail would fill a book. One day that book may be written, but for the moment I propose to deal with the important highlights as they appeared to me. Of course there was a large proportion of legal mumbo-jumbo, little chats between judge and counsel on abstruse points of law, all very punctilious and according to protocol, the sort of stuff that is included-out in television courtroom dramas as having no impact. I sat through all this with a feeling of unreality. Was this really happening to me? There was a middle-aged woman who always occupied the same seat in the public gallery, who smiled, nodded and mouthed a 'good-morning' every day. I never knew who she was or why she was there. One day Dolly fainted and had to be assisted from the court while I sat in the dock on my little chair, powerless to do anything to help her. Next morning the papers carried a story 'Charles Kray sits impassive as wife is carried from court . . .' Had I done or said anything, it would have been 'Charles Kray in dock outburst . . .' Heads you win, tails I lose.

The prosecution was a model of its kind, smooth, efficient and obviously well-rehearsed. The witnesses trooped in and out of the witness box, said their pieces under the skilful guidance of the diminutive Welshman with a voice too big for his body, submitted to cross-examination by the various counsel for the defence and went their ways. Billy Exley repeated his dying swan act. Limehouse Willie, whom I had known and trusted for the greater part of my lifetime and who, while visiting us in Brixton, was in constant contact with the Nipper, spoke of my brothers as brutal and sadistic men, creatures of violence who would stop at nothing. This man, himself an ex-Fascist, had stood beside Oswald Moseley when violence against the Jews erupted in the East End, had eaten meals with us at Vallance Road, and had owed his standard of living to the twins' generosity over many years. Harry Hopwood, smartly dressed in one of Ronnie's discarded suits and looking sleek and well-fed on the fillet steak bought by his wife out of money provided by the Old Bill, lied like a trooper about a telephone call he was supposed to have made to me in the early hours of the morning following the killing of McVitie. This Hopwood, who had professed to be a friend of my father for many years, testified against me and my brothers not out of principle or a sense of public duty but purely for a sum of money well in excess of the thirty pieces of silver paid to the original Judas who was called Iscariot.

Perhaps the most important factor lending veracity to Hopwood's evidence was that he and his daughter and son-in-law were given a home and a living at the Carpenter's Arms when the twins bought it. Talk about nurturing a serpent in the bosom . . .

One thing that surprised me was the appearance of 'Scotch Jack' Dickson as a witness for the prosecution. This man had been concerned in Frank Mitchell's escape from the Moor, for which he was sentenced to nine months, a very light punishment indeed for such an offence. Somewhere along the line he had done a deal with the Old Bill, but I would have thought he was the last man in the world to try to avoid the consequences of his crimes by becoming a grass. Which just shows how mistaken one can be. He did have the grace to say that he felt sorry for me personally, a rather back-handed favour since his evidence helped to put me away for ten years.

There were many other witnesses, some of whom I had never seen before, a few that I vaguely remembered. They all told the same story, painting the picture of a pair of malevolent monsters who held the East End in terror. I found it hard to reconcile this with what I knew of my brothers who, whatever crimes thay had committed, were men of generous impulses who were always ready to help those in need and never raised a hand against the innocent, whether man, woman or child, which is more than can be said for bomb terrorists who received a lighter punishment for more serious crimes. Let me hasten to say that I know nothing of the Irish problem and have no comment to make on the methods adopted by those who think the solution lies in bombs, bullets and bloodshed, but I am comparing the sentences passed on my brothers with those recently passed on men who were responsible for the wholesale slaughter of ordinary people.

As I see it, my brothers committed crimes, but what were those crimes? They benefited at the expense of those who could well afford to part with money, and who had probably acquired it by doubtful means in the first place. They profited from the gaping holes in the Companies Acts, carved up a few villains and were concerned in ridding society of a pair of useless parasites in the persons of George Cornell and Jack McVitie. Some realists, aware of the facts of life, said they should have been awarded medals. I make no such claim. My brothers took their chances and their punishment, but whether or not Justice was seen to be done will be decided by posterity.

Back at the Old Bailey the trial dragged on. The prosecution produced its star witness in the shape of Ronnie Hart, the man who wielded the knife in the basement at Evering Road. His uncorroborated evidence had twin results. It provided the main plank in the fabric of the case of the prosecution. It also enabled this guilty man to walk out of the Old Bailey to freedom. That he later confessed to having lied under oath is a matter of academic interest. Persons better qualified than myself to pass an opinion on the subject have already expressed themselves as disturbed that a criminal may escape the consequences of his misdeeds by giving testimony (whether it be true or false) leading to the conviction of others.

One thing that I noticed from my seat in the dock – an excellent vantage point from which to view a trial, but not to be recommended – was that Hart seemed to speak very slowly and had some difficulty in articulating. It was later mentioned that he had been given tranquillising drugs to enable him to face the long hours he spent in the witness box. I know it's an offence to drive a car while under the influence of drugs but maybe giving evidence on oath comes under another set of rules. Anyway, Hart had to take some stick. He was referred to as a confessed extortioner, a hired assassin, the most unspeakable liar in the case, a violent man and a blackmailer.

No wonder he needed tranquillisers.

The case for the prosecution inevitably came to an end. It was clear that, no matter what efforts defence counsel might make, the result was a foregone conclusion. To put it in a nutshell, the Old Bill weren't in business to lose this kind of case after all the painstaking work they had put into it. They intended to secure convictions – and they did. The defence witnesses were duly paraded, eminent counsel did the best they could with the material provided, but it was all easy meat for Mr. Kenneth Jones Q.C. He had himself a ball. One female, called for the defence of Ronnie Bender, was quite needlessly forced to declare that she was the sister-in-law of Reggie's deceased wife. What might have followed was forestalled by Reggie, who jumped up in the dock and presented the small and rotund Welsh gentleman with a torrent of abuse in the course of which he used the expression 'fat slob'. Jak, the cartoonist on the Evening Standard, captured the description for posterity in the following day's edition of that journal. He depicted a courtroom where a judge (with a remarkable resemblance to Mr. Justice Melford Stevenson) looks down on a short, fat barrister (the image of Mr. Kenneth Jones). The caption reads 'Would you clarify that last point again, you fat slob!'

It wasn't all that funny. Murder trials aren't usually noted for the humour of the proceedings, though there must have been a few giggles when the judge, in the course of summing-up, referred to Hart as a sneak. That was the understatement of the century, a very innocuous description indeed of a man who was a ruthless and bloody murderer.

On Tuesday the 4th of March 1969 the twelve good men and true, after seven hours of deliberation, brought in verdicts of guilty against all the men in the dock with the exception of Tony Barry, who was acquitted, even though he had admitted taking a gun to Evering Road and handing it to Reggie. Whether he told the truth or not was immaterial. That he did a deal with the Old Bill was very apparent. He had been on bail since the Bow Street hearing, even though the charge against him was accessory to murder. The facts speak for themselves. Curiously enough, Barry was ordered to pay £138 towards the cost of his defence.

Back in my cell in Brixton, through the long evening and a sleepless night, I tried to sort out my impressions of the trial and make a guess at what the morrow would bring. I had to admit that the prospect looked pretty grim for my brothers and not too cheery for me. I went over the various stages of the trial, comparing the cocksure confidence of Mr. Kenneth Jones Q.C. with the desperate attempts of defence counsel to convince the jury of discrepancies in the evidence, the calm assurance of Nipper Read as he moved quietly in and out of the courtroom marshalling his witnesses and wondered if I had been wrong in not calling my wife and my son to give evidence in my defence. I thought about Limehouse Willie and Harry Hopwood, men I had known for the best part of a lifetime, and accepted the bitter lesson that every man has his price whether it be paid in silver or other forms of currency.

I felt nothing but contempt for Dickson and Donaghue. They were villains who lived in a world peopled by their own kind, a world from which they had now been excluded, branded as police informers along with a number of others who tried to hide behind a wall of anonymity and police protection but who were known by name to those whose business it was to be aware of these things. But when I considered the treachery of Ronnie Hart, I felt sickened. Nobody expected him to stand up and confess to the murder of McVitie, but had he been any kind of a man he would have taken his chance in the dock with all of us. Significantly when Ronnie stood in the witness box, the only one of us who elected to do so, he steadfastly refused to name Hart as the man who used the knife on that fateful October night. What I am talking about has nothing to do with innocence or guilt, which is decided by judges and juries. I am talking about honour, which is every man's private and personal business. Hart is now in Australia, but wherever he goes his conscience will go with him. If he should read these words he will know what I mean.

The morning came, the morning of the 5th of March 1969. Each man was escorted to the dock separately to hear sentence pronounced together with the judge's comments. When my turn came, I mounted the stairs to face Mr. Justice Melford Stevenson, presiding over a court which seemed more crowded than it had ever been during the course of the trial and in which every eye appeared to be fixed on me. Although the duties of the jurymen had been completed the day before, they were present in force to hear the verdicts. I learned later that they had spent the previous evening dining together at the Mount Pleasant Hotel. They didn't pay the bill, but I can make a shrewd guess who did. However, that's by the way. The public gallery was packed.

I looked at the judge, his head bent over the papers before him, and wondered what was going through his mind. This was the man who was to dictate my immediate future, this learned and eminent figure who had celebrated his sixty-seventh birthday exactly seven days before the twins had reached their thirty-fifth anniversary in the October of 1968. Through my mind flashed a description I had read somewhere referring to Mr. Justice Avery who, towards the end of his career 'seemed to prolong his life by the infliction of misery on others'. There was complete silence which lasted for what appeared to me to be minutes but was probably only seconds.

Mr. Justice Melford Stevenson raised his head and looked me full in the face. I had never realised before the meaning of the words 'absolute power', but in that one moment I knew for certain. So did the man facing me.

He said, 'Charles James Kray, you have been found guilty of being an accessory to murder. It may well be that you were not a member of what, in this case, has been called The Firm, but I am satisfied that you were an active and willing helper in the dreadful enterprise of concealing traces of the murder committed by your brother. I sentence you to . . .'

He paused. I saw his lips beginning to frame the word 'life'. I went cold.

It was Kenneth Jones, of all people, who sprang to his feet and interrupted the judge.

He said, 'The maximum sentence for this offence, m'lud, is ten years, and . . .'

This time it was the judge who interrupted Mr. Jones.

'That's enough,' he said sharply. He turned to me. He said, 'I sentence you to ten years imprisonment.'

I shall always believe that Jones was going on to say that the prosecution would not press for the maximum sentence.

The judge said 'Take him down', and down I went.

Less than fifteen minutes later, in a cell below the Old Bailey, I was charged with the murder of Frank Mitchell.

TEN

Back in Brixton once more, but this time with a difference. I was now a convicted felon, beginning a sentence of ten years imprisonment and with a murder charge hanging over my head. No more wearing my own clothes, smoking as many cigarettes as I wished, eating food sent into the prison from the outside and receiving frequent visits from relatives and friends. I was a prisoner, and not an ordinary one at that. I was on what is known as the 'A' book, a convict under special security who must be watched at all times, regarded as a potential danger to himself, to other prisoners and society at large.

I heard how my brothers had fared. They had been sentenced to life imprisonment with a recommendation that they serve not less than thirty years. Ian Barrie and Ronnie Bender got life with a recommendation that they serve twenty years, the Lambrianou brothers also got life sentences with a fifteen year recommendation. Freddie Foreman was sentenced to ten years and Cornelius Whitehead, already serving a two-year sentence for currency offences, found himself with another seven years on top of that.

So ended the circus, the criminal trial which went into the Guinness Book of Records as the longest (and the most costly) ever to have taken place at the Old Bailey. Now I had to face the fact that, for the next several years, my home would be a prison. Notices of appeal had been lodged, but I had no great hopes of success in that direction and indeed my pessimism was justified when the appeals were turned down in July. Before that, however, there was a further trial at the Old Bailey before Mr. Justice Lawton when me and my brothers stood accused of the murder of Frank Mitchell. Also accused of the murder was Freddie Foreman, who had received a sentence of ten years for complicity in the murder of Jack McVitie. 'Big Pat' Connolly and Wally Garelick were charged with helping Mitchell to escape from the Moor, to which Garelick pleaded guilty. Dickson and Donaghue, both of whom gave evidence for the prosecution, were not subject to any charges, even though the Old Bill were well aware that they had both actively assisted in the escape, had taken care of Mitchell subsequently in Lennie Dunn's flat in Barking and that Donaghue, on his own admission, was the last person to see Mitchell before his final disappearance.

What puzzled me about this case was that it was ever brought at all. I had been cleared of a charge of murdering Mitchell in a lower court, when evidence was given that I had been confined to bed with influenza during the period of Mitchell's freedom. Now I was brought to the Old Bailey on a voluntary bill of indictment (there was nothing voluntary on my part, rest assured of that) to answer the same charge. My brothers had already been sentenced to long periods of imprisonment, so there was nothing more the Law could do to them. The only feasible explanation was that Somebody Up There had decided that I should be given a further helping of porridge. Fortunately for me, Mr. Justice Lawton didn't see it that way. He directed the jury to acquit both Ronnie and myself. After the strain of the past fifteen months it was too much for me, and my relief was so intense that I found myself weeping in the dock.

Reggie, as a reward for his considerable contribution to the Frank Mitchell Escape Fund, received five years with a bonus of nine months for harbouring Mitchell. This sentence made not the slightest difference to the time he would have to serve since it was concurrent with the life sentence he had already received. For his role as ministering angel to Mitchell's sexual needs Tommy Cowley, who had taken Liza Prescott from Winston's Club to the flat in Barking, was awarded nine months. Cornelius Whitehead got a similar sentence, Wally Garelick got eighteen months and 'Big Pat' Connolly was acquitted.

Donaghue and Dickson, both members of the escape team, were not charged, but they did appear in court as witnesses for the prosecution, when Donaghue swore on oath that Freddie Foreman and another man had shot Mitchell. This evidence was without corroboration but it was significant that Ronnie Hart, in the McVitie case, had pointed the finger at Foreman as the man who arranged the disposal of McVitie's body. This evidence also was uncorroborated. Did these men lie, and if so, why did they lie?

The answer is that they lied, and the reason (apart from being granted immunity) was, in this particular instance, not far to seek. Hart and Donaghue bore a grudge against Foreman. In the course of their small-time extortion activities, in which they terrorised publicans into handing over comparatively minor sums of money, they attempted to put the bite on Foreman. They picked on the wrong man. Foreman threw them out of his pub, the Prince of Wales in Lant Street, just off the Southwark Bridge Road, in the course of which action Hart and Donaghue suffered blows to their bodies and their pride. Mr. Justice Lawton (unlike his fellow judge Melford Stevenson) placed on record his opinion of perjurors by directing the jury to acquit Foreman. There the Mitchell case ended.

I was thinking only the other day that, if Mitchell were to turn up out of the blue sometime in the future, there would be a lot of red faces around.

I don't want anyone to run away with the idea that, by drawing public attention to the various discrepancies in the evidence presented against them, I am trying to present my brothers as whiter than white. They would be the first to say that they took their chances while making a lot of money and were under no illusions about the possibilities of retribution that lay in wait around the corner. What I do stress, however, is that a lot of people who committed acts far worse than my brothers were not so heavily punished, nor did their alleged crimes receive the enormous volume of adverse publicity which surrounded Ronnie and Reggie like a cloud of poison gas.

Shortly after the conclusion of the Mitchell case, the three of us were separated. Ronnie went to Durham and Reggie to Leicester. Special security arrangements existed in both these places. I was transferred to Chelmsford to settle into the dreary monotony of life in prison, to think of the years that stretched ahead and to tell myself every day that I must not give way to self-pity or whiningly protest my innocence. Yet there were many people outside who knew the facts. One of them was my wife, Dolly, who could have testified that the telephone did not ring in the early hours of the morning following the killing of McVitie. To give her her due, she did everything in her power to bring about the re-opening of my case, writing letters to influential persons, making representations to members of Parliament (among them Ian Mikardo and Tom Driberg) and, as late in the day as August of 1972, attempting to enlist the help of Lord Hailsham. That all her efforts ended in failure was not due to want of trying but to the impenetrable barrier raised by officialdom against the assaults of anyone by the name of Kray.

Mum, God bless her, tore into the fray like a champion, and like a champion she refused to accept defeat. Turned down in one quarter she bobbed up again in another, going to see solicitors, consulting private enquiry agents, bombarding officials from the Home Secretary downwards with letters and phone calls, yet still finding time to visit us whenever permitted to do so. It was an astonishing performance considering that she was over sixty. Lord knows where she got the energy.

There was a ray of hope for me in June of 1970 when Hart made a statement to solicitors admitting that he committed perjury at the Old Bailey, after which belated act of contrition he attempted to take his own life. For a short period I lived in expectation of a re-hearing of the charges against Freddie Foreman and me and perhaps my brothers, but I had not reckoned with the Home Office. This all-powerful arm of Government, a law unto itself, takes its decisions and is under no obligation to give reasons for them. At about the same time as the Home Secretary finally set the seal of approval on Hart's perjury, I was transferred from Chelmsford to Albany on the Isle of Wight.

Towards the end of my stay in Chelmsford I received a visit from a barrister by the name of Shulman. A friend of mine had told him that I was doing ten years for nothing, and the legal gentleman put on a great show of indignation, agreed that I had received less than justice and departed after promising that he would take immediate action. I never saw or heard from him again, but I believe he is now in South America, having fled to escape the consequences of forging a will. The lady at the receiving end of his unprofessional attentions was a Mrs. Raphael, better known to the public as Penny Brahms. She later married 'Dandy Kim' Waterfield, one of the patrons of the old Double R club. Small world, isn't it?

Parkhurst was reckoned to be one of the toughest jails in the country with a high percentage of hard cases in the care of equally hard prison officers. I was a bit apprehensive when I was told I was going there, especially when I discovered that I would not be in Parkhurst prison proper but in Albany, the high security building which was its next door neighbour. It was a bit of a blow. I expected that, after having been a model prisoner for a couple of years, I would enjoy some relaxation of the rules, but there again the Home Office moved in a mysterious way its wonders to perform. An added irritation was that my visitors would have to undertake the long journey to Portsmouth and the ferry crossing to the Isle of Wight. For Dolly, with the responsibility of a five-year-old child, it was no joke.

There are many who will say that this is all part of the punishment for committing crimes against society. I could wish that some of them had been in my place on one occasion which I will remember all my life.

Dolly and Nancy had paid me a visit, we said our goodbyes and I went back to my cell, which seemed lonelier than ever, feeling a bit down in the mouth. It was nothing to my feelings later in the day when the news came through that the Isle of Wight ferry had overturned outside Portsmouth harbour and a woman and a little girl were reported as among those missing. There are no words to describe my utter desolation at that moment in time when my world came to a dreadful stop. There are also no words to describe how I felt when I was told by the prison authorities that Dolly and Nancy were safe. They had just missed the fateful ferry and had crossed the Solent on the next one.

What I would call the second phase of my sentence could not be described as joyful. My brothers were in the same building but I was not allowed to communicate with them or have any contact at all. In neighbouring Parkhurst there were demonstrations against the food and conditions, reports of riots and disturbances to which the press gave maximum publicity, inferring that the Kray brothers had some hand in the mischief. For the record, we were in a separate prison and, for all practical purposes, might just as well have been in Timbuctoo. In fact we could well have done without this sort of thing, which had its repercussions in a general tightening of security in Albany.

For my part I kept my nose clean, did the menial jobs that were allocated to me as well as I could, took advantage of the educational facilities and kept fit by weight-lifting and such exercise as was permitted. Although it would have been all too easy to sink into idleness and become an institutionalised cabbage, a state of mind and body which prison life tends to encourage, I had made up my mind that this was not to be my fate. When my time came I would leave prison a whole man, ready and able to take up my life where it left off on that morning of the 9th of May 1968. Or at least that was what I thought. But the Fate that had landed me in jail for a crime I did not commit still had a few cards up its sleeve.

Some old sage or other once said, so far as I can remember the exact words (which made a considerable impression on me at the time) that however impossible life might be there are compensations which make it tolerable. It seemed to me that it was all a question of adapting to circumstances, deriving every possible personal advantage from any given situation and, within limits, never accepting defeat. Imprisonment breeds an insidious disease which saps the soul and spirit, but there is an antidote in mental and physical activity, which I took in large doses. There was an interesting by-product of this self-diagnosis and treatment. I found that my normal sex-urge, to which I had given free rein on the outside, could be directed into other channels of physical expression. Hence, unlike many other of the inmates, I did not contract any liaison with members of my own sex and only infrequently practised the habit which has been described as hygienic, satisfying but very lonely.

Actually, prison life was not an endless grey monotony, even under conditions of maximum security. The surroundings were grim, but they could have been worse and the human animal is not only adaptable but sometimes very durable. There were times when I saw the funny side of the most trivial incidents and thanked God for the sense of humour which helped me to maintain my mental equilibrium. Most of all I was supported by the knowledge that I had friends and loved ones on the outside who were making strenuous efforts on my behalf. I am convinced that it was their constant sniping at the bastions of the Home Office which resulted in my being transferred from Albany to Maidstone, known as an 'easy' prison where keen but kindly vigilance and some attention to rehabilitation replaced the tough oppression of the harder jails.

Her Majesty's Prison, County Road, Maidstone, opened its doors to me shortly after Christmas of 1973 which, incidentally, was the twenty-fifth anniversary of my marriage, known as the Silver anniversary. I got no gifts of Silver, not even a visit from Hymie Silver whom I had known quite well on the outside. What I did get was a new feeling of freedom for, though I was still a prisoner, the irksome restraint of being an 'A' man was removed. The prison governor, Mr. Skrine, was a man of liberal views whose influence made itself felt right through the hierarchy and down to the warders who, with few exceptions, treated the inmates as men and not the unwanted dregs of society.

For the first time since I had started my sentence, I really began to enjoy my visits. These were held in the large hall which was also used for entertainments and film shows. The inmates could sit with their visitors at small tables in comparative privacy, which was occasionally broken, but not unpleasantly, by the intrusion of some toddler who had come to see Daddy and then decided on further exploration. In one corner of the hall was a tea bar and somehow the place had a homely atmosphere with cups and saucers on the tables and kiddies running around. In theory visits were limited to half-an-hour, but in practice visitors arrived at one-thirty and were allowed to stay until three-thirty.

The transfer to Maidstone had the further blessing that it removed some of the strain of travelling for Mum and Dad and Dolly and the children. London was only thirty miles away, just over an hour's journey by road, and I was told that parking facilities outside the prison walls were plentiful and cheap. There's a moral in that somewhere if you look for it. Anyway, I found it much easier to talk to Mum and Dolly when they were not exhausted after a long journey, and the pleasure of sitting my little daughter on my knee and holding her close made me realise how much I had missed her.

On the face of it, everything was fine and dandy, or as fine and dandy as it could be considering that I was still locked up. But I had served almost five years of my sentence with a clean record and I could look forward to the possibility of parole in the not too distant future. I reasoned it out this way. Although I had been convicted of a serious crime, it was my first conviction, and the evidence against me had been, to say the least, very suspect in the light of Hart's confession. Even though a review of my case had been turned down, the facts must have been noted on the dossier in the files of the Home Office. Another factor that contributed to my optimism was that Vassall, the Admiralty spy, was granted parole from Maidstone. If the Parole Board saw fit to release a man like that, then my chances looked pretty rosy. I should have known better. Grim old Fate still had a few blows in store for me.

On the 21st of May 1973 my wife, Dolly, the mother of my two children, the woman in whom I had trust and faith over twenty-five years, stood in the witness box at Chelmsford Crown Court and publicly acknowledged that she had spent a night with a man in our home while my daughter slept in the next room. The night in question was the night before Guy Fawkes night of the previous year. The man was George Ince, who stood in the dock charged with murder.

The explanation of how this situation arose is as follows. In the early morning of November 5th 1972, in a house at the rear of The Barn restaurant in Braintree, Essex, a woman had been shot and killed by one of two men engaged in armed robbery. Her name was Muriel Patience and she was the wife of the owner of the house and the restaurant, a man by the name of Bob Patience. Their daughter Beverly was also shot and seriously injured. Patience himself suffered a superficial head wound. The gunman and his accomplice escaped with the loot and, during the police investigation that followed, both Patience and his 20 year-old daughter identified the gunman from photographs as George Ince.

Those, briefly, were the facts, but there was more to it than that. When I read the news of the murder the name Patience rang a bell. I had never met the man but heard mention of him as a very wealthy and enterprising gent indeed, who had been mixed up in the club and restaurant business for many years. At one time he owned the Ranch House in Ilford, and as I remember there were a few incidents of a violent nature there, one of which ended in murder. I didn't pay too much attention to rumours. I had had enough of them in connection with me and my brothers to cause me to regard rumour as nothing but a lying jade. However, it did occur to me that Patience might have been marked down as a suitable bird for plucking by certain interested parties'. Other than that, I didn't pay much attention.

All this is largely by the way. I read about the murder and also read that George Ince had been charged and brought to trial at Chelmsford Crown Court before Mr. Justice Melford Stevenson, whose name and appearance I will never forget. I don't need to say that I followed the reports of the trial with great interest, because, as I have mentioned earlier, there was some suspicion that Dolly and Ince had been having an affair many years ago: and even though I was under the impression that it had died a natural death, I was still curious. It was, in any case, difficult to avoid reading about the case. It made banner headlines for several days, and a lot of dirty washing received a public dowsing. It was almost inevitable that the name of Kray should crop up: even though we were in prison the wagging tongues managed to probe the bars – but I had no idea that I was soon to be involved, albeit in a roundabout way, through the agency of my wife.

The trial ended on the 9th of May, when the jury failed to reach a verdict. They were out for a total of almost seven hours. It was said in some quarters that the result reflected Melford Stevenson's handling of the case. I doubt that. The noble and upright gentleman did a very efficient job on us. It's true he came in for his share of abuse from the dock, to which he must have been accustomed, and he didn't seem too pleased with some of the remarks made by Victor Durand Q.C. who appeared for Ince, and this may have had some effect on the jury. Anyway, there was nothing for it but a re-trial under another judge. This began surprisingly quickly five days later, still at Chelmsford Crown Court but this time presided over by Mr. Justice Eveleigh.

Before I say anything about Dolly's appearance in the witness box seven days after the opening of the trial, I would like to make one fact plain. After I had been sentenced, and when it became clear that there was no chance of my early release, Dolly changed her name to Gray by deed poll and with my full agreement. I don't intend to disclose the reasons here. They were very personal and private. Suffice it to say that the witness who was described by the judge as Ince's mistress and who provided the alibi which was to clear him of a murder charge, was called to the box in the name of Mrs. Doris Gray. When I read the report of the proceedings on the following day I went cold with fury. Not only had my name been dragged into this sordid business while I was locked away in prison but, more important than that, my wife had taken her lover into the home that I still looked upon as mine – I had no other – and paraded her infidelity before my eight-year-old daughter.

Looking back after a lapse of more than two years I can remember how my guts twisted into knots. I was never a violent man, but had Ince been in front of me at that moment I would have torn his fucking head off. I had a vivid mental picture of the man entering my home, taking off his coat, playing games with my innocent little daughter, helping in putting her to bed, then, in the adjoining bedroom, coupling with my wife to the accompaniment of grunts and groans that must surely have been heard by the wondering child. Pacing up and down in my cell I was tortured by doubts. Had my little Nancy been taught to call this man 'Daddy'? Did he walk about the flat only partly clothed, as I had so often done? Deepest agony of all, had my Nancy witnessed the sight of her mother in the throes of passion, the two naked bodies thrashing about on the bed . . . ? I am not a religious man, but more than once in the course of my sleepless nights I called on God to help me.

Time, it is said, heals all wounds. It also wounds all heels, a slightly facetious comment I cannot resist making since it is apposite. Dolly means nothing to me now. We are divorced, she has custody of our daughter and I have what is known as 'reasonable access'. The home we once shared is now in her name and she is financially secure on the proceeds of the story she gave to one of the sensational Sunday papers added to the comparatively small sum she obtained by selling all my possessions just before my release from prison. Her lover is serving a sentence of fifteen years for his part in the Mountnessing silver bullion blag. If they should marry after his release, my only comment is that they richly deserve each other.

There is a strange irony in the fact that, had I called Dolly as a witness at the Old Bailey in 1969, she would have testified that I never left home on the night McVitie was killed. I wished to spare her the ordeal of cross-examination. The absence of her testimony together with Hart's confessed perjury and a few words from Mr. Justice Melford Stevenson destroyed my business, my home, my family and seven years of my life. They didn't destroy me.

One more thing before I draw a line under this shameful episode. Shortly after he went to jail, George Ince was attacked by another prisoner and cut about the face. Immediately the scream went up 'The Krays are at it again'. In fact, the cutting was done by an old lag called Harry Johnson who had reason to be grateful to my brothers. It was on his own initiative that he chose this way of showing his loyalty. It was a pity he did not realise that he was doing more harm than good.

To return to life in Maidstone, I was now waiting for an interview the outcome of which would determine whether I was suitable for release on parole. In the meantime I kept myself occupied. My duties in the prison kitchen, where I was in charge of the hotplate, were not onerous, but I immersed myself in the day-to-day life of the jail, organising a volleyball team, attending French lessons, swimming when the weather permitted, doing work-outs in the gym and anything else to keep boredom at bay.

The interview, when at last it came along, was a definite non-starter. The supercilious gent who saw me opened up the proceedings by telling me that of course I wouldn't get parole, after which hopeful beginning I was supposed to give my reasons for applying. I thought I would have a go. I said that I was doing ten years for nothing, pointed out that the evidence on which I was convicted was anything but positive and that some of it was false. I also drew attention to my blameless prison record. It was a waste of time. Had I been a rapist, a child molester or a spy, said I had been a naughty boy, sorry, they would have probably let me out to continue my raping, child molesting or spying. Bitter words, but I was bitter.

Parole is a carrot dangled in front of a donkey. I have discussed the question with friendly prison officers, who are themselves baffled by the unpredictability of the decisions reached by the officials. At least I learned one important lesson, which was to expect nothing and then I wouldn't be disappointed. I went back to my cell in the wing that housed, among others, no less than seventy men serving life sentences, accepting that my earliest date of release, taking into account full remission for good behaviour, would be January of 1975. Thankfully there was one small privilege that could not be taken from me. I was entitled to a week-end leave shortly before my final discharge, three whole days in which I would be free to do exactly what I wanted to do, drive a car, have a few drinks with friends, see streets and houses and people in ordinary clothes, all in the surroundings of freedom, short-lived though it might be. I could hardly wait. After more than six years incarceration, it would be like winning the pools.

Nobody writes his life story more than once in a lifetime, which is pretty self-evident. One of the problems is deciding what should be left out, and I am conscious of the fact that not enough has been said about our mother, who by rights should have pride of place on every page. By any standards she has always been a remarkable woman. She was born into a proud and respectable East End family, a pretty child who became a beautiful woman and a mother in a million. Though she never knew real poverty she saw it all around her and was always ready to come to the aid of those less fortunate than herself.

She had all the warmth and heart that tradition associated with the close-knit families of the East End where the man goes out to earn the bread and the woman stays home and looks after the kids. And we were well looked after, make no mistake about that.

Actually, it wasn't until I had been subtracted from the rat race and added to the prison population that I thought about family matters in any depth. It's part of the character of the East End male to take his womenfolk for granted. To the twins and me, Mum was always there, on the spot, dishing up the grub, listening to our problems and providing solutions based on her own quiet philosophy. On many a night, in the loneliness that began at nine o'clock when the cell door closed, I wondered what Mum was doing and tried to raise a mental picture of her in the little flat high above the silent streets of the City. I thought back to the times when me and my brothers used to return from school to the house in Vallance Road that Mum had made a home, and realised why the twins always came back to the one person who had been the centre of their lives for so long. We are all children, no matter how much we try to behave like adults. Emotional security, the greatest gift a parent can bestow on a child, was provided by Mum in full measure and brimming over.

It has been said that our mother was over-protective, particularly with the twins, and that may well have been true. In life there's always a choice between falling flat on your face or leaning too far over backwards, so you pays your money and you takes your pick so to speak. I will say this for Mum, she didn't make a habit of falling flat on her face. There were times, however, and I admit this freely, when she was a bit too forgiving, which probably led to the twins loving her more and others less. In a department of life that puzzles so-called experts I would be a brave man indeed to be dogmatic.

One thing which gave me a certain amount of pleasure was Mum's attitude to events when the twins began to hit the jackpot and it was mink instead of musquash, fashionable West End salons in place of Peggy's hairdressing shop round the corner. She didn't change one iota, put on no airs and graces and never tried to pretend that she was anything but herself. Dukes and dustmen, peeresses and publicans' ladies, they were all the same to her. She behaved with a calm dignity that won the respect of all who met her, no matter what their position in the social scale. She may not have been a dab hand at intellectual conversation but she said what she had to say with simple honesty. We were proud of her.

While on the subject of family, I have given a lot of thought in the still watches of the night to the root causes of my brothers' activities. Experience and reading have taught me that we live in an acquisitive society where wealth is a measure of worth and greed is mistaken for ambition. Show me a man who has achieved great riches starting from scratch and, in nine cases out of ten, somewhere along the line, he has made considerable dents in the law. In the moral climate which surrounds us all, the cardinal sin is not the commission of crime – it's being found out.

Granted all that, what were the reasons that led my brothers away from the normal respectability of East End life, into which they were born and in which they were reared? Both of them could have made their mark (and probably quite a lot of money) in the boxing ring. It happened to the Cooper twins, Henry and George, who came from a similar background. Any ambition they may have had in that direction, of course, was brought to an abrupt end when they took on the Army as an opponent. They came out on top in a few minor skirmishes but the final victory fell to Army authority when the twins were enrolled as students in that well known school of brutality, the detention barracks at Shepton Mallet. While still in their teens they were thrown into a maelstrom of repression and violence which, I am firmly convinced, brought out in them the ruthlessness and reckless disregard of consequences which they displayed in later years.

The ways of Fate are strange and unpredictable. In all our lives there exists the eternal 'if'. If Ronnie had not slung a right-hander at P.c. Baynton on that Saturday afternoon in the October of 1950, he would not have qualified for the beating he took in Bethnal Green nick. Had it not been for a minor disagreement with a corporal in the Royal Fusiliers, the two of them might have completed their military service, taken advantage of their standing as professional boxers (always welcome in the Services), and emerged into Civvy Street to take up careers in the ring. But this was the turning point in two young lives, a few steps in the wrong direction that took them further and further along the road that led to the Old Bailey. Try as I might, there was nothing I could do to prevent it. When they were released from Shepton Mallet the damage had been done. No matter what the psychiatric pundits may say about inherited tendencies, the spark of rebellion which exists in every boy was, in the case of my brothers, fanned into fierce flame by their reaction to what they considered injustice. They suffered violence and offered violence in return. It's true that they brought it upon themselves to a great extent, but that doesn't alter the facts.

Though they were identical in appearance ·in their childhood and youth, and shared many common characteristics, my brothers were quite different from each other in many ways. Ronnie was the flamboyant one, the first in any enterprise and, naturally the first to get into serious trouble. Had Reggie been with him in Wandsworth jail there might have been a very different story to tell, for Reggie was the cautious one who thought before he acted and rarely allowed his heart to rule his head. As it turned out, Ronnie did his nut one day, he had to be restrained in a strait jacket and the prison doctor opened a door into what was to become Ronnie's private nightmare by treating him with a drug which has kept its hold over him right up to the present day. How far this drug was a contributory factor to Ronnie's sexual aberrations is a matter of opinion. There is little doubt, however, that Stemetil was responsible for his sudden and violent outbreaks, when he was completely out of control.

It may seem strange to say of Reggie that he always hankered after respectability and the quiet life, but it is true.

By the time he was able to see his way clear to realising that state of affairs it was too late. The goods had been acquired and the account was due for payment in full, with no discount for prompt settlement.

My brothers, in their early manhood, selected the stage on which to play out their roles. They were determined to make a lot of money and, like many others, were not too scrupulous about the methods they employed. I've no doubt they were aware that the day of retribution would come, but power comes with money and power breeds a reckless disregard of consequences. That I played an active part in some of their enterprises was only to be expected. As the elder brother I was trusted, but outside that I had only a minimal influence on them. Their success in their chosen walk of life caused them to be unmindful of anyone's opinion but their own. When they started out on the road that led to prison they created the circumstances in which they operated, but later on those circumstances took control of them, easy street became a steadily steeper downward slope and, finally and inevitably, the crash.

I would like to make one thing clear. My brothers have been represented as mindless thugs with a propensity for violence and little else. It is a completely false picture. They lacked higher education, true, but they more than made up for that in personality and they possessed a native East End wit which is known and appreciated in many more places than Bethnal Green. They met with the famous and the notorious and were able to hold their own in any company. They dealt with their problems decisively and effectively, a phrase which may serve as a fitting epitaph some time in the distant future.

Everything comes to he who waits. The morning of January the 9th, 1975, turned up bang on time and I walked out through the little door in the heavy gates of Maidstone jail to comparative freedom. I was exchanging one set of fetters for another, but I was delighted to do so. There's a place for everybody in this world, but prison is no place for anybody.

I did my best to dodge the press and photographers without much luck. I knew from experience the sort of publicity they could give me, and I needed it like a hole in the head. All I wanted was a bit of peace and quiet. What I got was a barrage of questions. I made my getaway a bit sharpish, ending up in a modest house in an outer suburb of London as guests of my very good friends George and Susan Dwyer. There I was able to take my time in adjusting to the strange feeling of being a free man after the years of imprisonment.

It's not easy to describe one's emotions at such a time. For quite a while everything seems unreal and slightly out of focus. Simple things like having money in one's pocket or taking out a packet of cigarettes and handing them round, lying in a hot bath, scented toilet soap, open doors, going up to a bar and ordering a round of drinks, all these things assume a great importance. Gradually, however, the novelty of freedom wears off and it's down to the hard reality of living once more.

There were a few shocks waiting for me. Some joker had decided to make threatening phone calls to the Dwyers telling them I had not long to live which didn't worry me overmuch but caused my friends some distress. Then, when I paid a call on my ex-wife, it was to find that she had disposed of all my clothes and personal possessions and taken over the tenancy of the flat that had once been the place I called home. This was a facer, but there was nothing I could do about it.

There was some small consolation. Dolly's family, her mother, four sisters and two brothers, were very much on my side. They had always accepted me as one of the family and their attitude hadn't changed while I had been away, if anything they treated me with more than their usual kindness, which was a good thing because the break-up of my marriage had affected me more deeply than I cared to admit. The French have a saying 'Un homme sans femme n'est pas complet', a more subtle way of expressing the same sentiment in English. My home, my wife and my children were my world. Now I had to start from scratch.

Coming toward the end of my story and looking back over the colourful years that have gone to make up my life this far, I have much to be thankful for. This may seem a peculiar remark from a man who has just spent several years in prison and emerged into the outer world dead skint, homeless and with only the clothes he is wearing. Yet, counting my blessings, I have Mum and Dad and the ever-open door of their little flat not far from the Bank of England (upon which I have no designs, by the way), my son Gary shows no signs of the harrowing period he must have gone through during the formative years of his life and I am, and always will be, the father of my little Nancy.

I don't recommend prison as an ideal retreat in which to form a philosophy, and you can bet your boots that I haven't the slightest intention of touching porridge for the rest of my life. Nevertheless I learned some valuable lessons during my cribbed and cabined confinement which I intend to put to good use in the future. If there were any finishing touches needed in my education they were provided at the academies of Brixton, Chelmsford, Albany and Maidstone where a man is taught patience, fortitude and the ability to endure what Hamlet referred to as 'the slings and arrows of outrageous fortune'.

I have not yet completely severed my links with prison authority, since I pay regular visits to Parkhurst to see my brothers. They are model prisoners (there's not much point in being anything else) who look forward to the day when a humane and enlightened Home Secretary will take the view that they have been adequately punished for their misdeeds. For my part, I maintain that if they were released now the community would be in no danger from them, and I am not alone in that belief.

When I say that I have much to be thankful for, I am not referring to one area in my life which I shall always recall with considerable bitterness. When I stood in the dock at the Old Bailey and listened to the evidence that was to send me to jail for a very long time, I wasn't able to grasp fully the reality of the situation. I was in such a confused state that I failed to untangle in my mind the fine and intricate web that had been constructed to enmesh me and my brothers. Later on everything fell into place. I was reading a play written in the late thirties by a chap called Stephen Spender, entitled 'Trial of a Judge'. At one point in the play this judge, a tool of a totalitarian regime, says: 'The dumb public, fed with lies and living in crazed darkness, believes the least credible lie as the most true.' Goebbels, the little limping evil genius of Nazism, said more or less the same thing when he proclaimed: 'Make the lie big enough and it will be believed.' There is one man who will know what I am saying. He is Ronald Hart, who will have to live with his conscience for the rest of his days.

So much for that. I'm not parading my innocence nor do I ask for sympathy. I played my part in some of my brothers' operations and took my share of the easy money, but I was never involved in killing or in any violence whatsoever. The truth will be resolved by due legal process in the course of time. I hold that Justice exists not only to punish the wrongdoer, but also to right the wrongs perpetrated in her name.

To turn to more pleasant topics. I remember the good times and the many friends I made, people who to this day accept me as what I am and have always been and do not pass by on the other side of the street. People who know the truth, such as Francis Wyndham of the 'Sunday Times', a great journalist and a true gentleman, have been of great assistance to me. On both sides of the Atlantic there are prominent figures in theatrical and sporting circles who were the guests of me and my brothers and who still speak well of us. From the world of boxing came Rocky Marciano, Joe Louis, Sonny Liston, Barney Ross, Henry Armstrong and many others from the United States. Jack 'Kid' Berg and Ted 'Kid' Lewis were personal friends, and we were helped in our work for charities by Terry Spinks, Henry Cooper, Billy Walker and many others who had graduated from the East End via the boxing ring and were not ashamed of their beginnings.

I watched the fight between John H. Stracey and Jose Napoles on television recently. I was particularly interested, not only because I fought as a welter during my professional career, but also because John comes from my home manor of Bethnal Green, was a contemporary of my son Gary at Daneford Street school and is a perfect example of the poor boy who, through dedication and hard work, has risen to the top. I was pleased and very proud when this young fighter brought a world championship back to Great Britain. I remembered vividly the time when my brothers represented Daniel Street school (the name by which Daneford Street was then known) in the London Schoolboys' Championships. I also remembered the cheers and shouts of the crowd at the Albert Hall when Reggie notched up his seventh professional victory in a row by demolishing Bob Manito. It's speculation without profit, but who knows what might have been had not National Service and a corporal in the Royal Fusiliers intervened in the lives of the twins. However, that's all water under the bridges now . . .

There are many responsible and worthy people, some of them in high places, who still hold me and my brothers in personal esteem. There are also ordinary folk, the inhabitants of the manor of Bethnal Green who know what it's all about and who face the harsh realities of life in the East End every day. Walk down Bethnal Green Road, talk to some of the older residents, and you will find men and women who have nothing but praise for the Kray brothers and remember them with affection.

For the other side of the picture one looks to men such as Leslie Payne, fraudsman and informer, Alan Bruce Cooper, specialist in the manufacture of paper hats for others to wear, the motley crew of witnesses at the Old Bailey including Harry Hopwood, Billy Exley, Jack Dickson, Albert Donaghue, Ronnie Hart, men who lied for financial gain and the promise of immunity from prosecution, clothing their actions in hypocritical concern for public order and protesting a moral conscience which none of them possessed. A special place in this gallery of public-spirited citizens must go to Charlie Mitchell, well known in Fulham, who in return for his services as an informer was permitted to spend nights in the comfort of his own bed while ostensibly being held in custody in Wandsworth.

As these words are being written, Christmas is approaching, my first Christmas as a free man in eight years. I shall spend the festive season of goodwill with my mother and father and my son Gary, looking forward to that future Christmas when the family circle will be completed by the presence of my brothers, Reggie and Ronnie. There will be one other person present, the woman who has done more than anyone (apart from my mother) to sustain and encourage me since I was released from jail. Diane and I propose to make our life together and she will be proud to be known as Mrs. Kray, unlike certain people who believe that a rose by any other name would somehow smell differently. She has given me her trust and loyalty, my mistakes lie in the past and the future is ours to make of it what we will.

A late comment is one for which I am indebted to the 'Evening Standard'. Leonard 'Nipper' Read is in line to be interviewed for the job of deputy chief constable for Staffordshire, the annual salary for which is in the neighbourhood of £9,000. In these days of rising unemployment, it is good to know that one man at least will not have to face the threat of redundancy.

One last note. When the news leaked out that I was writing the story of my life I was asked if some revelations might be expected. This is not the Book of Revelations, and I don't propose to end it with the word AMEN.

My final words are few, and directed to any young East Ender who thinks to make a fortune by pitting himself against the forces of law and order. Leave it out, son. My brothers won a few battles, but the police have won the war.

INDEX

Abraham, Harry, 86
"A" Book, 231, 238
Air Training Corps, 45, 48
Albany Prison, 93, 235
Albert Hall, appearance of the Fighting Krays 66-70: 251
Allen, Jack, boxer, 48, 57
Anderson, Gordon, Enugu 145-8: Brixton 215
Armstrong, Henry, boxer, 250
Astor Club, 119, 176
Aubrey-Fletcher, John, Metropolitan magistrate, Bartlett affair 123
Aunts May and Rose, sisters to Violet Kray, 9, 18-20, 26, 28, 35, 38-9, 56, 99
Avery, Mr. Justice, 228

Bagga Tor, Dartmoor, 180
Bill Bailey, 220
Bailey, David, Incident at the Horns, 158: Reggie's wedding 159
Baker's Arms, pub, 176-7, 184
Barn Restaurant, Braintree, 8, 239
Barrie, Ian, 120, 222, 231
Barry, John, 184
Barry, Tony, 184, 222, 226
Bartlett, Det. Con. 122-3
Batt, Col. W. E., magistrate, 74
Baynton, P.c. Donald, 62-5, 245
Bebber, Ted, 60
Bender, Ronnie, 198, 222, 231
Berg, Jack 'Kid', 32, 250
Berry, Harry 'Kid', 70
Bethnal Green Hospital, Rheumatic fever, 40-1
Bethnal Green Junction, tragedy at, 34
Betting and Gaming Act, became law, 128
Bildeston, Suffolk, 37, 203
Blind Beggar, pub, 170
Bloom's Kosher Restaurant, 163
Booth, James, 135
Boothby, Lord, 132: Sunday Mirror case 142-4: 155
Brahms, Penny, 235
Brightlingsea Buildings, 90
Britannia, pub, 81-2
British Tourist Board, 166
Brixton Prison, 214-5, 231
Brooke, Henry, Home Secretary, Boothby case, 144
Brooks, The, 203-4
Brown, George, 205
Brown, Tommy 'The Bear', 120
Bruno, Angelo, 166
Bryant, escaped detention with twins, 75
Bunhill Row, 206-7

Bunnett, Ted, 44
Burns, director Esmeralda's Barn, 127

Cambridge Rooms, 138: Party at 150-1
Cappell, Jack, boxing promoter, 69
Capstick of the Yard (Charlie Artful) 153
Carpenter's Arms, pub, shooting of Ginger Marks, 174: meeting with Paul Elvey 189: 224
Carston Group, 138
Carter, Johnny, 169-70
Caruana, George, 205
Cater, Insp. Frank, 206
Cedra Court, 161
Challoner, Det. Sgt., 101
Charlie Brown's, restaurant, 88
Chelmsford Crown Court, 8, 240
Chelmsford Prison, 234
Clare, Barry, 87-8, 108
Clark Brothers, 135, 158
Clark, Nobby, 212
Collins, Jackie, 88
Colony Club, 166
Connolly, 'Big Pat', 88, 120, 122, 232, 233
Cooney, Steve, boxer, 67
Cooper, Alan Bruce, first appearance, visit to U.S. 164-5: weaponry 189: Spain 190: 195: Harley Street 204-5: 218, 251
Cooper, Henry, 51, 72, 245, 250
Corbett, Billy, 34
Cornell, George, (real name Myers), shooting of 170-3: 176, 196, 204, 222
Coronet Youth Club, 42
Cowley, Tommy, 164, 172-3, 181, 189, Harley Street 204-5: 210, 233
Crowder, Petre, Q.C., McCowan case 155
Crowley, Dave, 67, 70
Crown and Manor Youth Club, 42
Cummings, Det. Sup., Mr. Smith's Club 169

Dale, John, 171
Daily Express, Boothby case, 144
Daniel Street School (later Daneford Street), 43, 45, 48, 50, 251
Daniels, Billy, 135
Dartmoor Prison, 179
Darvil, Albert, boxer, 44
Darwin, Charles, 29
Davis, Jimmy, Albert Hall, 66
Davis, Wally, 67
de Faye, Stefan, 127
Diane, 252
Dickson, George, 184
Dickson, 'Scotch Jack', 180-1, 184, 224, 227, 232, 251

253

Dimes, Albert, (Alberto Dimeo), 100
Donaghue, Albert, 180-3, 198, 222, 227, 232, 251
Dors, Diana, 88
Double R Club, 86-7, 90, 110, 121, closed 128: 149
Downes, Terry, 135, 151
Driberg, Tom, M.P., 234
Drummond, Commander, 127
Dunn, Lennie (Books), 180, 232
Durand, Victor, Q.C., 240
Durham Prison, 21
du Rose, Commander John, 206, 210, 218
Dwyer, George and Susan, 248

East London Advertiser, 48
Effingham, Lord, 136, 151
El Morocco Club, 156, 163
Elvey, Paul, meeting Carpenter's Arms 189: 205, 218
Enugu, Nigeria, 141
Esmeralda's Barn, 124, 126-8, 132, 138, 148, 194
Evans, James, Ginger Marks' shooting 174-5
Evans, Vice-Admiral Sir Charles (Evans of the Broke), 151
Eveleigh, Mr. Justice, 8, 240
Evering Road, 197, 199, 203, 225, 226
Exley, Billy, 180-2, 217-8, 223, 251

Farson, Daniel, 136
Firm, The, 8, description of 121
Fisher, John, P.c., 'Three-half-crowns' 74, 78
Fitzroy Lynn Club, 44
Foreman, Freddie, 183, 198, 222, 231, 232
Foreman, George, 174-5
Foster, Rev. Edward, McCowan case 155-6: Reggie's wedding 159
France, Gilbert, Hideaway Club 154: 156
Fraser, 'Mad Frankie', 100, 169, 170, 192, 218
Fraser Ronald, 151
Frost, Johnny, 201
Fullerton, Jimmy, 81

Galton, Sir Francis, 28, 30, 46-7
Garelick, Wally, 232-3
Garland, Judy, 145
Gerrard, Det. Chief Sup. Fred, Boothby case 143: McCowan case 154-5: 164
Gibbins, schoolmate, 23
Gill brothers, 44
Gipp, Billy, 122-3, 135
Glenrae Hotel, 138, arrest of twins at 153
Goddard, Lord Chief Justice, 111
Gold, schoolboy boxer, contest with Reggie, 48-9
Goodsell, George, boxer, 67-8
Gore, Freddie, 126-7, 130, 132, 138, Enugu 145-8
Gorsuch Street, 7, 15
Grange, The, club, 108
Grave Maurice, pub, 153, 193
Great African Safari, beginning of 138-9: 141-2, 153
Green, Danny, 108
Green Dragon Club, 157
Grundy, Bill, 59

Guinness Book of Records, 231

Hadleigh, Suffolk, 9, 32, 35-7, 203
Hagate, 'Patsy', 67
Hailsham, Lord, 234
Hare, Bob, 134-5
Hart, Richard, 169-70, 184
Hart, Ronnie, 184, killing of McVitie 198-202: 222, Old Bailey 225, 227: Confession of perjury 234-5: 250, 251
Hawkes, schoolmaster, 16
Hertzberg, Mrs. Lillian, 124
Hetherington, Rev., (vicar St. James the Great), 61
Hicks, Colin, (brother of Tommy Steele), 136
Hideaway Club, 154, 156
Hill, Billy, 99, 173
Home Office, 235, 237, 239
Hopwood, Harry, 174, 210, 223, 227, 251
House of Peacocks, 175
Hoxton Baths, 16
Humphreys, porn-peddler, 101
Hutton, Johnny, 125
Huntman, Benny, 71

Ince, George, 8, 157, Barn murder 239-242
Irani, Freddie, 132

Jenkins, Roy, Home Secretary, 181
Johnson, Harry, attack on Ince, 242
Johnson, Ron, boxer, 66
Jones, Billie, 81-3
Jones, Kenneth, Q.C., 222, 'fat slob' 226: 227, 229
Jordan, Jack, 9, 67, 76
Joyce, William, (Lord Haw-Haw) 24-5
Junkets, 166

Kaufman, Joe, visit in Spain 190-1
Kennedy, arrested 212
Kensit, Jimmy, 122-3
Kentucky Club, opening 133: 135-6, Donkey incident 136-7: closed 137-8: 149
King, Cecil H., Boothby case 144
King, Freddie, 44
King, Ronnie, 44
Kray, 'Big' Jimmy, grandfather of twins, 16, 26, 31, 50
Kray, Charles David (Dad), 7, 9, 11, 15-17, deserter from Army service 38, 39: Bunhill Row 203: The Brooks 206: 252
Kray, Dolly, nee Moore, wife of Charles, 13-15, marriage 57: 71, marital trouble 85-6: 90, 92, 134, affair with Ince 157-8: visit to Spain 191: incident Old Bailey 223: efforts to re-open Charles' case 234: Isle of Wight ferry 236: alibi for Ince 239-242: final break 248
Kray, Gary, Charles' son, 13-15, 86, 134, 157, 249, 252
Kray, Nancy, Charles' daughter, 13-15, 241, 249
Kray, Reggie, 7, 9, 10, 11, birth of 18-20: 21, amateur boxing 44-46: 48-9, 60, trouble with the law 62-65: Albert Hall 66-7, 69, 70: reported for military service 72-3: desertion 74: prison and Shepton Mallet 75-6: Regal billiard hall 78: acquitted Old Bailey 83:

254

Double R club 86-7: trouble with hooligans 88-9: opened 'spieler' 91-2: assisted Ronnie's escape from Long Grove 95-7: thrashed blackmailer 108-9: Podro affair 116-7: charged with burglary 124: trips to Enugu 141: Chemmy losses 150: McCowan case 153-6: marriage 159: El Morocco 163: Townsend case 177-8: met Frank Mitchell 178: Mitchell's escape from Dartmoor 179-81: reaction to Richardson trial 192: Frances' suicide 193-4: police surveillance 194-6: McVitie's killing 197-202: bought The Brooks 203: arrested 9th May 1968 207: lower courts 213-8: Old Bailey 219-29: sentenced 30 years 231: Leicester prison 234: 235-7, looking back 251: looking forward 252

Kray, Ronald, 7, 9, 10, 11, birth of 18-20: 21, 26, amateur boxing 44-46: 48-9, 60, trouble with the law 62-5: Albert Hall 66-7, 69, 70, reported for military service 72-3: desertion 74: prison and Shepton Mallet 75-6: Regal billiard hall 78: affray at Britannia pub 81-3: sentenced three years 83: Wandsworth prison 87-8: fought warders, transferred Winchester, certified insane 92-4: escaped Long Grove 95-7: period of liberty and re-arrest 101-4: time served 105: Bartlett affair 122-3: Esmeralda's Barn 126-7: Boothby affair 122-3: donkey at the Kentucky 136-7: trips to Enugu 141: Boothby affair 143-5: bought Solway Cross 150: McCowan case 153-6: drugs 160-1: visit to U.S. 165: shooting of George Cornell (Myers) 170-3: Townsend affair 176-8: 188, 191, reaction to Richardson trial 192: police surveillance 193-6: McVitie's killing 197-202: bought The Brooks 203: arrested 9th May 1968, 207: lower courts 213-8: Old Bailey 219-29: sentenced thirty years 231: Durham prison 234: Parkhurst 236: 245-7, looking back 251: looking forward 252

Kray; Violet, (Mum) 7, 9, 11, 18-21, 25-7, 161, Bunhill Row 203: The Brooks 206: efforts on behalf of sons 234: appreciation of 243-5: 252

Laburnum Street School, 16, 17, 22
Lagos, 141
Lambrianou brothers, Chris and Tony, 198, 200, 222, 231
Lange, Dr. 28-31, 46-7
Lavenham, Suffolk, 201
Lawton, Mr. Justice, 182, Richardson trial 192: Mitchell trial 232
Lazar, Lew, boxer, 69, 70
Lee Jimmy, 'Southpaw Cannonball,' grandfather of twins, 20, 21, 28, 31, 33, 34, 39-40, 50
Lee, Johnnie, 21, 28
Le Monde club, 120
Lethbridge, Nemone, 179
Levacq, Roy 'Chopper', 135
Lewis John, M.P., 71
Lewis, Ted 'Kid', 16, 32, 135, 151, 250
Limehouse Willie (Alf Willey), 111, 120, 210, 212, 223, 227
Liston, Sonny, 72, Cambridge Rooms 151: 250

Little Hank, midget entertainer, 136-7
Littlewood, Joan, 135, 151
London Schools Boxing Contests, 45
long firm frauds, 130
Long Grove Mental Hospital, 96, 104, 160
Louis, Joe, 72, 250
Lowson, Sir Denys, 81
Lucas, Norman, 96, Boothby case 143: 152

Mafia (Syndicate), 149, 165-7
Magpie and Stump, pub, 220
Maidstone Prison, 10, 93, 187, transfer to 237: open visits 238: existence in 242: release from 247
Mallett, Eddie, 48, 71
Mancini, Alf, (jun), 67
Mancini, Tony, Esmeralda's Barn 128
Manito, Bob, boxer, 70, 251
Marciano, Rocky, 72, 250
Marks, Thomas 'Ginger', shooting of 174-5: 176, 184
Marshall, Eric, landlord Baker's Arms, 177
Martin, Charlie, 81
Martin, Terry, 82
Magistrate's Court, Bartlett affair 123: Frank Mitchell 178-9
Mathew, John, barrister, McCowan trial 155: Townsend trial 177, 191
Meadows brothers, 132
Melvin, Murray, 151
Mendoza, 32
Mikardo, Ian, M.P., 234
Mile End Hospital, 135
Milton, Frank, Metropolitan magistrate, 111
Mitchell, Charlie, 184, 211, 252
Mitchell, Frank, (Mad Axeman) met Reggie 178: escape from Dartmoor 179-183: 198, 201, 217, 224, 229, 232
Mooney, Det. Sup. Harry, 206, 211, 218
Morgan, Dickie, 75
Moseley, Oswald, 24, 223
Mr. Smith's Club, 168, 175, 192
Mountnessing Silver Robbery, 242
Mount Pleasant Hotel, jury party 228
McCowan, Hew Cargill, 142, Old Bailey 153-6: 178
McGovern, Tommy, 44, Albert Hall 66
McVitie, Jack 'The Hat', 7, killing of 197-202: 222

Napoles, Jose, 251
Nash brothers, 132
National Sporting Club, 68
Naylor, R. H., 184
Neill, A. S., 161
Newgate Prison, 221
New Statesman & Nation, comment on Boothby affair 152
North London Magistrates' Court, 111

O'Connor, Jimmy, 179
Oh, what a lovely war, 136
Old Bailey (Central Criminal Court), 7, 11, 65, 83, 153-6, 213, 219-229
Old Street Magistrates' Court, 64, 177
Osborne, Georgie, 116-7, 120
O'Sullivan, Dickie and Danny, boxers, 44

Parkhurst Prison, 21, 235-6

parole, 238, 239, application for, 242-3
Patience family (Bob, Muriel, Beverley), 8, 239
Payne, Leslie, first meeting with 125: Esmeralda's Barn 126-7: 132, 138-9, 141, 145-8, 199, 218, 251
Payne, Reginald, 144
Pearson, John, 28-30, 97, 204
Perkoff, solicitor, 104
Peters, Lennie, 135
Peter Pan Society, 150, 151
Platts-Mills, John, Q.C., 221
Podro, Murray, 116-7
Port Harcourt, 147
Prescott, Lisa, 181-2, 233
Presidential Hotel, 141
Private Eye, 144
Profumo scandal, 144
Prospect of Whitby, 88

Queen Elizabeth Hospital for Children, 135

Raft, George, 166
Ramsey, Bobby, attack on Terry Martin, conviction at Old Bailey 79-83: 135
Ranch House, Ilford, 239
Raymond, Paul, 132
Read, Det. Insp. Leonard 'Nipper', 65, McCowan case 153-6, transfer to Great Train Robbery team, 163: 164, 196, 206, 211, 218, 227, 252
Regal billiard hall, twins take over 78: Ronnie and Bobby Ramsey 79-81: 110, 149
Regency Club, 111, 121, 199
Repton Boys' Club, 135
Richardson, Charles, 118-9, 176, 184, 191, 192
Richardson, Edward, 118-9, 169, 176, 184, 191, 192
Richardson, Jean, 192
Robert Browning Institute, 44, 48, 51
Ross, Barney, 250
Royal Fusiliers, twins report for service 72-3: 246, 251
Royal Navy, boxing for 47: discharge from 48

St. Clement's Hospital, Ronnie becomes patient 115
St. James the Great, 50, 61
Scawfell Street School, 22, 23
Scribham, amateur boxer, 44
Sewell, George, 135, 151
Sharpe, John, 69
Shaw, Sebag, Q.C., Richardson trial 192
Shay, Danny, 116-7
Shea, Elsie (Frances' mother) 159
Shea, Frances (later Reggie's wife), wedding 159: suicide 193
Shea, Frank (Frances' father), 159
Shepton Mallet Military Prison, 75, 76, 79, 80, 245-6
Sherlock, boxer, 68
Shinwell, Ernest, 139, 142
Shulman, barrister, 235
Simmons, Dave, 212
Simpson, Sir Joseph, Boothby case 143-4
Sims, Charlie, 44-5, 51
Sliney, Bill, boxer, 67, 69, 70
Snowdon, Lord, 136

Smith, 'Mad' Teddy, McCowan case 154: 201
Solomons, Jack, 48, 71
Solway Cross, 150, 151
Sparrows can't sing, 135-6
Spender, Stephen, 'Trial of a judge' 250
Spinetti, Victor, 135, 151
Spinks, Terry, 135, 151, 250
Spot, Jack, (Comer), 99, 100
Stafford, Frank, 218
Stean Street, 7, 18
Stemetil, 95, 97, 160, 161, 246
Stevenson, Mr. Justice Melford, 7, 8, 221, 222, 226, 228-9, 240
Stracey, John H., 251
Stratford Magistrates' Court, 77
Streeter, Insp. Vic, 211
Sturge, Harold, Metropolitan magistrate, 64
Styles, Mrs., 9, 35-37
Sulky, proprietor Astor Club, 119
Sunday Mirror, 132, Boothby case 143-4

Tanner, Allan, boxer, 66
Theatre Royal, Stratford-atte-Bow, 135, 151
Thompson, schoolboy boxer, 48
Thurston, Gavin, Westminster coroner, 171
Tintagel House, 206
Townsend, Det. Sgt. Leonard, corruption case 176-7: 184, 188, 191
Townsend, Det. Sup. Ronald, 176, 184
Tucker, Charlie, 44
Tunney, Gene, 43

Upton Park mob, 89

Vallance Road, No. 178. 9, 26, 32, return from evacuation 36-7: twins return from Shepton Mallet 76: 128, 244
Vassal, Admiralty spy, 239
Vaughan, Sidney, 155
Vowden, Desmond, Q.C., 221

Walker, Billy, 72, 135, 250
Ward, Henry 'Buller', 66, 197
Waterfield, 'Dandy Kim', 88, 235
Watney Street, mob 54-56; 78, 81-2
Watts, Queenie, 88-9, 136
Webbe Boys' Club, 48
West End Central Police Station, 209-213
Whitehead, Cornelius, 198, 222, 231, 233
Wilde, Jimmy, 16
Wilde, Oscar, 93, 98, 131
Willey, Alf (see Limehouse Willie)
Winchester Prison, 94-5, 159
Windsor, Barbara, 135, 151
Winston's Club, 181, 233
Wolfenden, Sir John, 98
Wood, Albert, 171
Wood, Bobby, 68
Wormwood Scrubs Prison, 80
Wrightson, Paul, Q.C., McCowan case 155: 221
Wyndham, Francis, incident at the Horns 158: 250

Yeardye, Tommy, 88
York Hall, Bethnal Green, Reggie's promotion 135
Yutke, model, 131